NEW RECIPES

from

QUILT

COUNTRY

Marcia Adams

NEW RECIPES
from
QUILT
COUNTRY

More Food & Folkways
from the Amish & Mennonites

CLARKSON POTTER/PUBLISHERS

NEW YORK

Published by Clarkson N. Potter, Inc., 201 East 50th
Street, New York, New York 10022. Member of the
Crown Publishing Group.

Random House, Inc. New York, Toronto, London,
Sydney, Auckland

http://www.randomhouse.com/

CLARKSON N. POTTER, POTTER, and colophon are
trademarks of Clarkson N. Potter, Inc.

Printed in China

Design by Jill Armus

Library of Congress Cataloging-in-Publication Data
is available upon request.

ISBN 0-517-70562-1

10 9 8 7 6 5 4 3 2

To Denise Kisabeth, WBGU, Bowling Green, Ohio, former director of all my television cooking series; to Pam Krauss, editor of all my books; and to agent Christine Tomasino, guardian angel for writers. Thank you for introducing me to a whole new professional world. I have loved it. Most of the time.

[Contents]

❖

❖

GOOD MORNING: GUD MARYE

❖

DINNER TIME: MIDDAAGESSE

❖

SUPPER TIME: NACHTESSE

❖

GOOD NIGHT: GUD NACHT

❖

The thing about farming is there is nothing

between you and the world. Everything

you touch either wounds or responds.

Everything you love touches back

with food or with poison . . .

❖

The thing about farming is you work

most of your life alone

for better or worse . . .

no enemy but the weather and the wind, the wind, the wind.

❖

The thing about farming is you are responsible

for a small portion of the planet.

You keep it or you lose it and it changes,

no matter what, according to your efforts.

But what's important is

when you wake and pick blueberries,

not only are they good—they're yours . . .

❖

From "The Thing About Farming"
by Iowa poet Michael Carey

[*Acknowledgments*]

❖

At the Academy Awards, the winners stand at the podium, clutching their Oscars tearfully to their hearts. Then they list, in a seemingly interminable fashion, everyone who has helped them along the way, including their dog, to achieve their goal.

It wasn't until I started writing books that I understood this sometimes long recitation of names. Now I know that creating a film or video series or a book requires lots of people. And behind many a food world personality is a skilled group of professionals making us look good. I am no exception.

I am blessed to be surrounded by talented people with whom it is a pleasure to work. Dick, my husband, handles our oddly organized life with great tolerance. I lean heavily on his business and marketing skills. Susan Raver, my assistant and friend, brings organization and calm to the office. My niece, Mary Ellen Zeiger, has intrepidly stood by me during all the testing of these 230 recipes (some, over and over again until we got them right) and keeps the house running efficiently. In addition, she has a great sense of humor, a most helpful attribute.

Now is the time to mention the cats, Emily and Edith, who accompany me at 6 A.M. every morning to the study and computer, without complaining about the time. We start the day together in a most companionable way over cups of Earl Grey tea; the cats have yum-yums. Their sometimes intrusive and humorous demands for affection lighten my day.

Laura McCaffrey, at the Allen County Library, cheerfully locates obscure research books for me. Rebecca Haarer, who is the owner of Arts and Antiques in Shipshewana, Indiana, as well as an Amish quilt collector and Amish culture consultant, has been a constant help in the preparation of this text and its photography, as was Marge Stock, at the Inn at Honey Run. Alexandra Avakian, whose photographs appeared in *Cooking from Quilt Country*, was again available to work with us. Knowing her has enriched my life and my work. Chris Tomasino, my agent, steers me through the business complexities of publishing, and miraculously stays calm and cheerful. Friends Elaine and Cliff Shultz graciously assisted with out-of-town guests, which I so appreciated.

At Clarkson Potter, I am so lucky to have had Pam Krauss as my editor for all five of my books. She is a good friend and so very skilled. Could there be such a thing as a female Max Perkins? If so, that is what Pam is. Jill Armus is responsible for the very handsome layout.

At Maryland Public Television, in Owings Mills, I have been privileged to work with John Potthast, Margaret Sullivan, John Alan Spoller, Marlene Rodman, and Gordon Masters to bring the haunting images and food style of another culture to the television audience. Friend and food stylist Lois Hamilton was, as always, an important part of bringing the recipes to the screen. Bruce Chaney collects and researches all the marvelous antiques we use at the end of every show; he truly finds treasures to share with the viewers.

To all, as they say at the Academy Awards, "thank you, thank you so very much." Over and over again.

[Introduction]

❖

WHEN COOKING FROM Quilt Country was published in 1989, the first printing was 15,000 copies, an ambitious quantity for such an esoteric subject. However, something about this book's subject and recipes captured the interest of the cooks and collectors. Now, eleven printings later, interest in these isolated farm communities dotted across just twenty-one states seems to grow day by day. It's apparent the public is fascinated by the Amish and their culture, and likes their uncomplicated, provincial recipes.

People ask me why a cookbook describing a small rural religious group that fearlessly consumes three hearty meals a day and never counts a calorie or fat gram would be so popular in today's health-conscious climate. I offer several reasons. First, it was timing; many recipes published in food magazines, newspapers, and cookbooks had become a tad impractical for the home cook in charge of preparing family meals. That person no longer had the time or willingness to run about to four separate supermarkets looking for exotic ingredients. The public wanted simpler recipes. Second, there were lots of mutterings about the cute, overpriced food being served in restaurants; our jaded palates longed for food that was statisfying and familiar. Third, few among the new generation of cooks

have had the opportunity to learn about cookery from the oral tradition, as was common before dispersal of extended families and working mothers became widespread. In the last few decades, many family recipes were lost because no one prepared them. Today, many people remember tapioca pudding and pot roast as satisfying, easy-to-prepare dishes but can't find a recipe that matches their memories. I've been overwhelmed by the letters I've received from grateful cooks who've finally been able to re-create the meals they ate with parents and grandparents.

Most important, though, the simplicity of Amish life seems ever more appealing as our daily life becomes increasingly peculiar. Random violence happens anywhere, and there is little any of us can do personally about acid rain, chemical pollution of our environment, drug dealers, or political situations in countries with new names. We yearn for that period in our lives when the populace seemed a bit more stable, our children seemed safer, and we seemed more in control of our lives. The nineteenth-century folkways of the Amish and their recipes are nostalgic reminders of what seems to many of us a better time in America.

For nearly a decade now, the trend was and is to retreat into the sanctuary of our homes. And for a little while, in the privacy of our kitchens and dining rooms, through food and recipes from our past, we can evoke better times. This accounts for the renaissance of interest in old recipes and also explains why we once again quilt, do crafts, and garden with such zeal. These are creative pursuits that reestablish us as rational human beings and foster family traditions.

OPPOSITE: **Amish come from miles around to attend local auctions. Auctions are combined business and social outings, enjoyed by the whole family, even the tots.**

To gather the recipes and stories collected in this book, my husband Dick and I once again took to the road, this time widening our travels to include Amish and Mennonite communities outside of Indiana and Ohio. When we revisited some of the sights we chronicled in *Cooking from Quilt Country*, we were immediately struck by the changes that had taken place in the past ten years. With their belief that they must live separately, that they are stewards of God's earth, it is to be expected the Amish will always manage to live on the land. But as farmland prices escalate and with encroaching urbanization, the Amish with their large families are finding it more and more difficult to survive on a farm that averages only ninety acres. The goal of every Amish farmer is to provide a farm for each of his sons, thus ensuring that their families will carry on Amish traditions. Achieving this is becoming harder and harder—and in some cases, impossible. Many have stopped farming altogether, becoming entrepreneurs and creating their own successful small businesses. They still live on the land, but they are a people in transition. As they now try to achieve a profit, the question is: Can they also retain their culture?

My interviews with the Amish people were always enlightening and fascinating. In some cases, I had names of scribes—those people who write weekly news columns for *The Budget*, the very popular Amish and Old Order Mennonite newspaper. I would call on them first, and they in turn referred me to others who would allow themselves to be interviewed. You will find quotes from columns in *The Budget*, with the names and communities changed, used throughout this book. Their own words express the diversity and richness of their lives.

I was told once, "You should see Elizabeth Zook; she likes to talk." I would come to discover my best sources were always those women who liked to talk! No one ever refused to share recipes with me, but of course food is very nonthreatening—unless you don't have any; then there is apt to be a war. But that is another story.

The recipes in the pages that follow show that twentieth-century influences have begun to make inroads in Amish cooking, as the women are beginning to use some of the convenience foods so many "English" cooks rely on. But most of them pointed out that they used very little store-bought food, for they considered it too costly when they could raise and preserve their own.

The recipes in this book are authentic, just as I found them. In some cases, if I felt the addition of an herb truly enhanced the dish, I added it, but I've also indicated that the ingredient is optional when it was not in the original recipe. Since I wanted to avoid duplication of recipes used in the first book, there are no recipes for mush, noodles, funeral pie, and the like. If you can't find an Amish or Mennonite recipe you'd like in this book, check the earlier one. I have not attempted a low-fat, low-sugar Amish cookbook; as a culinary historian, I believe the recipes should be published as they are cooked and enjoyed today. The average Amish farmer expends nearly 8,000 calories a day, and his spouse, around 4,000; their bodies obviously burn a lot more calories than ours do. Of course, there are ways to lower the fat and sugar content in these recipes, and I hope the reader will feel free to do so. These recipes are not holy writ; they are suggestions and guides. Change as you please, with my blessing.

And with my interest—indeed, passion—for saving old recipes for posterity, I did want to save these old, unusual recipes that I discovered, as strange as some of them may sound to our English ears. These women cook from an oral tradition and don't record most of their recipes; with Amish culture evermore threatened by the increasing contact with their English neighbors and the inevitable crossover of cooking trends, I felt a renewed sense of urgency to publish this collection. I hope that by preparing them for your family and loved ones you may create in your home the comforting sense of tradition, harmony, and the love of the land that is such a palpable presence in every Amish and Mennonite home I've visited.

Essen gut! Eat good!

[Brief History of the Amish and Mennonites]

❖

BOTH THE "PLAIN PEOPLE," as the Amish call themselves, and the Mennonites were part of the Church of the Brethren and have roots in the Swiss Anabaptist movement that began in 1525 during the Protestant Reformation. Their leader was an ordained Dutch priest, Menno Simons, and his followers were known as Mennonites. They believed in separation of church and state and in adult baptism. Dressing simply, rejecting worldly trappings, they were also against taking political oaths and remain pacifists to this day.

In 1693, Joseph Ammann, a Swiss Mennonite elder who thought the church congregations were straying from the purity of their original philosophy, broke away from the Mennonites and formed his own group, later called the Amish. Ammann and his followers migrated to Alsace Lorraine in France and there the group flourished.

When we look at engravings of the clothes of this period, it is obvious that the unadorned fashions favored by the Amish have changed little since that time. Nor has their horse and buggy transportation and their avoidance of most of society. To them, society at large is lumped collectively under one word,

the "English," meaning anyone outside their faith.

Ammann believed that by their austere lifestyle the Amish could best fulfill the Scripture that teaches that true believers should be separate from the world. Today the Amish are still more conservative than the Mennonites, worshiping in their houses and rejecting electricity and automobiles.

Because of widespread religious persecution in Europe, an invitation in the 1800s from William Penn to come to Pennsylvania was a godsend. Today, Pennsylvania is home to the second largest group of Amish in the world. The Holmes County area in Ohio is the largest, and the third largest group is in northern Indiana. Other Amish and Mennonite settlements are scattered over nineteen other states and abroad.

Rules of conduct are strictly codified. Amish businesses are always closed on Sundays, and they observe some Christian holidays on dates other than those chosen by other religious orders. Many Amish celebrate "Old Christmas" on January 6 instead of December 25. Many of their traditions come from a literal interpretation of the Bible and the verses, "Be not conformed to this world" and "Be not equally yoked together with unbelievers."

Vistiors to an Amish house will notice the absence of mirrors; any large ones attached to dressers may be partially covered, as physical vanity is frowned upon. Rag dolls (*lumba babba*) are made without faces, and there are no pictures of people in an Amish home because of the Bible verse from Exodus, Chapter 20: "Thou should not make unto thee any graven images of any likeness or anything that is not in heaven above or that is on the earth beneath or that is in the water under the earth."

The Amish conduct church services every two

weeks in their homes, on a rotating basis, hence the term "house Amish" for Old Order Amish. This practice dates back to Europe in the 1700s, when the Amish were subject to religious persecution. Rather than come together in one designated meeting place, where they might be captured by troops who would imprison and torture religious dissidents, they moved from home to home for safety.

Ministers are chosen by lot from the male membership, though the women do have a vote concerning church matters. Three-hour-long services are conducted in German and include scriptural readings, preaching, hymn singing, and prayer. No collection plate is passed and no records are kept. Both the Amish and the Mennonites reject infant baptism and are conscientious objectors, though the Mennonites find alternate service opportunities through the Mennonite Central Committee and serve two- to three-year assignments in more than fifty countries.

I do not want to leave the impression that the Amish and Mennonites live a utopian life. They face harsh realities like the rest of us—illness, financial reversals, worries concerning children—but they handle these problems within their sustaining group with a unified code of reactions. To the Amish, our life is bewildering and threatening because we have so many choices. These people insist on a stability other societies might find shackling. However, when baptized as adults and entering the church, they recognize the compromise, the tradeoff, if you will, that they have made. To those of us who exist in English society, which loves change and eagerly anticipates new trends, the Amish culture can seem unrealistically static.

Today, the Amish as a whole are also a culture in transition, though this might not be obvious at first to the casual eye. Entrepreneurs and artisans are becoming more and more visible in their rural communities, developing new businesses in order to survive the shrinking of affordable and available farmland. Many young people will apprentice in established shops, then start up their own businesses

when they marry. Moses Knepp, in Sherman, New York, started out making plain buggies for fellow Amish people, but rapidly expanded his business after the City of New York hired him to make the decorative horse-drawn carriages we see lined up at the entrance of Central Park, near the Plaza Hotel.

"You know, these special buggies are so pretty when they are finished, I almost hate to sell them," he laughs. He also fills orders for Mackinaw Island and the Ringling Brothers Circus. He has eight employees (all part-time); his wife oversees the upholstery production, assisted by two grown daughters and two friends. One corner of the workshop is strewn with faceless dolls and small wooden animals; the mothers bring their tots with them when they come to work.

Getting good help for these small Amish businesses is not difficult and the problems of absenteeism, alcohol, and drug use are nonexistent. The work ethic is strong and positive; slackers in the workplace are frowned upon.

No wonder so many of us look at the Amish and Mennonite lives with respect and a degree of longing. They have been able to keep intact the very values so many of us revere. Hardworking, thrifty, kind, and supportive of one another, with tightly knit loyal families, they seem to be an island of sanity in our crazy world. They have a strong consciousness of their unity and identity through their religion, customs, and language. Their culture is a commonwealth. And it works—for them.

As I drive back to the city in the winter's pink twilight, I muse that my own interest in the Amish, their lifestyle, and their recipes never abates. Constantly changing and evolving, they have always been part of my life. And I know they always will be. Working with them and writing about them has always been a most satisfying privilege.

After a successful day at the auction, an Amish couple returns home for supper.

[Some Notes on Techniques, Ingredients, Cookware]

❖

IN THE RECIPES THAT FOLLOW, you will notice I have suggested some very non-Amish tech-niques—such as using electrical ap-pliances like the food processor and microwave, which speed up the prepa-ration process for non-Amish cooks. In other cases, I suggest some appliances that you might not have in your kitchen for space reasons, such as electric skillets and slow cookers. In those instances, I have given alternative instructions.

I often suggest using a sauté pan; these deep frying pans with lids are extremely versatile and time-saving —my favorite obsession. The pans can be used for steaming, sautéing, braising, or roasting, all in the same pan, and they are also deep enough for prepar-ing sauces. I have both the 10- and 11-inch size.

Times given for cooking in the oven may be slightly different for you, for all stoves have their own temperature idiosyncracies; all of these recipes were tested with electric appliances. Also, the varia-tion in utensils makes a great difference in the way heat is conducted. Do invest in a good set of cooking and baking pans; it will make such a difference in your pleasure in cooking, not to mention the food itself. Restaurant supply houses are a good source

for sturdy, long-lasting, and economical cookware.

One item that I especially like to use is a cookie scoop, which comes in various sizes. These truly speed up the process of dropping cookies and are ideal for many other uses such as muffins, mashed potato patties, and fritters. An aluminum pastry fork (available at Yoder's, in Kidron, Ohio; see Mail-Order Directory, page 286) is perfect for cutting fats into flour; there are times when the food processor just doesn't give me the texture I want. This slanted-tined heavy-duty fork is also ideal for mashing strawberries and blueberries just a bit, to release the juices. Actu-ally, I use this fork a lot, for many things.

For baking, using parchment paper to line baking sheets also is my preference. The paper can be used for several batches and the cookies never stick. Parchment paper is now available in most supermarkets and at baking specialty supply stores. For greasing pans and baking dishes, I now use the nonstick cooking sprays; again, they cut down on motion and save time.

An instant-read thermometer is a terrific boon for the bread baker. The old technique of knocking on the bread and hoping for a hollow sound to indicate that the bread is done has never been totally fool-proof. Instead, insert an instant-read thermometer into the bread when it is presumably finished baking; if it registers 200°F., the bread is indeed done.

My favorite timer is the Terrillon model that is to be worn around the neck; it has saved me from many a disaster. It is available through my newsletter (page 286).

As for cooling most cakes and some breads, I use an old-fashioned way, but it assures a very moist cake. As soon as you take the cake out of the oven, cover it with foil, then a heavy terry cloth towel. Let it cool completely. The steam caused by the covering will help give you a moist cake every time.

In a couple of recipes, lard is listed as an ingredient. If you simply can't tolerate that, substitute butter. The flavor and texture won't be quite the same, but the recipe will be very good, nonetheless. I also use butter-flavored shortening in many of my pastry crusts, as do the Amish, who appreciate the economy and convenience of this product. However, if you want true authenticity, use butter. The other ingredients you'll encounter in these recipes are quite uncontroversial.

To ensure the best possible results for your efforts in the kitchen, be sure to read through the recipe from the beginning to the end before you start preparation. Be careful to observe if there is divided usage of any of the listed ingredients, which will be indicated in the body of the recipe. Do measure ingredients accurately; this is most important for baking. "Approximate" isn't good enough. And if you see you are running short of an ingredient, write it down immediately on the weekly shopping list so you won't be caught short the next time.

If baking, preheat the oven at least 10 minutes for best results. When creaming fats and sugars together, first beat or whip the fat a few seconds to further break it down (it is generally at room temperature, unless otherwise instructed), then *gradually* add the sugar. Dumping in the sugar all at once will not give you a smooth, creamy emulsion.

To ensure that the bottom crust of a pie is baked thoroughly, the slash in the top crust should have bubbles of juice or filling coming up through it, or the top of a one-crust pie should show bubbles on the surface. This indicates the heat within the pie has reached the maximum temperature to thicken the pectin or eggs and the bottom crust is thoroughly baked. If the crust is getting too brown, "tent" or cover the pie very lightly with a piece of foil that completely covers the pie, but still lets the hot air into the pie itself.

Occasionally an Amish recipe will call for Milnot.

In this canned milk product, vegetable oil replaces the milkfat found in whole milk, removing the saturated fat and cholesterol. The product still performs well in baking because there is fat present, producing a creamy moist product. One of the company's slogans was "If cows could, they'd give Milnot." The product was developed in the 1930s and is available today, mostly in the Midwest. It can be ordered by the case (you also pay the postage) from the Milnot company in St. Louis. Call (314) 436-7667 and ask for customer service.

Above all, when cooking don't worry about achieving perfection. These recipes have been carefully written to move you through the preparation with ease and reassurance, trying to anticipate every question a cook might have about them. And most of the imperfections or failures (if you have any) will be unnoticeable (if you don't mention it) and are still quite edible. Cooking, like tennis, improves with practice. And I personally think it's a lot more fun.

WEIGHTS OF COMMON INGREDIENTS

INGREDIENT	WEIGHT PER CUP
All-purpose flour, sifted	5 ounces
Butter or solid shortening	8 ounces
Cake flour, sifted	3½ ounces
Cheese, grated	4 ounces
Honey	12 ounces
Nuts, coarsely chopped	4 ounces
Sugar, granulated	7 ounces
Sugar, brown, packed	7½ ounces
Sugar, confectioner's	4 ounces

OVERLEAF: An August early-morning fog presents a surreal landscape.

GOOD
MORNING
[G U D M A R Y E]

❖

IN THE BEGINNING, there is an early mist shrouding the landscape. Then the sun rises, the mist burns away, and the world is still for a short time. The air is intoxicating with the mingled fragrance of the wild roses, violets, and lilies of the valley. Gold finches begin trilling in the cherry trees; the roosters crow. In the haymows, the cats sleepily stretch. In the still damp garden, a pair of robins dip and dart for worms between the rows, stopping, stretching their necks, listening, then move quickly on, dipping and darting again. The orchard is like the psalmist's joy that "cometh in the morning," as the birds fill the trees in a concert of song. Cardinals serenade with the tit-mice, and wrens join in. This time of day, there is magical light and sound on the farm, and all things are possible.

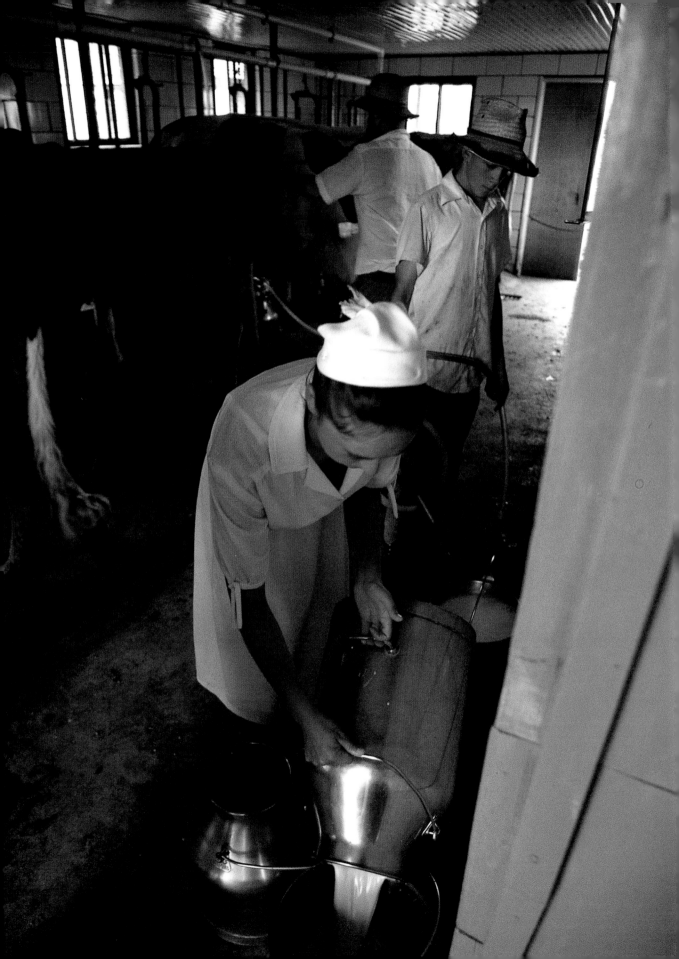

1
FAMILY
BREAKFAST

Golden Brown Sautéed Yellow Corncakes ❖ Nutty Nutritious Granola ❖ Baked Oatmeal Porridge ❖ Swiss Oatmeal with Dates and Honey ❖ Breakfast Cornmeal Pudding ❖ Creamed Eggs on Toast ❖ Country Grits with Eggs on Top ❖ Pepper-Coated Breakfast Bacon ❖ Quick Amish Panhaus (Scrapple) ❖ Pecan Cinnamon Biscuits ❖ Sautéed Apples and Onions ❖ Mustard Fruit Bake ❖ Apricot Almond Coffee Cake ❖ Mrs. Miller's Breakfast Crumb Pie ❖ Mrs. Klob's Coffee Cake ❖ Raised Raisin Coffee Cake

THE CHORES, THE CHORES. For an Amish farmer and his family, the chores are with them always and never ending. It is impossible to ignore a barn full of cows impatient to be milked, a pen of pigs snuffing and snorting about for corn, or a chicken coop filled with clucking birds who skitter up and down in front of the windows, waiting

for their buckets of feed. To the Amish, these creatures are part of God's kingdom and are their responsibility. Even the thought of skipping chores is a luxury no farmer can afford.

However, there are tangible compensations for this daunting workload. Their isolated rural lifestyle enables these hardworking people to pursue their religious family life and to live in a community that shares their beliefs. They have a genuine affection for their animals, even allowing themselves a bit of worldly pride in their horses. The fragrant hay-filled barns in August, the groaning cribs of corn, the inevitable batch of spring kittens that romp about the yard and barns, the calls and swoops of the martens as they dive about their

FROM 'THE BUDGET'
SPRING ISSUE

The martens are back from their winter quarters. The first scouts arrived on Tuesday, the third. I don't class myself as a bird watcher, but their annual arrival is always a blessing, sort of a benediction of the spring season.

—MIDDLEFIELD, OH

birdhouses—all of these contribute to a satisfying farm life and provide a setting for a family that functions well within the community.

"It's hard to roll out of bed in the winter at 4:30 or 5:00 A.M., I'll admit," shrugs Ezra Miller. "But after a lifetime of farming, I don't bother thinking about it too much. It has to be done, so get it done, and you don't have to worry about it, I tell the boys."

Ezra's family of three teenage sons and four daughters is typical of the Amish today. The boys all bicycle into the nearby town of Berlin, Ohio, to work in the RV (recreational vehicle) factories. If the weather is really bad, the factory sends around a mini-van to pick them up. Three of the girls also work in Berlin, two in a large Mennonite restaurant that serves Amish food and the other as a companion to an older "English" lady. The restaurant picks up all three girls at 6:30 A.M. and they won't return until after 3:00 P.M. The

PRECEDING PAGE: At milking time, the whole family pitches in to help. Most milk from Amish farms is sold to local cheese makers.

youngest daughter, Ruth, is physically disabled and remains at home with her mother, Naomi. The work on this ninety-acre farm is done by all the men, with the girls pitching in when necessary, such as during threshing season.

Naomi gets up about a half-hour after her husband. "He likes to be by himself when he first gets up," she says, "and that's fine with me. He makes a big pot of coffee, has a cup while he reads a bit in the New Testament, then goes out to the barns. The boys come down next, have their coffee, and go out too, then we girls come down and start our day."

Wash day begins early, even before sunrise, and in the Lancaster area the clothesline, which is on a pulley, stretches seventy-five feet or more from the house to the barn. It is pulled up on a steep angle, low at the house, then up at least forty feet at the barn end; this gets the drying clothes up and out of the way and the buggies can drive underneath without getting tangled in the wet wash. In Amish settlements everywhere it's common to see long lines of washing, dark pants, pastel dresses, and white aprons dancing in the winds as they dry.

The beds are made, the bedrooms' and living and dining rooms' hardwood floors are dust-mopped, and enough coal is carried in from the back porch to last the day and keep the big pot-bellied stove in the living room stoked, as well as the black iron cooking stove, which was in use during my wintertime visit.

> The farmers are plowing and getting ready to sow alfalfa. Also dairy setups are being built yet this spring. Abe Hershberger finished concreting in the barn and plans to get cows on Saturday.
> **—PARADISE, PA**

> Today was a nice sunny day after yesterday's rain, then snow all day. Temperature is 42° and will likely go lower overnight, which makes good maple sugaring.
> **—SALEM, IN**

In the summer months, it stands idle and the cooking is done on the bottled-gas stove in the adjoining summer kitchen. "The women decided that if the men could have propane gas in the barn to help them milk the cows, the women could have it in the house," laughs Naomi.

Breakfast is ready by 6:00 A.M. and the men return from the barns, still carrying kerosene lanterns to light their way; in the winter months it won't be light until close to 7:00 A.M.

Naomi likes to cook, so breakfast is always generous. "Corn flakes in the morning just isn't enough to last this bunch until noon," she insists. Scrambled eggs with ham or bacon along with granola or oatmeal made from scratch is considered a quick meal. Most Amish families still raise a few chickens so they can be assured of fresh eggs year-round without having to use store-bought eggs, an almost unheard-of extravagance if you live on a farm. If you are accustomed to eggs from chickens on a natural diet, it is hard to accept commercially produced eggs. Sometimes there are pancakes or fried mush topped with the Millers' own maple syrup. And there is always thick toast made from homemade bread, slathered with jam or honey from a neighbor's hive. After breakfast and Bible reading, the fortified young people leave for their work among the "English" and Naomi, Ezra, and Ruth, aided by her walker, begin their day.

Golden Brown Sautéed Yellow Corncakes

Makes 32 small pancakes or 6 generous servings

YOU'LL HAVE REQUESTS for this recipe, a delightful golden pancake with a distinct corn flavor. The pancakes absorb quite a bit of oil during frying, so we skip the butter and just serve them with maple syrup or molasses. This recipe is from a Mennonite community in Bruceton, Tennessee.

> 1 1/3 cups buttermilk, at room temperature
> 1 teaspoon baking soda
> 3/4 cup yellow cornmeal
> 1/4 cup all-purpose flour
> 1 teaspoon salt
> 1 teaspoon sugar
> 1 egg
> 1 tablespoon corn oil or melted bacon fat
> Corn oil, for skillet or griddle

In a 2-cup measure, whisk together the buttermilk and baking soda, then set aside for 5 minutes; it will foam up. In a medium mixing bowl, whisk together the cornmeal, flour, salt, and sugar. In a large mixing bowl, beat the egg slightly and stir in the oil. Add the buttermilk mixture and combine well. Add the dry ingredients all at once and beat until blended with a rotary beater or electric mixer. The batter will be very thin.

Preheat an electric skillet to 360–375° F. or heat a griddle over medium-high heat and lightly grease. Drop in the batter by heaping tablespoons and cook the pancakes for 1 to 1 1/2 minutes on the first side, or until the pancake batter begins to bubble on the top. With a metal spatula, flip the cake and cook the other side for 1 minute or until the bottom is lightly browned.

Remove to a heated platter, cover lightly with foil, and repeat until all of the batter is used. Serve the corncakes hot with syrup.

Most Amish housewives will wash twice a week, and the clothes are dried outside, even in cold weather.

Nutty Nutritious Granola

Makes 2 quarts

GRANOLA HAS REPLACED homemade graham nuts as the cold cereal of choice in many Amish homes, and this nut-heavy version is especially good; it is a best-seller at the roadside stand where I first tasted it. Amish families buy all of the ingredients at a local bulk food store, making six batches at a time in a large dish pan reserved for that purpose. Serve the granola with milk and sliced bananas.

> 6 cups old-fashioned oats (not instant or
>   quick-cooking)
> ¾ cup coarsely chopped English walnuts
> ¾ cup whole almonds
> ¼ cup light or dark brown sugar, packed
> 1 cup sesame seeds
> 1 cup sunflower seeds
> ½ cup vegetable oil
> ½ cup honey

■ Preheat the oven to 350° F. In a large bowl, combine the oats, walnuts, almonds, brown sugar, sesame seeds, and sunflower seeds. In a small bowl, whisk together the oil and honey. Drizzle the honey mixture over the cereal and combine well.

■ Transfer the mixture to 2 jelly-roll pans coated with nonstick spray, and spread out evenly. Bake the granola for 10 minutes, stir, and bake 10 more minutes. Remove from the oven and stir again. Cool completely, break up larger pieces, if necessary, and store in an airtight container.

NOTE: Nuts and seeds turn rancid if stored at room temperature any length of time, so you might want to freeze any extra granola if it is not to be eaten within a week or two.

Baked Oatmeal Porridge

Serves 6

IT'S RECIPES LIKE THESE that cause me to so admire Amish cooks who can create something really delicious and unusual by combining the simple ingredients they (and we) all have in the pantry in different ways. This is one of the best hot cereals I've tried; the baked oatmeal is quite firm and nutty, and the warm milk accompaniment is important. I first saw this being prepared by a cook in Charlotte Hall, Maryland. It was baked in a large, deep black roasting pan, and made enough to serve eighteen people. Warm milk was passed around the blue and white checkered oilcloth-covered table in ironstone pitchers. Note: this recipe must be started the night before.

> ⅓ cup butter
> 2 eggs
> ¾ cup dark brown sugar, packed
> 1½ teaspoons baking powder
> 1½ teaspoons vanilla extract
> 1 teaspoon grated nutmeg
> ¼ teaspoon salt
> 1 cup plus 2 tablespoons milk
> 3 cups quick-cooking oats (not instant)
>   Warm milk, for serving

■ Melt the butter and set aside. Grease a 1½-quart casserole, and drop in the eggs. Beat slightly. Add the brown sugar, baking powder, vanilla, nutmeg, and salt. Mix well, making sure there are no brown sugar lumps. Whisk in the melted butter and milk, then stir in the oats. Cover and refrigerate overnight.

■ Preheat the oven to 350° F. Uncover the oatmeal and bake for 35 minutes or until the top is brown. Remove from the oven, transfer to serving dishes (or let diners serve themselves), and pass warmed milk.

Swiss Oatmeal with Dates and Honey

Serves 6

CHEWY DATES, ORANGE JUICE, and honey dress up this basic cereal, and it is really appealing. The recipe came to me from a Swiss Mennonite woman who says it is served as a cold cereal in the summer and as an alternative to hot oatmeal in colder weather. I did try it that way, but prefer to reheat it with milk in the microwave for a couple of minutes.

This is a wonderful way to start the day, and I admit, I sometimes have a small bowl late in the afternoon for a shot of extra energy. It does need to stand overnight in the refrigerator, so plan accordingly.

> 3 cups plus $^1/_3$ cup quick-cooking oats
>   (not instant)
> 1$^3/_4$ cups plus 2 tablespoons milk
> 1$^1/_4$ cups chopped dates or raisins
> $^3/_4$ cup orange juice
> $^1/_3$ cup honey or molasses
> $^1/_4$ teaspoon salt
>   Milk, for serving

In a large mixing bowl, combine all of the ingredients. Cover tightly and refrigerate overnight or up to 4 days. Scoop into cereal dishes and serve cold with milk, or reheat individual servings in the microwave for 2 minutes with additional milk.

Breakfast Cornmeal Pudding

Serves 4 to 6

THIS IS ONE of the creamiest, most warming of the Amish and Mennonite hot breakfast cereals. The cornmeal is cooked in milk and honey, and just before serving, beaten eggs are added. Topped with more milk, it makes a healthy, happy way to start the day.

I have made this with frozen egg substitute, skim milk, and reduced-fat butter and it works perfectly. Alas, it does not reheat perfectly—a bit lumpy, I'm afraid, though I have been known to reheat leftovers in the microwave with milk, and ignore the lumps. Don't try to fry this as you would mush; it simply won't work.

> $^1/_2$ cup honey or sugar
> $^1/_2$ teaspoon salt
> 3 tablespoons butter
> 4 cups milk
> 1 cup yellow cornmeal
> 3 eggs
>   Milk, for serving

In a large saucepan, combine the honey, salt, butter, and 3 cups of the milk. Bring to a boil over medium heat. Meanwhile, in a small bowl, whisk together the cornmeal and remaining 1 cup milk. Add the cornmeal mixture gradually to the milk mixture, whisking smooth. Reduce the heat to low, cover, and cook, whisking occasionally, for 5 minutes.

In a small bowl, beat the eggs. Stir 1 cup of the hot cornmeal into the eggs and whisk smooth. Gradually stir the cornmeal-egg mixture back into the saucepan. Cover, and cook on low heat for 5 more minutes. Ladle into serving bowls and serve immediately with milk.

Creamed Eggs on Toast

Serves 6

EGGS RAISED ON AMISH farms have a full, rich flavor and deep yellow-orange yolks due to the healthy diet of greens, bugs, and grains the chickens enjoy.

Some Amish cooks will store extra eggs in the root cellar, first coating the unwashed eggs with petroleum jelly. This seals the pores of the egg-shell, keeping air out and flavor and moisture in. Eggs prepared in this way are sometimes kept for six months; however, the yolks will be apt to break and the whites are runnier.

Do make this recipe with fresh eggs. Though it is considered a breakfast dish in the country, we often have it for Sunday night supper.

> 6 tablespoons ($^3/_4$ stick) butter
> 2 tablespoons minced onion
> $^1/_4$ cup plus 2 tablespoons all-purpose flour
> $^1/_2$ teaspoon salt

> Scant $^1/_2$ teaspoon white pepper
> $^1/_4$ teaspoon grated nutmeg
> 4 cups milk
> 12 thin slices toast, buttered
> 6 hard-cooked eggs
> Paprika
> Finely minced fresh parsley

■ Melt the butter in a large, heavy saucepan. Add the onion and sauté over medium heat until translucent, about 3 minutes. Whisk in the flour all at once, and cook and stir until the flour bubbles up thoroughly in the bottom of the pan. Stir in the salt, pepper, and nutmeg, then add the milk all at once. Continue cooking and whisking over medium-low heat until the mixture thickens. Remove from the heat.

■ Meanwhile, place 1 slice of toast in the middle of each of 6 dinner plates. Cut the remaining 6 slices in half diagonally, and place the halves on either side of each whole slice. Slice an egg and arrange over each whole toast slice. Top with the white sauce, sprinkle with a bit of paprika and parsley, and serve immediately.

BELOW: The chickens eagerly await their breakfast.

Country Grits with Eggs on Top

Serves 6

THOUGH THIS RECIPE is most often served at breakfast time in southern Amish communities, I also present it as a meat accompaniment, omitting the egg and the milk topping (the amount of bacon could also be halved for this version). The bacon and the grits base can be prepared in advance, making it a very convenient dish to prepare as well.

12 *slices regular or turkey bacon*
1 *cup quick-cooking grits*
4 *cups water*
1 *teaspoon salt*
$\frac{1}{4}$ *teaspoon coarsely ground black pepper*
$\frac{1}{2}$ *cup (1 stick) butter, cut into 8 pieces*
1 *cup grated extra-sharp Cheddar cheese*
8 *eggs*
$\frac{3}{4}$ *cup milk or cream*
   Paprika

Fry the bacon until crisp and drain well on paper towels. With scissors, cut the bacon into 1-inch pieces and set aside. Cook the grits with the water, salt, and pepper according to package directions. Whisk in the butter and cheese, and continue cooking the mixture over low heat until the butter and cheese have melted. Remove the grits from the heat and allow to stand, covered, for 10 minutes.

Meanwhile, preheat the oven to 350°F. In a small bowl, beat 2 of the eggs. Add the eggs to the slightly cooled grits and transfer the mixture to a greased 2-quart casserole. For a breakfast dish, sprinkle the chopped bacon over the grits. Beat the remaining 6 eggs and milk and pour over the bacon. Drift paprika over the top. Bake for 50 to 55 minutes, or until the top of the mixture is a deep golden brown and slightly puffed. If using this as a meat accompaniment, stir the bacon into the grits, sprinkle with paprika, and bake for 40 to 45 minutes, omitting the additional eggs and milk.

BELOW: Livestock is available at local auctions.

Pepper-Coated Breakfast Bacon

Serves 4 to 6

DREDGING BACON IN MILK and peppered flour before sautéing gives this breakfast staple a whole new lease on life. It is important, however, to use a thick-sliced bacon (sometimes called country-style); if it's not available at your grocery store, you can order it from a meat market, or buy slab bacon and slice your own. I must say, this recipe spoils one for regular bacon. Count on 2 pieces per person conservatively, or 3, more realistically. The bacon doesn't shrink, and it's an outstanding addition to BLTs.

$^1/_2$ to 1 cup milk
1 cup all-purpose flour
$^3/_4$ teaspoon coarsely ground black pepper
1 pound thick-sliced bacon (12 to 13 strips)
1 tablespoon vegetable oil

◼ Pour the milk into a shallow dish. Combine the flour and pepper on a plate or piece of wax paper. Dip the bacon first into the milk, then dredge it in the flour mixture, covering the bacon completely.

◼ Heat the oil in a large skillet over medium-high heat. Add the bacon, 4 strips at a time, and fry about 3 minutes per side, turning with tongs. Because of the flour coating, the bacon does not pop or spatter while frying; it will be very crispy and golden brown. Remove to paper towels to drain and keep it warm in a 200°F. oven while frying the remainder. Serve immediately.

Quick Amish Panhaus

SCRAPPLE

Serves 6

IF YOU LIKE FRIED MUSH, you are very apt to like panhaus, a traditional breakfast dish of cornmeal, sausage, and a touch of buckwheat and liverwurst, which is sliced and fried like mush. The term "panhaus" is used interchangeably with "scrapple." The Amish have stripped this rather time-consuming dish down to a minimum of steps and ingredients, and it is still a hearty, satisfying breakfast entree. Serve it with bacon, if desired, and, of course, maple syrup, or even honey or sorghum. This can be made several days in advance before sautéing.

5 cups water
$^3/_4$ teaspoon salt
$^1/_2$ teaspoon freshly ground black pepper
2 cups yellow cornmeal
$^1/_3$ cup all-purpose flour
$^2/_3$ cup finely chopped braunschweiger or liverwurst, at room temperature
$^1/_3$–$^1/_2$ cup corn oil, for frying

◼ In a very deep saucepan, bring the water, salt, and pepper to a boil. Whisk the cornmeal and flour together in a small bowl. When the water comes to a rolling boil, very gradually sift in the cornmeal by hand, whisking all the while. In the beginning it will be quite foamy. Turn the heat down to medium. As the mixture thickens, use a wooden spoon for stirring. When all of the cornmeal has been added, turn the heat to low, and gradually beat in the braunschweiger until combined; don't worry if the pieces do not completely dissolve. Cook the mixture over the lowest heat for 10 minutes, stirring vigorously now and then.

◼ Transfer the mixture to a greased 9 × 5-inch loaf pan, and allow the loaf to cool uncovered. Transfer to the refrigerator and chill completely, then cover tightly with foil. (Any condensation will water down the mixture and it won't hold together properly when fried.) Refrigerate the loaf overnight.

◼ To serve, preheat an electric skillet to 375°F. or a sauté pan over medium-high heat. Tip the loaf out onto a cutting board and cut into 1-inch slices. Add 1$^1/_2$ to 2 tablespoons cooking oil to the pan, and with a spatula, transfer 4 to 6 slices to the hot fat; do not crowd the pan. Sauté for 5 minutes on one side, then flip and sauté 3 minutes longer, until the panhaus is a crusty, irresistible brown and gold. Remove to a heated platter and cover while you fry the remaining slices. Serve hot.

Pecan Cinnamon Biscuits

Makes 24 two-inch rolls

THIS IS A MOST UNUSUAL breakfast quick bread; the rich, cinnamon-fragrant rolled biscuits melt in your mouth. They are soft and tender with a caramel and nutty topping, and they are very quick to make. You may think a 2-quart pan (12 × 7 inches) sounds too small, but it works —a larger pan is too big. Trust me. And be prepared to share the recipe. Pecan extract is available at baking specialty shops.

CINNAMON BISCUITS
1 cup heavy cream
1$\frac{1}{2}$ cups all-purpose flour
4 teaspoons baking powder
$\frac{1}{2}$ teaspoon salt
2 tablespoons melted butter
2 tablespoons ground cinnamon
$\frac{1}{2}$ cup light brown sugar, packed

TOPPING
$\frac{1}{2}$ cup light brown sugar, packed
$\frac{1}{2}$ cup finely chopped pecans
2 tablespoons heavy cream
1 teaspoon vanilla extract
$\frac{1}{2}$ teaspoon pecan extract (optional)

▦ Preheat the oven to 425°F.

▦ MAKE THE BISCUITS: In a mixer bowl, whip the cream until stiff. In a small bowl, whisk together the flour, baking powder, and salt. Add to the whipping cream gradually and blend with a rubber spatula until a firm dough forms. Transfer to a lightly floured surface and knead the dough for 1 minute. Roll out the dough into a $\frac{1}{4}$-inch-thick rectangle approximately 13 × 16 inches. Using a pastry brush, spread the melted butter over the dough and sprinkle evenly with the cinnamon and brown sugar.

▦ Beginning with a long edge, roll up like a jelly roll and cut into $\frac{3}{4}$-inch slices with a serrated knife. Place close together in a greased 12 × 7-inch metal baking pan and bake for 15 minutes or until the tops of the rolls are very lightly browned.

▦ While the rolls bake, prepare the topping: In a small bowl, mix the brown sugar, pecans, cream, vanilla, and pecan extract until well blended. Remove the browned rolls from the oven and spread the top of each roll with some of the topping mixture. Return to the oven to bake for approximately 3 to 4 minutes or until the topping starts to bubble. Remove from the oven and serve warm.

Sautéed Apples and Onions

Serves 6

THIS IS A REALLY GOOD accompaniment to fried eggs and bacon for those mornings you prepare a late breakfast, but I have also served it as a partner to roast pork at dinner. I know using bacon fat is a luxury almost not to be considered, but if you dare, the smoky flavor is tops in this dish. The entire dish reheats well in the microwave.

3 tablespoons bacon fat or butter
2 large onions, thinly sliced
6 large apples, such as Jonathan or Gala, skin on, cored, and sliced $\frac{3}{8}$ inch thick
$\frac{1}{2}$ cup dark brown sugar, packed
1 teaspoon ground cinnamon
$\frac{1}{4}$ teaspoon coarsely ground black pepper
$\frac{1}{8}$ teaspoon salt (omit if using bacon fat)

▦ In a large sauté pan or deep skillet, melt the fat or butter. Add the onions and sauté over medium heat for 8 minutes, or until the onions begin to color. Add the apples to the pan atop the onions, then sprinkle on the brown sugar, cinnamon, black pepper, and salt if using; do not combine.

▦ Cover the pan, turn the heat to low, and simmer without stirring until the apples are almost tender, about 10 minutes. Uncover, raise the heat to medium (there will be a lot of juice and that must be reduced a bit), and toss the mixture lightly to combine. Continue sautéing until the apples are tender, about 10 more minutes, though that will vary from apple to apple, season to season and with the age of the apples. Serve warm.

Mustard Fruit Bake

Serves 4 to 6

THIS IS SO GOOD for any breakfast or brunch, but the Amish would serve it only for the most special of occasions, such as at holiday breakfasts or when visitors come to call. I like to add candied cherries for color, though the Amish do not. And I happen to prefer Dijon mustard to the more traditional horseradish mustard. Don't overlook this recipe for your next brunch party; serve it in an antique cut-glass bowl.

1 29-ounce can sliced peaches, drained
1 20-ounce can pineapple chunks, drained
$1/2$ cup pitted prunes, either soft or dried variety
$1/4$ cup halved candied cherries (optional)
$1/2$ cup light brown sugar, packed
$1/4$ cup ($1/2$ stick) butter
2 teaspoons Dijon or horseradish mustard
2 medium bananas, cut into 1-inch slices

▓ Preheat the oven to 350°F. In a lightly greased 8-inch square baking dish, combine the peaches, pineapple, prunes, and cherries if using; set aside. In a small saucepan, over low heat, combine the brown sugar, butter, and mustard, stirring constantly until the butter melts. Pour over the fruit and mix lightly. Bake uncovered for 45 minutes. Remove from the oven and stir in the banana slices and bake for an additional 5 minutes. Serve immediately or at room temperature.

Apricot Almond Coffee Cake

Serves 12

THIS SUPERB COFFEE CAKE is one of the fancier ones prepared by the Amish, not only to sell to the English but for themselves too, as a special treat. The almonds and apricot preserves fall to the bottom of the cake, creating a surprise layer of texture and flavor. Wrapped in foil, pieces of coffee cake might also be taken to the fields along with a thermos of coffee for a midmorning snack.

The Amish women have always worked side by side with their husbands and fathers in the fields when they were needed, but the first time I saw an Amish woman driving a tractor down a gravel road, the sight was so contrary to my image of the Amish woman, I was quite agog. But pleased. English farm women do it all the time; even I know how to drive a tractor.

1 cup (2 sticks) butter, at room temperature
2 cups sugar
2 eggs
1 cup sour cream, at room temperature
1 teaspoon almond extract
2 cups all-purpose flour
1 teaspoon baking powder
1 teaspoon ground cinnamon
$1/4$ teaspoon salt
1 cup sliced almonds
1 10-ounce jar apricot preserves

▓ Preheat the oven to 350°F. Grease and flour a Bundt pan or tube pan; set aside. In a mixer bowl, cream the butter with the sugar thoroughly, then beat in the eggs, one at a time. Stir in the sour cream and almond extract; combine.

▓ In a large mixing bowl, whisk together the flour, baking powder, cinnamon, and salt. Gradually add the dry ingredients to the butter-sugar mixture. Blend until just combined. (Don't overbeat or the cake will have holes in it when baked.) Pour one-third of the batter into the prepared pan. Sprinkle one-half of the almonds on top and smooth on one-half of the preserves. Spoon on the remaining batter and smooth the top, then top with the remaining almonds and preserves. Bake for 1 hour or until done.

▓ Remove the cake from the oven. To assure a moist coffee cake, cover the hot bread with foil and a terry cloth towel. Let it stand for 15 minutes, then remove from the pan and re-cover with the foil and towel until completely cooled. Slice into wedges and serve.

Harvesting grains is an arduous process, since the Amish do not use tractor-pulled combines. Here spelt is being shocked by hand.

Mrs. Miller's Breakfast Crumb Pie

Makes 12 wedges

WHEN I WAS A YOUNG BRIDE, I lived next to Lou Jane Miller, whose mother-in-law cooked in the old German Mennonite style. This crumb pie recipe of the elder Mrs. Miller was a family favorite for dunking at breakfast.

Like many old recipes, it has its peculiarities, for it is not a soft cake or pie. More like a firm, dark, and spicy biscuit, it was and is considered a food for dunking. And as inelegant as that sounds, it is terribly satisfying and delicious to dip the dark brown wedges in milk or coffee and nibble away. By the way, the term "dunk" is from the Pennsylvania German dialect for *dunke*, "to dip."

> 1/2 cup solid vegetable shortening
> 1 1/2 cups dark brown sugar, packed
> 1/2 teaspoon baking soda
> 3/4 teaspoon salt
> 1 1/2 teaspoons maple extract
> 1/2 cup hot water
> 3 3/4 cups all-purpose flour
> Ground cinnamon

▓ Preheat the oven to 375°F. In a mixer bowl, cream the shortening for 30 seconds, and gradually add the brown sugar. In a measuring cup, combine the baking soda, salt, extract, and hot water. Gradually add the water mixture to the sugar mixture, then add the flour a bit at a time. The dough will be soft but will not stick to your fingers.

▓ Grease a 10-inch pie or cake pan and transfer the dough to it, patting it out with your fingers; the surface should be rough and irregular on top. Sift cinnamon liberally over the top of the dough. Bake for 10 minutes, then lower the oven temperature to 350°F. and continue baking for 25 minutes more. Remove from the oven and cool (if desired) on a rack. Cut into wedges and serve with coffee, milk, or hot chocolate.

Mrs. Klob's Coffee Cake

Makes two 9-inch cakes; serves 18

THIS IS AN OUTSTANDING yeast-leavened coffee cake; warmed milk and half-and-half, which I heat in the microwave, has a lot to do with its tenderness. The dough must ripen in the refrigerator overnight, so plan accordingly.

> 3 cups all-purpose flour
> 1/2 cup (1 stick) butter
> 2 tablespoons plus 2 teaspoons granulated sugar
> 1 teaspoon salt
> 1/4 cup milk, heated to lukewarm
> 1 envelope active dry yeast
> 3 eggs, separated
> 1 cup half-and-half, heated to lukewarm

STREUSEL
> 1 1/2 cups granulated sugar
> 1 1/2 cups all-purpose flour
> 1/2 teaspoon salt
> 1 teaspoon grated nutmeg
> 3/4 cup (1 1/2 sticks) butter

ICING
> 1 1/2 cups confectioners' sugar
> 1/2 teaspoon vanilla extract
> 2–3 tablespoons warm milk

▓ In a large mixing bowl, combine the flour, butter, 2 tablespoons granulated sugar, and the salt with a pastry blender or pastry fork until the mixture resembles coarse crumbs; set aside. In a glass measuring cup, mix the warm milk with the 2 teaspoons sugar and the yeast until dissolved. Allow it to stand for 10 minutes, until the yeast is bubbly and foamy.

▓ Meanwhile, in a small bowl, beat the egg yolks (reserve the egg whites in the refrigerator) and lukewarm half-and-half together. When the yeast mixture has bubbled, pour it and the egg mixture into the flour mixture and beat well with a spoon until all the flour is mixed in. The dough will be very sticky. Cover and refrigerate overnight.

▓ The next day, grease two 9 × 9-inch baking pans. Divide the dough into 2 equal pieces and press each half into the prepared pans. (Dip your fingers in flour to keep them from sticking to the dough.) Brush the dough with the reserved egg whites; set aside.

▨ MAKE THE STREUSEL TOPPING: In a medium mixing bowl, whisk together the granulated sugar, flour, salt, and nutmeg. Using a pastry blender, cut in the butter until the mixture resembles coarse crumbs. Sprinkle evenly over the dough. Cover each pan with plastic wrap and let rise in a warm place for 45 minutes to 1 hour.

▨ Preheat the oven to 350°F. Bake the cakes for 25 minutes or until they are slightly brown around the edges. Cool slightly before removing from the pans.

▨ While the cakes cool briefly, make the icing: Mix the confectioners' sugar, vanilla and enough warm milk to make a thin frosting in a small mixing bowl. Drizzle over the warm coffee cake. Serve warm, or let cool and then reheat in the microwave for a few seconds before serving.

Raised Raisin Coffee Cake

Makes a 10-inch coffee cake; serves 8 to 10

BLUFFTON COLLEGE IN OHIO is a well-respected Mennonite college located in a strong Swiss Mennonite community. When lecturing at Bluffton, I stayed with my husband in the house that the college's home economics majors use to practice running a household and kitchen. For breakfast, we were served this moist raised coffee cake by rather terrified students—we were their first guests. They needn't have worried; the breakfast of a fresh fruit cup, eggs sunny-side up, crispy bacon, and coffee cake was just perfect.

SPONGE
2 cups all-purpose flour
1 teaspoon salt
1 cup milk, scalded and cooled to lukewarm
½ cup warm water
1 package active dry yeast
4 teaspoons granulated sugar

CAKE
1 cup (2 sticks) butter, at room temperature
2 cups granulated sugar
2 eggs
4 teaspoons milk
2 teaspoons vanilla extract
2 cups all-purpose flour
2 teaspoons baking powder
1 teaspoon ground cinnamon
1½ teaspoons grated nutmeg

¾ cup raisins, plumped (see page 270)
Confectioners' sugar

▨ Preheat the oven to 350°F. Coat a 10-inch Bundt or tube pan with nonstick cooking spray.

▨ MAKE THE SPONGE: In a large bowl, combine the flour, salt, milk, water, yeast, and granulated sugar. Mix well, cover, and let stand for 30 minutes, or until the mixture is bubbly.

▨ MEANWHILE, MAKE THE CAKE: In a large mixer bowl, at slow speed, cream the butter and granulated sugar until fluffy, about 2 minutes. Add the eggs one at a time, beating well after each addition. Add the milk and vanilla, and beat again. In a medium mixing bowl, whisk together the flour, baking powder, cinnamon, and nutmeg. Add to the sugar-butter mixture, mixing until the batter is well moistened and integrated.

▨ Add the sponge mixture, mixing only enough to incorporate, then stir in the raisins. Pour into the Bundt pan, smooth the top, and bake in the center of the oven for 50 to 60 minutes or until an instant-read thermometer registers 190°F. Remove from the oven, cover with foil and a terry cloth towel, and cool on a rack for 10 minutes. Turn the cake out of the pan, and cover again with the foil and towel. When completely cool, dust with confectioners' sugar.

NOTE: I like to drizzle a thin frosting (use the frosting in Mrs. Klob's Coffee Cake, page 26, made with a dash of vanilla extract) over this cake, then sprinkle ⅓ cup sliced almonds. Plain confectioners' sugar is also nice. This cake requires only one rising.

2
BAKING
DAY

Sauerkraut Apple Cake ❖ Amish Cake ❖ Apple Cake with Black Walnuts, Coconut, and Raisins ❖ Chop Suey Cake ❖ Mincemeat-on-the-Bottom Pumpkin Pie ❖ Applesauce Pie ❖ Buttered Toffee Apple Pie ❖ Brown Sugar Chess Pie ❖ Shoofly Pie ❖ Deep-Dish Apple Date Pie ❖ Amish Vanilla Pie (Montgomery Pie) ❖ Mighty Easy Molasses Bread ❖ Easy Onion Kuchen (Zwiwwelkuche) ❖ Kentucky Cornmeal Bread ❖ Best Ever Biscuits ❖ Four-Grain Walnut Bread ❖ One-Month Shredded Wheat Date Muffins ❖ No-Knead Country Oat and Raisin Loaf ❖ Sage Caraway Herb Bread ❖ Amish Friendship Bread

I N ALL MY interviewing and research with Amish women, I never heard one say she didn't like to bake. All of them prepare quick and yeast breads, pies, cookies, and cakes as naturally as breathing. And in enormous amounts. Many of the Amish and Mennonite families that migrated to the

United States have lived in wheat belts—those areas of the country where grains flourish.

Mennonites from Russia arriving in Canada in the 1870s brought with them seeds of a winter wheat that flourished in the steppes of their homeland. And so it did on the plains of America and Canada. Called Turkey Red, it was a dark hard wheat, excellent for baking. In the United States, it has been replaced by other varieties, although it can still be found in Canada, where it is used in hot cereal blends. Consequently, good flour has always been available and economical, two characteristics common to all staples of provincial cookery, and the Amish are justly famous for their baked goods.

In the Miller kitchen, the bread is Ruth's responsibility. She has used the same recipe for years: "I think I got it off a yeast packet, but I've fiddled with it. I make about twenty-four loaves of bread a week to sell. My brothers take lots of sandwiches in their lunch pails to work. And we

FROM 'THE BUDGET'

SPRING ISSUE

The weather is so unpredictable we won't make much comment on it except to say it is 70 degrees today and windy. Today my sisters will meet to clean the house for Freda and John in preparation for their move after the wedding. While Jeff Gingerich is here, he is doing some work on finishing the cupboards and trim work in Joel Mast's house.

—PANAMA, NY

have it for every meal, too." Although she experiments with different kinds of bread recipes brought home from the restaurant by her sisters; those are to sell to the English. "We like the plain white bread best," she explains.

Naomi makes the pies, and both women share the cookie and cake baking. "Those boxed cake mixes at the grocery store are pretty good, but they cost a lot, so we don't use them," says Naomi. Pie pastry is made with either lard or vegetable shortening and stirred up in a large dish pan. Divided into balls large enough for two-crust pies, the balls are kept chilled on the back porch. In the summer, they are stored in the cool root cellar.

The English folk living in Berlin and Millersburg drive out weekly to pick up orders they've left the week before; there are no phones in the Millers' house. (The nearest one is a quarter of a mile away, outside the local feed mill, and is shared by several families for business and emergencies.) "I do lots of cakes for birthdays; a favorite is the sauerkraut apple cake and the chop suey cake. The folks put on their own decorations," Naomi says as she rolls out the pastry for the first of twenty pies she'll prepare that morning.

In the Midwest, sugar pies or milk pies are popular, and Naomi also makes Pennsylvania shoofly pies, vanilla pies (similar to a Bob Andy pie), and applesauce pies. Muffins and quick breads are also made to sell, as well as for the family when the kitchen's bread supply runs low.

The wood range is roaring and the heat cozily warms the room on the chilly March morning of my visit. A handsome black, white, and orange dappled tabby cat stretches out on the rag rug in front of the stove.

From the glass-fronted cupboard that holds the collection of tea cups Naomi has collected at auctions over the years, she pulls out a shoebox where she keeps track of her clients and their requests. "Today, we've got orders for six loaves of bread, one coffee cake, three mincemeat pies (lots of people don't make their own mincemeat anymore, so we sell lots of those, especially in the winter months), plus peach and apple. And a couple of apple cakes, too." No wonder the world beats a path to her door.

Later I visited three unmarried sisters who live together and support themselves by bak-

> The Perry Goods moved into their grandpa's house last Saturday. They want to put hardwood flooring in the part of the big house before son Ben and family move over from the little house they live in now.
>
> —MILTON, IA

> There's a farmer here who is feeding out a herd of bulls and steers to sell. Having a bank barn, he had them penned in the haymow. On Sunday morning, several broke through a gate and one fell out of the other side of the haymow, down onto the front part of a buggy, breaking off a headlight, but leaving the fiberglass shafts unharmed. The bull was walking around below, shaking his head, apparently in disbelief.
>
> —REXFORD, MT

ing and quilt making, and have done so for nearly thirty years. The conversation flowed easily and warmly among the three women as they talked about their life.

They used to get up at 3:00 in the morning, but now that they are getting older, they are getting lazy, they say, and they don't rise until 5:30 A.M. Each makes her own breakfast, then they read the Bible and are ready to start their day. The baking, done by Malina and Sarah, begins in the large kitchen. The pies, cookies, and quick breads are baked in a wood-fired oven, and the bread is baked in a kerosene-fired oven that holds twenty loaves at a time.

The women are from a family of eleven children, and from the beginning, these three daughters were considered good bakers. Esther became a full-time quilter when they discovered that the English wanted not only homemade pies and breads but quilts as well.

Finishing the interview along with an apple date pie, I asked, "Do you think of yourselves as career women?" The women looked at each other and hooted with laughter. Then Sarah turned to Malina. "Malina, are we career women?" Malina mulled this over. "Yes, we just might be."

"That settles it," says Sarah. "If Malina says we are, I guess we are."

Sauerkraut Apple Cake

Makes a 9 × 13-inch cake; serves 12

SAUERKRAUT IS ANOTHER GIFT that Pennsylvania Germans have given to American cuisine. Commercially made sauerkraut of very good quality is now available in all supermarkets, the majority of it originating in the Fremont, Ohio, area, where the cabbages grow as big as basketballs.

Being so fond of kraut, I am always willing to try odd-sounding recipes using this ingredient and have never been disappointed. So when I came across this one, I just knew it was going to be really good, and it is. It's very moist, with a satisfying texture, like a good carrot cake. And it freezes well, too.

The original recipe indicates that the batter should be stirred by hand; I cheat and use the electric mixer, but in short bursts, being careful not to overbeat.

> 2 cups all-purpose flour
> 2 teaspoons baking powder
> 2 teaspoons ground cinnamon
> 1 teaspoon baking soda
> 1 teaspoon salt
> 1/2 teaspoon grated nutmeg
> 1 cup granulated sugar
> 1/2 cup light brown sugar, packed
> 4 eggs
> 1 cup vegetable oil
> 1 16-ounce can sauerkraut, rinsed and
>   thoroughly drained
> 1 apple, peeled, cored, and finely chopped,
>   preferably Gala or Yellow Delicious
> 1 cup coarsely chopped walnuts or pecans

FROSTING

> 1 8-ounce package cream cheese, at room
>   temperature
> 1/2 cup (1 stick) butter (no substitutes), at
>   room temperature
> 1 pound confectioners' sugar
> 1 teaspoon vanilla extract
> 2 teaspoons ground cinnamon
> 1 tablespoon grated orange zest
> 1/8 teaspoon salt

▦ Preheat the oven to 325°F. In a large mixing bowl, whisk together the flour, baking powder, cinnamon, baking soda, salt, and nutmeg; set aside. In another large mixing bowl, combine the sugars and whisk in the eggs and then the oil; blend well. Stir in the drained sauerkraut, apple, and nuts. Add the dry ingredients and stir until just moistened. Pour into a 9 × 13-inch glass baking dish and bake for 35 minutes, or until the top of the cake springs back when touched with your finger and the cake is just beginning to pull away from the sides of the dish. Cool the cake completely before frosting.

▦ PREPARE THE FROSTING: In a large mixer bowl, beat the cream cheese and butter until blended. Gradually add the confectioners' sugar, then the vanilla, cinnamon, orange zest, and salt; beat well. Spread on the cooled cake. Keep the cake refrigerated until serving time or the frosting becomes too soft.

NOTE: Because of the cream cheese in the frosting, the cake should be refrigerated, but the flavor will be better if you bring it to room temperature before serving.

An Indiana farmer admires some of the apples ripening in his orchard.

Amish Cake

Makes a 9 × 13-inch cake; serves 10 to 12

MARTHA LEHMAN OF ARTHUR, Illinois, gave me this recipe. She is a scribe for *The Budget* newspaper, is unmarried, and lives in an electrified housetrailer in her parents' yard. This community is one of the more progressive ones; they do not have services in their homes, but rather meet in a two-storied church that can handle 600 people. "That is about the average number who come to funerals," she explains.

This cake is frequently taken to funeral meals. Rich and buttery, it has its own broiled nutty glaze on top. It is very nice reheated in the microwave and served in a pool of English Pouring Sauce (page 275).

> 1 cup (2 sticks) butter, at room temperature
> 1 cup granulated sugar
> 1 cup dark brown sugar, packed
> 2 teaspoons vanilla extract
> 3 cups all-purpose flour
> 1½ teaspoons salt
> 2 cups buttermilk, at room temperature

> TOPPING
> 6 tablespoons (¾ stick) butter, melted
> 1 cup dark brown sugar, packed
> ¼ teaspoon grated nutmeg
> ¼ cup milk
> ½ cup chopped pecans or black walnuts

▪ Preheat the oven to 350°F. In a mixer bowl, cream together the butter, sugars, and vanilla for 2 minutes. In another bowl, whisk together the flour and salt. Add flour to the butter mixture, alternating with the buttermilk, beginning and ending with the flour. Transfer to a greased 9 × 13-inch glass baking dish and bake for 35 minutes or until the top springs back when touched with your finger.

▪ While the cake is baking, prepare the topping. In a mixer bowl, combine the butter and brown sugar. Add the nutmeg and milk, and mix well, then stir in the nuts.

▪ When the cake is done, remove it from the oven and turn the temperature to broil. Immediately spread the topping over the hot cake, then place in the broiler, 6 to 8 inches from the heat source. Place the cake on the rack and broil for approximately 3 minutes, or until the topping begins to bubble and brown slightly. Remove to a rack to cool.

Apple Cake with Black Walnuts, Coconut, and Raisins

Serves 16

THIS IOWA VERSION of apple cake is sturdy with lots of flavor and a firm texture, and it keeps well. I add some apple brandy to the glaze, but that is very non-Amish.

Iowa has a great many Amish and Mennonites, and there is an especially large group around Kalona. The land is fertile in that region and it is a progressive, prosperous community. Many Amish run thriving shops in their homes, with both husband and wife working in the business. One of the bishops I interviewed was not sure all of this success was good. "I worry sometimes that we are getting *too* prosperous," he said. Most of us would not consider that a worry.

> 3 cups all-purpose flour
> 1 teaspoon salt
> 1 teaspoon baking soda
> 1 teaspoon ground cinnamon
> ½ teaspoon ground cloves
> ½ teaspoon ground mace
> ½ teaspoon grated nutmeg
> 2 cups granulated sugar
> 1½ cups corn oil
> 3 eggs
> 2 teaspoons vanilla extract
> 4 cups peeled, cored, and chopped apples
> ½ cup chopped black walnuts
> ½ cup chopped English walnuts

1 cup sweetened coconut flakes
1 cup golden raisins
1 tablespoon grated orange zest

GLAZE

2 cups light brown sugar, packed
$\frac{1}{2}$ cup sweetened condensed milk
$\frac{1}{3}$ cup Calvados (apple brandy) (optional)

▪ Preheat the oven to 325°F. Grease a Bundt or tube pan or spray with nonstick cooking spray and set aside.

▪ In a medium bowl, whisk together the flour, salt, baking soda, cinnamon, cloves, mace, and nutmeg; set aside. In a large mixer bowl, combine the sugar and oil and blend. Add the eggs one at a time, mixing well after each addition. (This will look like lemon curd.) Add the vanilla. Using a sturdy, long spoon, stir in the flour mixture, then fold in the apples, nuts, coconut, raisins, and orange zest, making a stiff batter.

▪ Spoon the batter into the prepared pan and bake for $1\frac{1}{2}$ hours or until the cake is deep gold and just beginning to shrink away from the sides of the pan; don't overbake. Remove from the oven and cover with foil and a terry cloth towel and allow to cool for 20 minutes. Tip out onto a baking rack to cool completely before glazing.

▪ PREPARE THE GLAZE: In a small saucepan, combine the brown sugar and condensed milk and simmer for $2\frac{1}{2}$ minutes over medium heat. Remove the pan from the heat and stir in the apple brandy, if using. Immediately pour over the cooled cake and spread it evenly with a rubber spatula. Be sure the inside surface of the cake is also well glazed. Cool, cut into wedges, and serve.

Chop Suey Cake

Makes a 9 × 13-inch cake; serves 10 to 12

I HAVE NO IDEA why this is called a chop suey cake, for it certainly isn't a Chinese dessert. It *does* have an interesting definable texture and is very moist. No matter about its provenance; it's really good!

If you are making this in a flat glass baking dish, lower the heat to 325°F. and keep the frosted cake in the refrigerator. Since it is a butter cake, it will be more flavorful and softer if brought to room temperature before serving.

2 cups all-purpose flour
2 cups granulated sugar
2 teaspoons baking soda
2 eggs, slightly beaten
1 20-ounce can crushed pineapple in its own unsweetened juice, undrained
1 cup chopped nuts, such as pecans or English walnuts

FROSTING

1 8-ounce package cream cheese, at room temperature
$\frac{1}{2}$ cup (1 stick) butter, at room temperature
$1\frac{1}{2}$ cups confectioners' sugar
1 teaspoon vanilla extract
$\frac{1}{2}$ teaspoon salt
$\frac{1}{4}$ teaspoon mace

▪ Preheat the oven to 350°F. Grease and flour a 9 × 13-inch baking dish. In a large mixing bowl, whisk together the flour, granulated sugar, and baking soda. Add the eggs and mix well. Fold in the pineapple and nuts and combine gently. Pour into the prepared pan and bake for 35 to 40 minutes. Remove and cool completely before frosting.

▪ PREPARE THE FROSTING: In a large mixer bowl, blend the cream cheese for a few seconds, then add the butter and cream well. Add the confectioners' sugar, vanilla, salt, and mace; mix well. Spread on the cooled cake. Refrigerate until serving time, cut, and bring to room temperature.

INFORMATION ON BAKING INGREDIENTS

Like all scientific formulas, baking recipes require precise measurements and unadulterated ingredients. These guidelines will ensure a happy outcome to your baking efforts.

❖ Buy baking powder in small cans and date it immediately with an indelible marker. It loses its boosting power within a year. To test baking powder for potency, dissolve 1 teaspoon in ½ cup boiling water. It should bubble up vigorously.

❖ Baking soda, quick-cooking tapioca, and cornstarch should be used within a year of purchase. It is best to transfer leavening and thickening ingredients that are packaged in paper to airtight plastic, metal, or glass containers. And date them.

❖ Unsweetened chocolate is pure, ground, roasted chocolate in solid form. Since no sugar has been added, you get more chocolate flavor for your money. Flavors vary from one brand to another. In a pinch, you can substitute 3 tablespoons unsweetened cocoa plus 1 tablespoon butter for each ounce (square) of unsweetened chocolate.

❖ Dutch-process cocoa powder is European-style alkalized cocoa, in which the natural acidity of the cocoa has been neutralized, giving it a smoother flavor and a deep, rich color. If a recipe calls for Dutch-process cocoa, don't add baking soda even if the recipe calls for it; the acidity has already been neutralized. Hot cocoa mixes should never be substituted for cocoa powder in any recipe.

Mincemeat-on-the-Bottom Pumpkin Pie

Serves 6 to 8

THIS EXQUISITE DESSERT combines the best of two autumn pies, mincemeat and pumpkin. The recipe is from an Old Order Mennonite house-wife in Argos, Indiana, who happily shared it with me. Her house was exceptionally immacu-late, with shiny wooden planked floors and an enormous kitchen with handsome walnut cabinets.

African violets bloomed on her windowsills. Checkered oilcloth covered the commodious kitchen table; the table was set for eight people, and included paper napkins. The living room had two recliners and small painted rockers for the children, including a mini-kitchen set for her two little girls. This group lives with more luxuries than most Amish would permit—most families do not have any upholstered furniture in their living rooms.

> Pastry for a 1-crust 9-inch pie (page 270)
> 2 whole eggs plus 1 egg white, white slightly
>   beaten
> 2 teaspoons all-purpose flour
> $1\frac{1}{4}$ cups mincemeat (page 162)
> 1 tablespoon melted butter
> 1 tablespoon Angostura bitters (optional)
> $1\frac{3}{4}$ cups (16-ounce can) solid pack pumpkin
> $\frac{3}{4}$ cup sugar
> $\frac{1}{4}$ teaspoon ground cloves
> $\frac{1}{2}$ teaspoon salt
> $\frac{1}{2}$ teaspoon ground ginger
> 1 teaspoon ground cinnamon
> $1\frac{1}{2}$ cups (12-ounce can) evaporated milk
>   Whipped Cream Topping (page 271)

■ Preheat the oven to 425°F. Roll out the pastry and line a 9-inch pie pan. Brush the bottom with the egg white; sprinkle with the flour. Spread the mincemeat over the bottom of the crust and set aside while preparing the pumpkin layer.

■ In a large mixer bowl, beat the 2 whole eggs until frothy; add the melted butter and bitters and blend. Add the pumpkin, sugar, cloves, salt, ginger, cinnamon, and evaporated milk. Mix well and pour over the mincemeat; do not mix.

■ Bake the pie for 15 minutes, then reduce the oven temperature to 350°F. and bake for 45 to 50 minutes longer, or until the center of the pie is firm. Remove to a rack to cool. Serve in wedges and top with Whipped Cream Topping, if desired.

Applesauce Pie

Makes one 9-inch pie; serves 6

THIS RESEMBLES A SUGAR PIE and tastes just a tad cider-ish. The woman who gave me the recipe called it a "a pie to moon over." The Amish never gush, so that was high praise, though the pie does live up to that reputation, I do believe!

> Pastry for a 1-crust 9-inch pie (page 270)
> 2 eggs
> 1 cup sugar
> 2 tablespoons all-purpose flour
> 1 teaspoon grated nutmeg
> $\frac{1}{2}$ cup (1 stick) butter, melted
> 1 cup chunky unsweetened applesauce
> 1 teaspoon vanilla extract
> 2 tablespoons fresh lemon juice (unless the
>   applesauce is tart)

■ Preheat the oven to 350°F. Roll out the pas-try and line a 9-inch pie pan; set aside.

■ In a large mixer bowl, beat the eggs until just combined. In a small mixing bowl, whisk together the sugar, flour, and nutmeg. Add the sugar mixture to the eggs and blend. Add the butter, applesauce, vanilla, and lemon juice, if using, and combine gently, being careful not to overmix; you want to avoid adding too much air to the batter.

■ Pour the filling into the pastry shell and bake for 45 minutes or until the top of the pie is golden brown. Remove from the oven, cool completely on a rack, and serve.

Buttered Toffee Apple Pie

Makes one 10-inch pie; serves 8 to 10

THE TOFFEE TOPPING on this delicately flavored apple pie makes it most unusual. Be sure to use a 10-inch pie pan, or the pan juices will run over and really mess up your oven.

Some frugal bakers in this part of the country take the leftover apple peelings and cores, cover them with water, and boil them until tender, then strain it. The juice can be made into jelly and the peelings dried and steeped with tea.

Pastry for a 2-crust 10-inch pie (page 270)
1/3 cup light corn syrup
3 tablespoons granulated sugar
1 tablespoon melted butter
1 tablespoon quick-cooking tapioca
1 teaspoon ground cinnamon
1/2 teaspoon grated nutmeg
1/4 teaspoon salt
6 apples, such as Gala or Mutsu, peeled, cored, and thinly sliced

TOFFEE TOPPING
1/2 cup plus 2 tablespoons dark brown sugar, packed
1/4 cup chopped English walnuts
3 tablespoons light corn syrup
3 tablespoons melted butter
1 teaspoon vanilla extract
2 tablespoons all-purpose flour
1/4 teaspoon ground cinnamon

■ Preheat the oven to 425°F. Roll out half the pastry thinly on a floured surface and line a 10-inch pan, patting it in firmly. Set aside.

■ In a large mixing bowl, combine the corn syrup, granulated sugar, butter, tapioca, cinnamon, nutmeg, and salt. Allow to stand for 10 minutes. Add the apples and toss lightly to coat. Transfer the filling to the pastry shell.

■ Roll out the top crust, roll onto the top of the apples, and seal the edges; slash the top to let steam escape. Bake for 10 minutes, then reduce the heat to 350°F. and bake for 30 minutes more or until the crust is golden brown and juices are bubbling up through the top crust.

■ MEANWHILE, MAKE THE TOFFEE TOPPING: In a small bowl, combine the brown sugar, walnuts, corn syrup, butter, vanilla, flour, and cinnamon. Remove the pie from the oven, pour the topping over the crust, and immediately return it to the oven to bake 5 minutes longer. Transfer to a rack to cool completely before cutting into wedges and serving.

Brown Sugar Chess Pie

Makes one 10-inch pie; serves 10

HERE IS ANOTHER VERSION of the brown sugar pie—with its butterscotchy, smooth texture, it can hardly be improved on. Well, maybe a dollop of English Pouring Sauce (page 275) wouldn't hurt. It is quite different from the Old-Fashioned Brown Sugar Cream Pie on page 110. I hope you will try both of them.

Pastry for a 1-crust 10-inch pie (page 270)
2 1/3 cups (1 pound) light brown sugar, packed
1/4 cup all-purpose flour
3 eggs
3/4 cup (1 1/2 sticks) butter, melted
3/4 cup half-and-half
2 teaspoons vanilla extract
1/8 teaspoon salt
Ground cinnamon

■ Preheat the oven to 350°F. Roll out the pastry and line a 10-inch pie pan and set aside.

■ In a mixer bowl, combine the brown sugar and flour. Beat in the eggs, one at a time, then gradually add the butter, half-and-half, vanilla, and salt; mix until well combined but don't overbeat. Pour into the pastry shell and drift cinnamon liberally over the top. Bake for 1 hour. The top will be quivery but the center of the pie should be bubbly, which means the middle of the bottom crust is baked. The pie will set up as it cools. Remove to a rack and cool completely before serving.

SHOOFLY PIE

Without a doubt the best-known dessert in Pennsylvania Dutch country, shoofly pie was originally considered a breakfast treat to be eaten with coffee. Through the years it has evolved into a two-layer pie, with a tender cakelike gingerbread topping and a delicately gooey molasses layer.

The origin of the name has never been definitely established; one interpretation is that it is a corruption of the French *choufleur,* or cauliflower, since the texture of the crumb-speckled surface resembles the head of a cauliflower. Certainly we do observe some French usage of words and recipes creeping into this style of cookery, as many Amish and Mennonites migrated from Alsace-Lorraine.

A more satisfactory explanation is from William Woys Weaver, who writes in *Pennsylvania Dutch Country Cooking* that this confection made its first appearance in 1876 at the Centennial in Philadelphia and was called Centennial cake. It was called shoofly pie later on, possibly in reference to the Shoofly brand of molasses that went into the original recipes. One thing everyone agrees upon: molasses is a necessary ingredient.

Shoofly Pie

Makes one 9-inch pie; serves 8

THIS IS THE BEST shoofly pie I've eaten, and believe me, I've tried many. Some versions are dry and soft; others are quite gooey and moist. This one falls somewhere in between, and is thick and unabashedly pleasing. Shoofly is authentic American pie that comes to us from the Pennsylvania Amish and Mennonites and the Pennsylvania Dutch; we should be grateful to them forever.

Surprisingly, shoofly pie is not as popular in other Amish and Mennonite communities. It is found in Ohio; but in Indiana, if you ask for a piece of shoofly pie in a restaurant, the Amish girl who serves it will rather disparagingly tell you it's made only for the tourists—a thousand pities.

Pastry for a 1-crust 9-inch pie (page 270)
1 cup all-purpose flour
2/3 cup light brown sugar, packed
1 rounded tablespoon cold butter
1/4 teaspoon salt
1 egg
1 cup light molasses
3/4 cup cold water
1/4 cup hot water
1 tablespoon baking soda

▓ Preheat the oven to 350°F. Roll out the pie pastry and line a 9-inch pie pan; set aside.

▓ In a food processor bowl, combine the flour, brown sugar, butter, and salt. Remove 1/2 cup of the mixture and set aside. Transfer the rest to a medium mixing bowl. In a small bowl, beat the egg lightly. Add the molasses and cold water, and blend but do not beat; you don't want bubbles in the batter. Set aside.

▓ In a small bowl, mix the hot water with the baking soda and blend into the molasses mixture. Add to the flour mixture and mix well. Pour into the pie shell and top with the reserved crumbs. Bake for 35 minutes. The pie will appear quivery but will firm up as it cools. Transfer to a rack to cool completely before cutting.

Deep-Dish Apple Date Pie

Serves 6 to 8

LIKE DATES? LIKE APPLES? This is going to become one of your favorite pies. I found this delectable recipe during a visit at an Amish house.

6 cooking apples, such as Yellow Delicious or
    Galas, peeled, cored, and cut into eighths
1 tablespoon quick-cooking tapioca
1/2 cup granulated sugar
1/2 cup dark brown sugar, packed
2 teaspoons grated lemon zest
2 teaspoons grated orange zest
1/2 teaspoon grated nutmeg
1/2 pound sliced dates
2 tablespoons butter
    Pastry for a top crust (page 270)
    Milk or heavy cream, for serving

▓ Preheat the oven to 350°F. Spray an oval 11 × 8 × 3-inch baking dish (or any other 2-quart, 3-inch-deep baking dish) with nonstick cooking spray. In a large mixing bowl, toss together the apples and tapioca. Allow the mixture to stand for 10 minutes. In a small mixing bowl, combine the sugars, zests, and nutmeg.

▓ To assemble the pie, arrange half of the apple slices in the bottom of the prepared dish and top with half of the dates and half of the sugar mixture; repeat with the remaining ingredients. Dot with the butter. Roll out a thick pastry crust to fit the top of the dish and place the crust over the apples. Cut slits in the pastry to allow steam to escape. Bake for 40 to 50 minutes or until juices bubble up in the center of the pie and it is golden brown. Serve the pie lukewarm in bowls with a pitcher of milk or cream.

Amish Vanilla Pie

MONTGOMERY PIE

Makes one 9-inch pie; serves 8

AMISH VANILLA PIE is one of the many variations on shoofly pie. They all include brown or white sugar in the base and have a crumb topping. This recipe, also known as Montgomery pie, uses white corn syrup in the base and oatmeal in the topping and is really a very enticing pie.

> Pastry for a 1-crust 9-inch pie (page 270)
> 1 egg
> 1 tablespoon all-purpose flour
> $^1/_2$ cup dark brown sugar, packed
> $^1/_2$ cup light corn syrup
> 1 cup water
> 1 teaspoon vanilla extract
> $^1/_4$ teaspoon ground mace
> $^1/_8$ teaspoon salt

> CRUMB TOPPING
> 1 cup all-purpose flour
> $^1/_2$ cup dark brown sugar, packed
> 1 teaspoon vanilla extract
> $^1/_2$ teaspoon cream of tartar
> $^1/_2$ teaspoon baking soda
> $^1/_4$ teaspoon ground mace
> $^1/_8$ teaspoon salt
> $^1/_4$ cup ($^1/_2$ stick) cold butter

▦ Preheat the oven to 350° F. Roll out the pastry and line a 9-inch pie pan; set aside.

▦ In a medium saucepan, whisk the egg until frothy. Whisk in the flour. Add the brown sugar, corn syrup, water, vanilla, mace, and salt and mix well. Over medium-high heat, bring the mixture just to a full rolling boil, stirring occasionally. Remove from the heat and let cool to room temperature. (The filling will be slightly thickened.)

▦ While the filling is cooling, prepare the crumb topping. In a medium mixing bowl, combine the flour, brown sugar, vanilla, cream of tartar, baking soda, mace, and salt. Using a pastry blender or pastry fork, cut in the cold butter until the topping resembles coarse crumbs.

▦ Pour the cooled filling into the pastry shell. (The pastry will be only half full but the pie will rise as it bakes.) Sprinkle with the crumb topping. Cover the edges of the pastry with foil to prevent overbrowning. Bake for 25 minutes, then remove the foil and bake for an additional 20 minutes or until the top is a deep, golden brown. The filling will be a bit soft but will firm up as it cools. Remove to a rack to cool completely before cutting.

Mighty Easy Molasses Bread

Makes 2 loaves

SURPRISINGLY, THIS IS NOT a dark bread, though the molasses does give it a wonderful texture and a very rich taste. It is such an easy loaf to make that it might be a good one to try if your children want to learn to bake bread. Since playing with the dough (kneading) is a delightful sensation and just the kind of tactile thing kids enjoy, encourage them.

In the late 1800s in the Pennsylvania area, yeast breads were baked in standing outdoor bake ovens, a custom carried over from Europe's Rhineland and the Palatinate, from where many Amish and Mennonites came. The ovens had low roofs and side shelves to hold the bread and pies. Outdoor ovens were also prevalent in Ohio, but the Indiana Amish, who left Europe later, used wood-fueled iron stoves from the beginning, either inside in the kitchen or in attached summer kitchens.

> 7 cups all-purpose flour
> 1 tablespoon salt
> 2 packages active dry yeast
> $2^1/_4$ cups milk
> $^1/_4$ cup corn oil
> $^1/_4$ cup dark molasses
> 1 egg, beaten
>   Melted butter, for brushing

In a mixer bowl, whisk together 2 cups of the flour, the salt, and the yeast. Combine the milk, oil, and molasses in a small saucepan and heat until warm. Add to the flour mixture, along with the egg, and mix until just combined. Beat for ½ minute at low speed, then 3 minutes at medium speed. Gradually add another 4 to 5 cups of flour until a soft dough forms. Turn out onto a floured surface and knead for about 1 minute, or until the dough is elastic.

Place the dough in a well-buttered 2½-quart bowl, turning the dough to grease all sides. Cover and let rise in a warm place until doubled in size, about 1 hour.

Punch the dough down and divide in half. Roll one piece out into a 7 × 14-inch rectangle. Starting at one short edge, roll up tightly, jelly-roll fashion. Turn the ends under and seal before placing seam side down in a greased 9 × 5-inch loaf pan. Repeat with the remaining dough. Cover again and let rise in a warm place until nearly doubled, about 45 minutes.

Preheat the oven to 350°F. Bake for 45 minutes or until the internal temperature registers 200°F. when tested with an instant-read thermometer. Brush the top with butter and tip the loaf onto a baking rack. Cover with foil, then a terry cloth towel. Cool completely before slicing.

Easy Onion Kuchen

ZWIWWELKUCHE

Makes 12 pieces

A KUCHEN IS A TRADITIONAL German fruit- or cheese-filled, yeast-raised cake that is generally served for breakfast or dessert. This recipe breaks the rules, and with splendid results. First, the dough is made from frozen loaves. Second, the filling is a savory onion and bacon one. The end result can be served at any meal.

The Amish woman who gave me the recipe apologized that it is relatively costly to prepare, owing to the store-bought dough. I don't think most of us will object, for this shortcut also speeds the prep time. Check the package directions for how long it will take for the frozen dough to thaw, and plan accordingly.

1 1-pound loaf frozen bread dough
2 tablespoons (¼ stick) butter
2 tablespoons corn oil
6 cups sliced onions (3–4 large)
2 eggs
1 cup milk
½ teaspoon salt
¼ teaspoon coarsely ground black pepper
2 tablespoons honey
8 slices bacon, cooked until crisp and cut into
    ½-inch pieces
1 teaspoon poppy seeds
Paprika

Place the frozen bread dough in a greased 9 × 13-inch metal pan and grease lightly. Cover with plastic wrap and then a terry cloth towel. Let rise in a warm place until doubled in size—this will be several hours, but time will vary depending on the season and the warmth of your kitchen.

Punch down the risen dough and press it onto the bottom of the pan and approximately 2 inches up the sides. Cover with a towel and let rise again until double in size, 45 minutes to 1 hour.

Meanwhile, in an 11-inch sauté pan, melt the butter with the corn oil, over medium heat. Add the onions and sauté 20 to 30 minutes, uncovered, or until they are very soft but not browned. Spoon the onions over the top of the bread dough in an even layer.

Preheat the oven to 350°F. In a medium mixing bowl, combine the eggs, milk, salt, pepper, and honey; mix well but don't overbeat. Pour over the onions and sprinkle the top with the bacon and poppy seeds. Dust lightly with paprika and bake for 45 minutes or until the kuchen is puffy and golden brown. Immediately cut into squares and serve while hot.

NOTE: It is better to use a metal pan than a glass dish for this recipe.

NOTES
ON FLOURS

Producing cakes that are tender and light or biscuits that have a fine texture has a great deal to do with the flour used. The finished texture reflects the amount of gluten-performing proteins present in the flour. When liquid is added to flour, the proteins join together to form the gluten that makes superior baked products. How much protein you need in your flour depends on what you're baking. Bread makers want gluten in their flour so it will rise to the fullest, while pastry bakers prefer less gluten; one doesn't want a puffy pie crust!

Many grains are ground into flours, but only wheat is high in protein or gluten, and different types of wheat have different amounts. **All-purpose** flour is a blended flour, generally made from grains from many regions of the country. A grocery in Texas will have flour similar to what a grocery in Manhattan carries, so cooks across the country can achieve identical baking results.

Still, there are local variations among regional all-purpose flours. **Southern flours** are made from low-protein (9 grams per cup) soft winter wheat; White Lily is a well-known brand and can be mail-ordered (see page 287). Northern flours are made from high-protein (12 to 13 grams per cup) hard spring wheats; the King Arthur catalog (see page 287) is a good source for hard-wheat and other excellent flours.

Unbleached all-purpose flour hasn't been treated to remove color, and may be higher in protein than bleached all-purpose flour; for that reason, many home bakers prefer it. The flour package will indicate whether the flour is bleached or unbleached.

Bread flour, produced by the large flour processors and available in all large markets, is a very high-protein flour (14 grams per cup) and is ideal for yeast doughs. Bromated bread flour has been oxidized and produces lighter breads; it is found in most grocery stores.

Cake flour is the lowest in protein (8 grams per cup) and is very finely ground to assure tender and fine-textured cakes. It has also been bleached and chlorinated, which makes it slightly acid. The acidity also contributes to a finer-textured product.

To be sure you're using the best type of flour for your particular recipe, follow these rules of thumb when selecting flour:

❖ Steam-leavened items such as a moist sponge cake (*genoise*) need a low-protein flour.

❖ A low-protein flour is preferred for pie pastry and when preparing quick breads, biscuits, or cookies made with baking soda or baking powder.

❖ Cream puffs and mixtures such as Yorkshire puddings are leavened with eggs and the steam that forms during baking. These will be more successful if made with a high-protein flour for strong dough to push the mixture to its full height and volume.

❖ Breads and yeast-leavened products need high-protein bread flour.

Adapted from "Flour Power" by Shirley O. Corriher, *Fine Cooking*, December/January 1995–96.

Kentucky Cornmeal Bread

Makes 1 loaf

I DISCOVERED THIS SUPERB, fine-textured bread in a Mennonite community cookbook from Kentucky, and it is outstandingly good, either plain with butter or for sandwiches and toast. If you have some bacon drippings on hand, it is a great addition to this bread.

> 1/2 cup lukewarm water
> 3 tablespoons honey
> 1 package dry active yeast
> 2 tablespoons bacon fat, melted butter, or oil
> 1/2 cup lukewarm milk
> 2 teaspoons salt
> 2 cups all-purpose flour
> 1/2 cup yellow cornmeal
>   Melted butter, for brushing

▓ In a large mixer bowl, whisk together the lukewarm water and 1 tablespoon of the honey. Sprinkle in the yeast, combine, and let it stand for 10 minutes until the mixture is foamy. Stir until blended.

▓ Add the fat or butter, milk, remaining 2 table-spoons honey, and salt; mix until blended. Stir in the flour and beat until smooth, then add the cornmeal and mix. If the dough is not stiff enough to knead, add additional flour.

▓ Transfer the dough to a floured surface and knead for 10 minutes (or use an electric mixer with a dough hook). Place the dough in a large greased bowl, lightly butter the top of the dough, and cover with a terry cloth towel or plastic wrap, and allow the dough to rise in a warm place until doubled in size, about 1 hour.

▓ Punch down, shape into a loaf, and place the dough in a greased 9 × 5-inch loaf pan. Cover with a towel or plastic wrap and let the dough rise again until doubled, about 45 minutes.

▓ Preheat the oven to 375°F. Bake the bread for 30 minutes, until crusty and brown. The inner temperature should register 200°F. on an instant-read thermometer. Tip out onto a wire rack, brush with butter, cool, and wrap until serving time.

Best Ever Biscuits

Makes 16 large wedges

HONESTLY, I THINK THESE are more like scones, but the cook who gave me this recipe insisted they were biscuits. So be it. Whatever they are, they are superb and so easy to make, since they aren't cut-out biscuits (though you surely could if you wanted to). These also are a very good base for strawberry shortcakes.

Using cake flour instead of all-purpose flour, plus the butter here, gives these biscuits a most tender, cakelike texture with a delectable, deep buttery flavor.

> 5 cups plus 2 tablespoons cake flour
> 1/4 cup sugar
> 2 1/2 tablespoons baking powder
> 1 teaspoon salt
> 1/4 teaspoon grated nutmeg (optional)
> 1 cup (2 sticks) butter
> 2 eggs
> 1 cup buttermilk, at room temperature
> 7 tablespoons water

EGG WASH
> 1 egg
> 2 tablespoons milk
>
>   Grated nutmeg (optional)

▓ In a food processor bowl, combine the flour, sugar, baking powder, salt, and nutmeg. Cut the butter into 8 chunks and add to the bowl. Process the mixture briefly just until coarse crumbs form. Transfer to a large mixing bowl and set aside.

▓ In a small mixing bowl, beat the eggs with the buttermilk and water. Make a well in the dry ingredients and add the liquid mixture all at once. Using a pastry fork, toss and stir the mix-ture very lightly until the ingredients are just moistened and combined. Set the dough aside for 5 minutes.

▓ Preheat the oven to 400°F. Flour a pastry cloth liberally with cake flour. Check to see if the dough is stiff enough to handle; you may have to add a tablespoon or two more flour to make it firm enough to cut. Cut the dough in half, and transfer half of it to the cloth. With your fingertips, pat out the dough to a 7-inch round 1½ inches thick. Cut the round into 8 wedges and transfer the wedges to a parchment-lined or very lightly greased large cookie sheet. Repeat with the remaining dough.

▓ MAKE THE WASH: Beat the egg with the water. Brush the wash liberally on the biscuits and sprinkle very lightly with nutmeg, if desired. Bake the biscuits for 15 minutes, or until they have nearly doubled in size and are golden brown. Serve immediately.

Four-Grain Walnut Bread

Makes 3 loaves

AS THE AMISH BECOME more concerned about their young people leaving the church, many communities now have Sunday school for the young people on alternate Sundays, when there are no church services. Also, Amish parents are mindful that they provide recreation for their teenagers, so frolics and singings are scheduled almost every weekend. These events are held in barns in the summer and inside the homes when it becomes colder. The teens are always served food, such as sandwiches of homemade bologna, "squeaky" cheese (not aged), pickled beets and cucumbers, and all sorts of desserts.

This is substantial and nutritious bread from an Ohio Mennonite community that would also be served at youth affairs as a sandwich base. It has really robust flavor and makes delicious toast.

> 1 cup quick-cooking oats (not instant)
> 2 cups water
> 1 tablespoon salt
> ½ cup light or dark molasses
> ¼ cup (½ stick) butter
> 3 packages active dry yeast
> 1¼ cups lukewarm water
> 1 cup rye flour
> 1 cup whole wheat flour
> ½ cup wheat germ
> ½ cup bran flakes

> ½ cup fine-grain yellow cornmeal
> 5 cups bread flour
> 1 cup coarsely chopped English or black
>   walnuts
> Melted butter, for brushing

▓ In a medium saucepan, combine the oats and water and bring to a boil; remove from the heat. In a mixer bowl, combine the salt, molasses, and butter; add the oats mixture and stir to combine. Cool to lukewarm.

▓ Sprinkle the yeast into ½ cup of the lukewarm water and let stand until dissolved and bubbly, about 10 minutes. Add the dissolved yeast and remaining ¾ cup lukewarm water to the oats mixture, beating until smooth.

▓ Add the rye flour, whole wheat flour, wheat germ, bran flakes, and cornmeal and beat until smooth. Gradually stir in the bread flour until a soft dough forms, then work in the walnuts. Turn the dough out onto a lightly floured surface and knead until smooth and satiny, about 10 minutes (or use an electric mixer with a dough hook). Divide the dough into thirds and shape each portion into a loaf. Place into 3 greased 9 × 5-inch loaf pans. Cover and let rise in a warm, draft-free spot until doubled in size.

▓ Preheat the oven to 375°F. Bake the loaves for 35 to 40 minutes or until the internal temperature registers 200°F. on an instant-read thermometer. Remove the loaves from the oven and brush with melted butter. Let cool in the pan for 10 minutes and then remove and cool completely on a wire rack. Wrap tightly in foil or freezer paper and freeze the extra loaves, if desired.

One-Month Shredded Wheat Date Muffins

*Yields 3–3 1/2 quarts batter;
approximately 6 dozen muffins*

TO PREPARE THESE MUFFINS, you'll need to use a very large bread bowl, or even a turkey roaster. The batter may be stored in the refrigerator for up to one month. (Be sure to date the container.)

> 4 large shredded wheat biscuits
> 2 cups boiling water
> 2 cups chopped dates
> 3 cups sugar
> 3/4 cup solid vegetable shortening
> 4 cups bran flakes cereal
> 4 eggs, slightly beaten
> 5 cups all-purpose flour
> 1 1/2 teaspoons salt
> 1 quart buttermilk
> 5 teaspoons baking soda

▨ Crumble the shredded wheat biscuits into a very large mixing bowl and pour the boiling water over them. Add the dates and sugar and mix well. Whisk in the shortening until it is well combined. Add the bran flakes, eggs, flour, and salt, mixing thoroughly.

▨ Combine the buttermilk and baking soda, and stir until dissolved; the mixture will foam up. Slowly stir the buttermilk into the batter. Transfer the batter to large, tightly covered containers and refrigerate until needed.

▨ To bake, preheat the oven to 375° F. Prepare muffin cups by coating lightly with a nonstick cooking spray or lining with muffin papers, also sprayed. Fill as many muffin cups as desired half-full and bake for 20 to 25 minutes. They should be golden brown on top and stay firm when the top of the muffin is touched with your finger. Serve warm.

OPPOSITE: **The English flock in to buy these Amish-baked goods. The income derived from these items will be the women's "cookie jar money," stored in a cookie jar for her own personal use.**

No-Knead Country Oat and Raisin Loaf

Makes 2 loaves

IN THE EARLY 1800s, raisins were considered a luxury and to add them to a bread made that loaf special, indeed. This is a rustic bread, and the molasses gives the loaf great depth of flavor. And do try toasting this!

> 1 1/2 cups boiling water
> 1 cup quick-cooking oats (not instant)
> 1/2 cup dark molasses
> 1/3 cup vegetable oil
> 1 tablespoon salt
> 2 packages active dry yeast
> 1/2 cup lukewarm water
> 2 eggs, slightly beaten
> 1 cup raisins, plumped (page 270)
> 2 3/4 cups all-purpose flour
> 2 3/4 cups bread flour

▨ In a large mixer bowl, combine the boiling water, oats, molasses, oil, and salt and mix well. Cool to lukewarm. In a small mixing bowl, dissolve the yeast in the water and set aside until it foams, 5 to 10 minutes. Add the yeast, eggs, and raisins to the oats mixture; combine thoroughly. In a large mixing bowl, whisk together the flours. Gradually stir or beat the flour into the oats mixture. Cover and refrigerate for at least 2 hours.

▨ Grease two 9 × 5-inch loaf pans. Divide the dough into two equal parts. Roll one piece out into a 7 × 14-inch rectangle. Starting at one short edge, roll up tightly, jelly-roll fashion. Turn the ends under and seal before placing seam side down in a loaf pan. Repeat with the remaining dough. Cover and let rise in a warm place for 2 hours or until doubled in size.

▨ Preheat the oven to 350° F. Bake the loaves for 50 minutes or until the internal temperature registers 200° F. when tested with an instant-read thermometer. Cool in the pans for 10 minutes, then tip out onto a rack and cover with foil and a terry cloth towel to finish cooling. Slice thickly and serve.

Sage Caraway Herb Bread

Makes 2 braided loaves

ONE OF THE MOST distinctive social patterns of the Amish is the integration and acceptance of the older generation. When a couple enter their late fifties or early sixties, it is not uncommon for them to vacate their home and move into a *daudi house* or *grossdaudi house*, which may be built onto the main house or very close to it. The farm and the main house generally pass to the youngest child, who will physically care for the parents.

The older couple remain active ("I'd rather wear out than rust out," one senior citizen told me), helping about the house and farm as needed. It is largely thanks to all these extra hands in the kitchen that the Amish still have time to prepare yeast breads and rolls.

This bread requires three risings; it's no wonder the English prefer to buy it from an Amish or Mennonite bakery.

> 2 packages active dry yeast
> 1¼ cups warm water
> 6½ cups bread flour
> 1 cup milk, scalded and cooled
> 3 tablespoons sugar
> 1 tablespoon salt
> 3 tablespoons melted butter
> 2 teaspoons caraway seeds
> 1 tablespoon rubbed dried sage
> 1 teaspoon grated nutmeg
> ½ teaspoon coarse black pepper
> Melted butter and caraway seeds, for top

■ In a mixer bowl, dissolve the yeast in the warm water. Stir in 3½ cups of bread flour, the milk, sugar, salt, butter, caraway seeds, sage, nutmeg, and pepper. Beat until smooth, then add 2½ to 3 cups more bread flour to form a soft dough. Turn out onto a lightly floured surface and knead for 10 minutes (or use an electric mixer with a dough hook). Place the dough in a greased bowl and then turn the dough over to grease all surfaces. Cover and let rise in a warm place for 1 hour or until doubled in bulk.

■ When doubled, divide the dough in half and form into 2 balls on a floured surface. Cover with inverted mixing bowls and let rise again for 15 to 20 minutes. Cut each half into 3 equal pieces. (Or, at this point, you can use the method described in Mighty Easy Molasses Bread, page 42.) Roll each piece into a rope about 17 to 18 inches long. Braid 3 ropes together and seal the ends (see Note). Repeat with the remaining dough and place the braided loaves on greased baking sheets. Brush each loaf with melted butter and sprinkle with caraway seeds. Cover and let rise for 45 minutes.

■ Preheat the oven to 400°F. Bake the loaves on the lower rack for 25 minutes or until an instant-read thermometer registers 200°F. Remove from the oven and brush with melted butter again. Cool, slice thickly, and serve.

NOTE: If you don't want to bother with braiding the dough, just form it into two loaves.

Amish Friendship Bread

Makes two 15-inch loaves

"AMISH FRIENDSHIP BREAD is just sourdough bread that is passed around to the sick and the needy in our community," explains Elizabeth Coblentz, an Old Order Amish food writer in the Berne, Indiana, community. This authentic version needs five to seven days to prepare the starter, so you must plan in advance. Remember to replace every *cup* you dip out of the starter with ¾ cup bread flour *and* ¾ cup liquid—buttermilk, milk, or water. Stir the starter mixture and let it sit at room temperature one day, then cover and chill. If the starter is not used for more than two weeks, scoop out and discard one cup, and feed the starter again with ¾ cup bread flour and ¾ cup liquid.

This is a wonderfully responsive dough; the baked bread is soft and white, which reflects the preferred bread style among the Amish. I personally like to substitute 1 cup whole wheat flour for 1 cup of the bread flour for a bit more texture and flavor.

STARTER

1 package active dry yeast
1 cup warm water
1 cup buttermilk, at room temperature
1 cup bread flour
1 tablespoon sugar

SPONGE

1 cup sourdough starter
1½ cups lukewarm water
2 cups bread flour

BREAD DOUGH

2 tablespoons vegetable oil
1 tablespoon sugar
2 teaspoons salt
3½ cups bread flour
½ teaspoon baking soda
2 tablespoons butter, at room temperature

▓ MAKE THE STARTER: Dissolve the yeast in warm water in a warmed crockery or glass bowl. (You can warm them up by filling with hot water for a minute or two.) Whisk in the remaining ingredients and combine until smooth. Cover loosely with plastic wrap or cheesecloth. Allow the mixture to stand, at room temperature, for 5 to 7 days (I found 5 days to be plenty) or until the mixture is bubbly and has a sour aroma. A clear liquid (called hootch by early settlers who drank it) will form on the top of the starter 6 to 12 hours after the original mixing; that is just fine. Stir it down into the mixture every day with a fork. After it has become "sour," cover and refrigerate until needed.

▓ MAKE THE SPONGE: Measure out the required amount of starter and transfer to a large bowl; allow it to come to room temperature. Add the warm water, then whisk in the flour until smooth. Cover loosely with plastic wrap or cheesecloth and let stand at room temperature for 1 to 2 days. The longer you leave it, the more biting and "sour" the flavor of the bread will be.

▓ MAKE THE DOUGH: To the sponge add the oil, sugar, and salt and mix well. In a small bowl, combine 1 cup of the flour with the baking soda; add gradually to the sponge mixture. Continue to mix, adding the remaining flour ½ cup at a time. The dough will be soft, springy, and not sticky when enough flour is added; 3½ cups is right for me in my kitchen, but your dough might take a bit more or less flour. The feel of the dough will tell you when it has absorbed the right amount of flour.

▓ Add the dough hook attachment to an electric mixer and knead the dough (or do by hand) for 10 minutes. Butter or oil the top of the dough, cover with plastic wrap, and allow the dough to rise for 1 hour, or until doubled, in a warm draft-free place.

▓ Punch the dough down firmly and divide in half. Transfer one half to a floured surface and roll out to a 12 × 15-inch rectangle. Roll the dough up tightly, starting from the longest side. Seal the sides and ends by pinching the dough firmly together with your fingers. Pat and form into a smooth roll and transfer to a greased baking sheet that has been coated liberally with cornmeal. Repeat with the remaining dough, placing the second loaf on a second sheet. Cover, and allow the loaves to rise for an hour, or until doubled, in a warm draft-free place. Preheat the oven to 375°F.

▓ With a sharp knife, lightly score the top of each loaf with 4 diagonal cuts. Bake for about 40 minutes, or until an instant-read thermometer registers 200°F. Remove the loaves to a rack to cool and rub with the softened butter. Slice thickly and serve.

3
THE SCHOOL
LUNCH
BUCKET

Hearty Beef Barley Soup ❖ Sauerkraut Soup with Sausage ❖ Vegetable

Soup with Brisket ❖ German Dumpling Soup ❖ Tomato Corn

Chowder ❖ Zesty Horseradish Meat Loaf ❖ Tuna Cream Cheese

Sandwiches ❖ White Dropped Amish Church Sugar Cookies ❖ Crispy

Amish Peanut Butter Cookies ❖ Coconut Crisps ❖ Lucille's Molasses

Cookies ❖ Spicy Schnitz Pie (Schnitz Boi) ❖ Shoofly Star Cakes

ENSURING THEIR children learn the fundamentals of reading, writing, and mathematics is a priority for most Amish parents, who refer to the students as "scholars." Amish schools are taught by studious persons from within the community, primarily using texts printed in Canada by an Amish press. Mennonite children attend high school and have their own colleges, which are also attended by the English, and some even go to English-run schools and colleges. But not the Amish.

Physical education, where the students are expected to undress and shower with others, as well as such things as computer classes, are considered too worldly and impractical for most of the Amish.

The ability to have their own schools was not always their right. There were many disputes between Amish parents and local school boards in several states about their children not attending public schools. However, in 1972, the U.S. Supreme Court sanctioned their right to educate their children separately, and the Amish school system has stabilized across the country. Each student is required to pass a standardized achievement test before graduation. Schools are now being built quite a ways from the road for safety reasons, since there have been incidents of harassment of the Amish scholars.

One-room schoolhouses dot the Amish countryside since most of the scholars walk or bike to school. They are spacious, airy, many-windowed, surrounded by swing sets and teeter-totters, and always a well-worn volleyball field, a sport popular with both boys and girls. There is also a buggy rail for parents or students to tie their horses.

Frequently, the practical Amish build the schools next to cemeteries for ease of maintenance. When the volunteers pushing rotary hand mowers come to tend the cemetery, the school grounds are mowed at the same time.

Building expenses as well as education costs are supplied by donations and monies derived from quilt auctions and special community fundraising events.

School boards, comprised of the parents of the scholars, are responsible for the hiring of the teachers, providing the supplies and books, and collecting school taxes from the community. The board will number either three or five members, who each serve three to five years. Women are not considered for board members.

For the Old Order Amish and Mennonite scholars, school starts right after Labor Day and is

FROM 'THE BUDGET'

SPRING ISSUE

If the weather stays nice, Eli Bylers will have a wiener roast by their pond for the teachers and scholars today. If not, they will take lunch to school. **—GRANTON, WI**

dismissed the last of April; this enables the young people, especially the older boys, to help with the spring planting of the fields. However, these schools do not have long vacations during the rest of the year, and the scholars have as many days of school overall as do English students.

As I approach an Ohio schoolhouse, one of more than 100 in this state, there are patches of late snow still blotching the fields but the sun shines with determined persistence. An Amish farmer and his sons are thinning out fruit-bearing twigs in their apple orchard to encourage better apples on those that remain. In May, this orchard will be a bower of pink and white and abuzz with bees.

I knock at the schoolroom door, unsure of the etiquette, and am graciously welcomed inside. Effie Beachy is tall, slender, and merry-faced, with dancing, intelligent eyes. Her mother, Maud Beachy, had told me, "Effie has always liked to read; she was a real scholar from the beginning. So when the deacon asked her to teach, she didn't hesitate a minute. She really doesn't like housework; she'd rather grade papers than cook, I guess." She's taught in this school for eleven years.

The scholars at their desks all focus their attention on me, away from the scribbled blackboard. Kerosene lanterns dangle from the ceiling, coats and boots hang from pegs on one side of the room, and opposite, two church benches stacked one atop the other are lined with both metal and plastic lunch pails in bright colors. A glass

> Scholars had their Easter egg hunt yesterday. Parents also took a hot dish to school. —**GAP, PA**

> Recently David Wengard took the boys to Turin, where they had an enjoyable time together on the ski slopes. Dad had told the boys if they do as good or better the last half of the school term as they did the first half that he'd do something for them, so skiing was their reward. —**BELLEVILLE, NY**

mason jar of pussywillows stands on Effie's desk.

We chat quietly in a corner while the scholars finish their reading assignment. Are there any regrets that she went through only the eighth grade? "This kind of education suits us," she replies. "We have a local school board of parents that supervises each school and all the teachers are chosen because of their academic skills and religious attitudes about conforming to the Amish way of life. Our children just don't fit into public schools—so much television is used in the classroom. We really disapprove of that. And here, we teach both English and German—many of us speak German or a dialect between ourselves as we did originally in Europe."

Since I am "the recipe lady," I'm naturally curious about what the children bring to school in their lunch buckets.

"Lots of sandwiches, of course, made with leftover cold meat, such as beef roast or meat loaf, maybe homemade bologna or cheese and sometimes peanut butter," replies Effie. "In cold weather, hot soup is sent in thermos bottles, or maybe some leftover casserole dish in wide-mouthed thermos containers. Always dessert—cookies, pies, cake. I bring in a couple of gallons of milk every day, but not all the teachers do that. We break forty-five minutes for lunch, and that includes playtime outside."

To end my visit, I ask the scholars what they like best for lunch. Peanut butter and jelly, of course! Why should I be surprised?

Hearty Beef Barley Soup

Serves 8 to 10

THIS IS TYPICAL of the homemade soups that would be packed in vacuum bottles to accompany men to work and children to school. Or serve this in deep soup bowls on a cold day, accompanied by freshly baked bread and a dish of spicy pickles. It's hearty enough to be a one-dish meal and it freezes well, too.

> 2 pounds chuck roast, trimmed and cut into
>   1-inch cubes
> 2 tablespoons vegetable oil
> 1 large onion, chopped
> 2 quarts Beef Stock (page 267), or
>   4 16-ounce cans beef broth
> 1 16-ounce can diced tomatoes, undrained
> 1 cup chopped carrots
> 1 cup chopped celery
> ½ cup chopped green bell pepper
> ⅔ cup quick-cooking barley
> 2 teaspoons Worcestershire sauce
> ½ teaspoon black pepper
>   Salt to taste
> 1½ tablespoons minced fresh thyme, or
>   1 teaspoon dried (optional)
> ½ cup finely chopped fresh parsley

▨ In a large covered stockpot, over medium heat, slowly braise the beef in the oil for 5 minutes. Add the onion and continue browning for 15 minutes longer, stirring occasionally. Stir in the stock and tomatoes, cover, and simmer for 1½ hours. Add the carrots, celery, green pepper, barley, Worcestershire, pepper, and salt; cover and cook until the vegetables are tender, about 25 minutes. About 6 minutes before the soup is ready, add the thyme and parsley. Serve immediately.

Sauerkraut Soup with Sausage

Serves 8 to 10

SERVED MOSTLY in the winter, this soup is an immensely gratifying dish, and if you know someone who likes sauerkraut, it is sure to become one of their favorite recipes. Add some homemade bread, and this is a robust one-dish meal.

> 1 pound sage bulk sausage
> ½ cup chopped onion
> 2 garlic cloves minced
> 1 pound sauerkraut, undrained
> 6 cups Chicken Stock (page 267) or
>   3 16-ounce cans low-fat chicken broth
> 1½ tablespoons butter
> 1½ tablespoons all-purpose flour
> 1 teaspoon sugar

▨ In a large stockpot, over low heat, sauté the sausage, onion, and garlic until the sausage is brown, 7 to 10 minutes. Drain off the fat and discard. Add the sauerkraut and stock and cook, covered, for 40 minutes.

▨ In a small saucepan, over medium-low heat, melt the butter. Stir in the flour, cooking just until it bubbles, then pour in 1 cup of the soup stock and whisk together. Return this mixture to the stockpot, raise the heat to medium, and stir and cook about 10 minutes, or until it thickens. Add the sugar, blend well, and ladle into soup bowls.

ABOVE: Solemn little girls observe the activities in the barnyard from an out-of-the-way distance of a cart. BELOW: Volleyball is a popular recess activity for both the boys and girls.

Vegetable Soup with Brisket

Serves 10 to 12

BRISKET (FRESH, NOT THE corned kind) is a flavorful cut of beef, but it must be simmered a long time so it becomes tender. It is the perfect base for a hearty soup rich with vegetables. A chopped turnip or parsnip adds sweetness to a dish. Any kind of pasta can be added at the end of the cooking period; the Amish use home-made noodles.

The marrow in the soup bone adds important flavor. I cook the meat a day in advance in order to easily remove all the fat. It's best not to freeze this soup, because the potatoes will get mushy. This makes enough for a soup party—a nice way to entertain.

> 2 pounds fresh beef brisket
> 1 soup bone (beef bone with marrow)
> 4 quarts water
> 2 cups canned tomato puree
> ½ cup chopped onion
> 2 medium carrots, peeled and sliced
> 1 medium turnip or parsnip, peeled and cubed
> 1 cup shredded green cabbage
> 1 cup fresh or frozen cut green beans
> 1 12-ounce can whole kernel corn, juices
>   included
> 1 large potato, peeled and cubed
> 2 cups chopped celery
> ½ cup fresh or frozen baby lima beans
> ½ cup fresh or frozen green peas
> ¼ cup ketchup
> 1 tablespoon Worcestershire sauce
> 2 teaspoons salt
> 2 tablespoons minced fresh thyme,
>   or 2 teaspoons dried (optional)
> ½ teaspoon crushed red pepper flakes
> 1 cup dry egg noodles, preferably thin

◼ In a large stockpot, combine the brisket, soup bone, and water. Bring to a boil, skimming well, then reduce the heat, cover, and simmer for 3 hours or until tender. Remove from the heat, cool, and refrigerate the mixture overnight. Skim off the coagulated fat and discard.

◼ To the stockpot, add the tomato puree, onion, carrots, and turnip or parsnip. Cover and bring to a boil, then reduce the heat and simmer, partially covered, for 45 minutes. Add the cabbage, green beans, corn, potato, celery, lima beans, peas, ketchup, Worcestershire, salt, thyme, and red pepper flakes, and cook for 30 additional minutes. Discard the bone and shred the brisket, then return the meat to the soup. Stir in the noodles and cook for 10 minutes longer. Serve in deep bowls with a tempting quick bread.

German Dumpling Soup

Serves 6

I AM SO FORTUNATE that readers and viewers want to share recipes with me; in most cases they, too, want to see a beloved old recipe recorded for posterity. This soothing dumpling soup is a perfect example. It was given to me by attorney Kim Werner, who came to a book signing in Toledo specifically to deliver it. His German grandmother served this soup to him every day at lunch, and he said he never tired of it. He counseled that it should always be made with butter and purchased cracker meal, so that's what I do.

> 2 eggs, at room temperature
> ¼ cup (½ stick) butter, at room temperature
> 2 tablespoons finely minced fresh parsley
> ½ teaspoon celery seeds
> ¼ teaspoon celery salt
> ½ cup cracker meal
> 6 cups Chicken Stock (page 267), or
>   3 16-ounce cans chicken broth
> Chopped scallion greens (optional)

◼ In a medium mixing bowl, beat the eggs slightly; cut the butter into small pieces and drop into the eggs. Whisk a bit, then using your fingers, squeeze the butter into the eggs; it works much better using your fingers for this! Whisk in the parsley, celery seeds, and salt, and add the cracker meal gradually, mixing with your hands, if necessary. Form the mixture into about 20 large marble-size balls. Set aside to dry for 30 minutes.

Meanwhile, in a large saucepan, bring the stock to a boil. Reduce the heat to a simmer, and gently drop in the dried cracker balls. Cover and cook over low heat for 20 minutes. Don't lift the lid until the soup has simmered for 20 minutes. Serve immediately in large soup bowls. I like to sprinkle chopped scallion greens over the top for added texture, but that is surely optional.

Tomato Corn Chowder

Makes 8 cups

THIS IS ONE OF THOSE soups Amish women prepare very quickly from the canned foods they keep in their basements. We can use commercially canned vegetables and broth with equally good results. Serve this with grilled cheese sandwiches or "cheese toasties," as they are called in my part of the country.

If you use one can of broth, the soup is very thick and hearty. For thinner soup, use more. You could substitute turkey bacon for the regular, but I really think the real thing is better for this dish.

> 6 slices pork bacon
> 1 medium onion, chopped
> 1 28-ounce can crushed tomatoes
> 2 cups Chicken Stock (page 267) or
>   1 10½-ounce can chicken broth
> 3 13-ounce cans corn (not creamed),
>   undrained
> 1 tablespoon brown sugar, packed
> 2 teaspoons ground cumin
>   Salt and pepper to taste
> ¼ cup minced fresh parsley

Fry the bacon slices in a large sauté pan until crisp. Remove to paper toweling to drain. To the drippings in the pan, add the onion and sauté 5 to 8 minutes over medium heat until it begins to color. Add all of the remaining ingredients except the parsley. Cover and simmer for 10 minutes. Season to taste, then stir in the parsley and serve immediately.

Zesty Horseradish Meat Loaf

Serves 4 to 6

MOST PEOPLE ARE CRAZY about this zippy meat loaf. Some Amish housewives will cook this very slowly on top of the stove in a Dutch oven and they call it *falscher hase.* It takes less watching, though, if you bake it in the oven in the conventional fashion. Leftovers make great lunch bucket sandwiches.

> 4 slices dense-textured wheat bread, chopped
>   medium coarse in a food processor
>   (see Note)
> ¼ cup milk
> ¼ cup prepared horseradish
> 1 egg, slightly beaten
> 2 tablespoons Dijon mustard
> 2 tablespoons chili sauce
> 1½ teaspoons Worcestershire sauce
>   Salt and freshly ground black pepper to taste
> ½ cup finely chopped celery
> ¼ cup finely chopped onion
> 1½ pounds lean ground beef
> ½ cup chili sauce or catsup, for garnish

Preheat the oven to 350° F. In a large mixing bowl, soak the bread in the milk until soft. Drain off any excess milk, and stir in the horseradish, egg, mustard, chili sauce, Worcestershire sauce, salt and pepper, celery, and onion; mix well. Add the ground beef and combine thoroughly but lightly, using your hands, if necessary.

Shape into a loaf and transfer to a foil-lined 7 × 11 2-quart glass baking dish. Spread the additional chili sauce or catsup over the top and bake for 45 minutes to 1 hour, until the loaf is firm and browned. During baking, baste two or three times with the drippings. Let stand 10 minutes before serving. Slice and serve while hot.

NOTE: I have Brownberry Nut Bread on hand all the time and it is superb for crumbs. If this is not available in your grocery, substitute any whole wheat bread.

DISCIPLINE OF AN INDIANA CONGREGATION

[Name Withheld]

This is from a 1978 discipline of an Indiana congregation and expresses the common understanding of what constituted the rules of conduct in that community at that time. It is reprinted with permission from *Amish Roots, A Treasury of History, Wisdom and Love* by Johns Hostetler, Johns Hopkins University Press. Today, some of these rules have been relaxed, but not everywhere. And this was the philosophy of just *one* community out of many.

❖ No worldly insurance or Social Security benefits
❖ Farm with horses, not with power machinery in the field
❖ No rubber tires on implements or buggies
❖ No unnecessary lights on buggies except what is for safety
❖ No bulk tanks or milkers
❖ No registered cows or horses
❖ No one shall operate cars or trucks
❖ Clothing shall be plain and humble; no small rim or band on the hat. No cowboy style or creased hat. Hook-and-eye coats are required. No outside pockets on coat or shirt. No hip pockets or slit pants or double crease pants. No belt loops and no suspender clamps. No members shall go without suspenders or without shoelaces. After marriage, no oxfords shall be worn.
❖ No bright colors on shirts like pink, yellow, orange, or bright cloth. No quilted coats or jackets. No zippers. Dark plain stockings must be worn. No form fitting clothing in respect to sisters. Shawls shall be worn when going from home.

❖ The dresses shall be plain and not striped or made of luxury material, or with bright colors like pink, yellow, or orange or bright red. No large collars or large openings at the neck.
❖ The shoes shall have strings, be black and have no high heels.
❖ Aprons shall always be white as also the cape for church services. No wide bands on the apron. Hair shall not be combed over the ears.
❖ The young people shall not run after pleasure places, have radio or TV or watch movies. No wrist watches, bicycles, no drinking or tobacco.
❖ No ball playing on Sunday.
❖ No bed courtship or other shameful behavior. Couples are not to see each other excessively and shall be home by midnight. Foul speech and unnecessary language and bywords are not to be found among us.
❖ No electrical generators except for welding. No lightning rods. No white rings or overchecks on the harness of the horse. No Sunday milk is sold.
❖ Houses shall be plain with no large windows or push windows, no two-toned trimming.
❖ Kitchen work tables are to be plain with no trimming.
❖ No sinks, work tables or colored stool or colored tub in the bathroom.
❖ No decorative colors on bathroom floor.
❖ Laundry shall be washed at home, not at the laundromats.

Tuna Cream Cheese Sandwiches

Makes enough filling for 6 generous sandwiches

MANY AMISH USE CHEESE lavishly since they frequently are able to buy it at a reduced price from the local dairy where they sell their milk. (They are also free of our cholesterol angst!) One way they use it is in this nicely seasoned tuna and cream cheese sandwich. Canned salmon can be substituted for the tuna.

> 1 8-ounce package cream cheese, at room temperature
> 2 tablespoons bottled chili sauce or ketchup
> 2 tablespoons chopped fresh parsley
> 2 tablespoons finely minced onion
> 1 tablespoon finely minced fresh dill
> 1/2 teaspoon hot red pepper sauce
> 2 7-ounce cans water-pack tuna or salmon, drained

▓ In a small bowl, combine the cream cheese with the chili sauce, parsley, onion, dill, and hot pepper sauce. (I use an electric hand mixer.) Stir in the tuna or salmon, cover, and refrigerate. Spread on lightly buttered dark bread and serve cold.

White Dropped Amish Church Sugar Cookies

Makes 6 dozen

THE AMISH ARE CONSTANT cookie bakers and make them in enormous amounts. Two of their favorites are associated with church services, including this soft, cakelike sugar cookie that is often served with coffee after church. (The other cookie is the Bushel Cookie, page 191, a traditional oatmeal cookie that is indeed made by the bushel.) The dough for these sugar cookies can be kept in the refrigerator for three to four weeks and baked up a batch at a time. Do not use butter; the cookies will be crisp rather than soft.

> 1 1/2 cups (3 sticks) margarine
> 2 cups sugar
> 2 eggs
> 1 teaspoon vanilla extract
> 1 teaspoon almond extract
> 3 1/2 cups all-purpose flour
> 1 teaspoon baking powder
> 1 teaspoon baking soda
> 1 teaspoon grated nutmeg
> 1 teaspoon salt
> 1 cup sour cream
>   Sugar and raisins, for garnish

▓ Preheat the oven to 375° F. In a large mixer bowl, cream together the margarine and sugar for 3 minutes. Add the eggs and extracts and beat until well combined. In a large mixing bowl, whisk together the flour, baking powder, baking soda, nutmeg, and salt. Add to the creamed mixture and combine until the mixture is moistened. Stir in the sour cream by hand and blend well.

▓ Using a 1 1/2-inch cookie scoop or a tablespoon, drop the dough onto a parchment-lined or nonstick baking sheet, then top each one with sugar and a raisin, or two or three. Bake for 10 to 12 minutes or until the bottoms are lightly browned. Remove the cookies to a rack to cool. Store in airtight containers or freeze.

Crispy Amish Peanut Butter Cookies

Makes 8 dozen cookies

I THINK THIS is my favorite peanut butter cookie recipe. The cookies are crisp, and intensely flavored with brown sugar and peanut butter. The batter is very crumbly, but don't worry about it; the end result is perfect. The cookies are not perfect rounds when baked, but that's the way they are supposed to be. Believe me, no one will complain!

5 cups all-purpose flour
1 teaspoon salt
1 tablespoon baking soda
2 teaspoons baking powder
4 eggs
4 teaspoons vanilla extract
1 1/2 cups solid vegetable shortening
1 18-ounce jar creamy peanut butter
   (generous 2 cups)
2 cups granulated sugar
2 cups dark brown sugar, packed
1/2 cup or more granulated sugar, for garnish

▨ Preheat the oven to 375°F. In a large mixing bowl, whisk together the flour, salt, baking soda, and baking powder; set aside. In a small mixing bowl, beat the eggs thoroughly and blend in the vanilla; set aside. In a mixer bowl, beat the shortening briefly, then gradually beat in the peanut butter, then the sugars. Blend well. Add the beaten eggs a bit at a time, then gradually add the flour mixture and incorporate thoroughly. The batter will be very crumbly, but not to worry.

▨ Place the garnishing sugar in a small bowl. Using a 1 1/2-inch cookie scoop or by heaping tablespoon, dip out batter and lightly roll each cookie in the sugar. Transfer the cookies to an ungreased cookie sheet. With a fork, press each cookie down a bit in a crisscross pattern to flatten. Bake for 10 to 11 minutes or until brown. Remove from the oven and allow the cookies to cool on the pan. Transfer them to an airtight container or freeze.

Coconut Crisps

Makes 40 cookies

EVERY ONCE IN A WHILE a cookie comes along that makes you say, "This is the best one *ever!*" Right now, this is the cookie that has my heart. The very essence of coconut in flavor, it is elegant in appearance, with its crackly white exterior dusted with sugar. People will be standing in line for the recipe. Thanks to Anna Wickey of Pardeeville, Wisconsin, for this wonderful cookie!

1 cup (2 sticks) butter, at room temperature
1 cup sugar
1 egg
1 teaspoon vanilla extract
1 teaspoon almond extract
2 cups all-purpose flour
1/2 teaspoon baking soda
1/2 teaspoon salt
2 cups flaked coconut
   Additional sugar, for sprinkling

▨ Preheat the oven to 325°F. In a mixer bowl, beat together the butter slightly and gradually add the sugar. Add the egg and extracts; combine. In a mixing bowl, whisk together the flour, baking soda, and salt, then add to the egg mixture, combining thoroughly. Add the coconut and mix well.

▨ Using a 1 1/2-inch cookie scoop or by heaping tablespoon, drop the dough onto a greased or parchment-covered baking sheet. Sprinkle each cookie with additional sugar, then using the bottom of a sugar-coated drinking glass, press the cookie lightly to about 3/8 inch thickness. (They will rise slightly during baking.) Bake for 12 to 15 minutes and do not allow them to brown. Remove to a rack to cool and store in a tightly covered tin or freeze.

HINTS FOR GOOD COOKIES

The Amish are known for their outstanding cookies. The guidelines that follow will help you earn the same reputation! Generally, butter or solid vegetable shortening is used, though in a few cases (where specified), lard or vegetable oil gives the best results. Margarine will generally produce a softer cookie than butter. Do not use diet, whipped, or soft margarines; these are not intended for baking. If you use corn oil margarine or vegetable shortening and are making shaped or sliced cookies, chill the dough in the freezer for two hours or at least five hours (or even overnight) in the refrigerator.

Be sure to measure all ingredients correctly, using nested metal or plastic cups for the dry ingredients. Glass or plastic cups with a spout are to be used for measuring liquids only.

When measuring flour, stir it in the canister to lighten it (sifting is not necessary unless specified in the recipe) and gently spoon the flour into a dry-measuring cup clear to the top. Level off with a knife. Don't ever pack the flour into the cup or tap it on the counter.

Overbeating the cookie batter will make the cookies rise too much and as they cool, they will fall and have a cracked surface and a ridge around the outside edge. Mix the batter just enough to combine the ingredients thoroughly.

Cookie dough made with baking soda can be made up to three days in advance and refrigerated, or frozen up to three months. Don't refrigerate baking powder dough for long periods, since a chemical reaction takes place that alters the flavor and texture of the cookie.

The chilling time given in a recipe assures easy rolling, cutting, or slicing. If a dough is too firm to roll after chilling, let it stand a bit at room temperature until it softens enough to be workable. Roll out just a portion of the butter dough at a time, since it gets very soft very quickly. Chill the scraps again before rerolling. Twenty minutes of chilling in the freezer is equal to one hour in the refrigerator.

Less flour is needed for rolling out cookie (and pastry) doughs if a pastry cloth is used. These are available by mail from Fantes or Sur La Table (see page 286). When rolling sugar cookies, prevent tough rerolled cookies by combining equal amounts of confectioners' sugar and flour to sprinkle on the pastry cloth.

To ensure cookies of uniform size, use cookie scoops to portion out the dough. They also save an incredible amount of time over the old two-teaspoon method. Scoops in various sizes are available by mail (see page 286).

Bake one sheet of cookies at a time to ensure even browning. The sheet should be centered in the oven and there should be 1 to 2 inches of space all around the cookie sheet. If it is absolutely necessary to bake 2 sheets at a time, arrange the racks in the upper third and lower third of the oven, and switch positions of the pans midway during the baking time.

Avoid dark cookie sheets that absorb heat and may cause cookies to overbrown. Jelly-roll pans (10 × 15 inches) are not appropriate for cookies, except bar cookies. Use insulated baking sheets for larger cookies that require a longer baking time.

Allow the cookie sheets to cool between batches, or the cookies will spread too much on the warm sheets and brown too much around the edges.

Frost the cookies when cooled. For storage, layer them and other soft fragile cookies between wax paper, or they will adhere to one another.

To recrisp cookies that have turned soggy, reheat in a 300° F. oven for three to five minutes. To soften cookies that have become dry, place a few slices of apple in the airtight cookie tin.

Lucille's Molasses Cookies

Makes 3 dozen

LUCILLE EASH, who belongs to an Old Order Amish group, lives close to Windsor, Missouri, and is an avid reader. Fond of Laura Ingalls Wilder's and James Herriot's books, she especially likes Herriot's *The Lord God Made Them All* and his *Dog Stories*. *Black Beauty* is another favorite. Whenever she's in town, she goes to the secondhand bookstore, looking for more books about animals. Many Amish also order books from Pathway Publishers, the only Amish press, which is located in Canada.

I always think of our visit and our talk of books whenever I make Lucille's spicy cookies. They are a good size and crackly on top, dusted with cinnamon sugar, which gives them extra zip and style.

> ³⁄₄ cup solid vegetable shortening
> 1 cup sugar
> 1 egg
> ¹⁄₄ cup dark molasses
> 1 teaspoon vanilla extract
> 2 cups all-purpose flour
> 2 teaspoons baking soda
> 1 teaspoon ground cinnamon
> ¹⁄₂ teaspoon salt
> ¹⁄₄ cup sugar and 4 teaspoons ground
>   cinnamon, for topping

▓ In a mixer bowl, combine the shortening and sugar until blended, add the egg, molasses, and vanilla and beat well for 2 minutes. In another mixing bowl, whisk together the flour, baking soda, cinnamon, and salt. Gradually add to the sugar mixture and combine thoroughly. Refrigerate the dough for at least 1 hour or overnight.

▓ Preheat the oven to 350°F. In a small bowl, combine the topping ingredients. With a 1-inch cookie scoop or using your hands, form the dough into walnut-size balls. Place 2 inches apart on a parchment-lined or ungreased baking sheet (these will spread as they bake). Sprinkle the cookies with the sugar-cinnamon mixture and bake for 10 to 11 minutes or until the tops crack. Remove from the oven and allow them to cool on the baking sheet for 5 minutes before removing to a wire rack to cool completely. Transfer to airtight containers and store or freeze until needed.

Spicy Schnitz Pie

SCHNITZ BOI

Makes one 9-inch pie; serves 8

"SNITZ" OR "SCHNITZ" generally means "dried apples," and is derived from the German word *schnitz*, or *schneiden*, "to cut." In later summer and fall, apples gathered are peeled and sliced into quarters or eighths and dried. Stored in bags in a dry place for winter use, snitz frolics are still common, and this practical foodstuff makes an ideal pie filling. Drying concentrates the apple flavor, which lingers even after they are reconstituted. I buy dried apples at Amish markets or at the health food store.

Try this unusual pie served in a shallow bowl with milk or cream.

> 3 cups dried apples
> 3¹⁄₂ cups warm water or apple juice
>   Pastry for 2-crust 9-inch pie (page 270)
> ²⁄₃ cup granulated sugar
> ¹⁄₃ cup light brown sugar, packed
> ¹⁄₂ teaspoon ground cinnamon
> ¹⁄₂ teaspoon ground allspice
> 2 tablespoons butter, cut into small pieces

▓ Combine the apples and water in a deep saucepan. Bring to a boil, reduce the heat to medium low, and simmer the apples, uncovered, until they are tender and all the water has been absorbed. Check frequently to see that the water has not boiled away, or the apples will scorch, adding a bit more water from time to time if necessary. The total cooking time will vary, but count on 35 minutes at least. Drain off any excess liquid; there will be very little.

■ Preheat the oven to 425°F. Roll out the pastry and line a 9-inch pan with half of it, and set aside. Add the sugars, cinnamon, and allspice to the apples and blend. Transfer to the pie shell and dot with the butter.

■ Roll out the top crust, cover the filling, crimp the edges to seal, and slash to allow steam to escape. Bake for 15 minutes, lower the heat to 375°F., and bake 35 minutes longer, or until the pie is a deep golden brown. Transfer to a rack to cool. Serve warm or cold.

NOTE: Instead of using a top pastry, you could sprinkle on Quick Streusel Topping (page 274).

Shoofly Star Cakes

Serves 12

THIS IS AN EXCELLENT CAKE, reminiscent of the famous Pennsylvania Dutch pie, down to the crumb topping. The recipe came from a recently established Amish community in Georgia consisting of transplanted Pennsylvania Amish. Maple syrup and brown sugar were the indigenous sweeteners in the other states, though some molasses was used because it is economical.

The batter bakes nicely in 12 individual star molds (mine are made by Wilton; see page 286) or heart molds, but it can also be baked in a 9 × 13-inch flat glass dish (lower the oven temperature to 325°F. if using glass), then cut in squares and served with whipped cream or a hot lemon sauce, or both. Of course, it also makes a nice lunchbox treat.

This is mixed by hand and goes together very quickly; the batter is thin, but that's the way it's supposed to be.

3 cups all-purpose flour
1½ cups sugar
½ teaspoon salt
2 teaspoons grated nutmeg
⅔ cup cold butter
1½ cups hot water
⅔ cup molasses, light or dark
1 teaspoon baking soda
    Hot Lemon Sauce (page 273)
    Whipped Cream Topping (page 271)

■ If you are making individual molds, you will probably have to use 2 racks and stagger the baking pans, so place one oven rack on the second shelf from the top, the other, the fourth shelf from the top. Preheat the oven to 350°F.

■ In a medium bowl, whisk together the flour, sugar, salt, and nutmeg. Cut in the butter with a pastry blender or pastry fork, forming coarse crumbs. Reserve 1 cup of this mixture and set aside.

■ In a small bowl, combine the hot water, molasses, and baking soda; immediately but gradually add to the remaining dry ingredients, whisking well to smooth out any flour lumps. Butter and flour the molds or baking pans liberally. Fill the cups about three-fourths full; sprinkle with the reserved topping. Bake for 20 to 25 minutes, or until the top of the cake springs back when touched with your finger. Watch carefully and don't overbake, or the tips of the stars get a bit too crunchy. Remove from the oven, cover with foil and a terry cloth towel, and let stand for 10 minutes. Remove the stars from the pans, cover again with foil and a towel, and cool completely.

■ Serve these atop a pool of Hot Lemon Sauce and dolloped with Whipped Cream Topping.

NOTE: Bake the loaf cake 30 to 35 minutes or until the top of the cake springs back when touched with your finger.

OVERLEAF: Fragile white baby rabbits are treated with reverence and affection by these two brothers. The Amish permit themselves pets, since animals are God's creatures, too.

DINNER TIME

[MIDDAAGESSE]

❖

AT MIDDAY IN Quilt Country, the noon sun scrolls a hot yellow rinse over the land. Locusts whir their ancient song in the trees, and in the fields voluptuous rows of corn, with tassels like earrings, rustle in the gentle wind; you can hear the corn growing. The shorn meadows are heavy with the sweet scent of alfalfa and clover, the windrows forming long vertical clouds of soft brown hay interspersed with yellow rocket and daisy flea-bane. The heavy sweet scent of the hay mingles with the fragrance of the evanescent froth of the elderberry bushes in the fence rows and the bees carry pollen from flower to flower, assuring a har-vest. At home or in the fields, men and women alike are hard at work; their day is in full swing, and meals, accordingly, are hearty and sustaining.

4
LADY
FOOD

Pressed Chicken Salad ❖ Glazed Ham Balls ❖ Baked Chicken with Pudding on Top ❖ Crusty Salmon Cakes ❖ Hot Spiced Tea ❖ Tomato Cheese Bread ❖ Corn and Tomato Pie ❖ Strawberry Aspic ❖ Baked Pecan Cream Pie ❖ Brown-Eyed Susans ❖ Strawbery Tapioca ❖ Sour Cream Lemon Pie with Never-Fail Meringue ❖ Cottage Puffs with Cocoa Sauce ❖ Golden Geranium Loaf Cake ❖ Chocolate Glazed Pound Cake ❖ Delicate Mini— Angel Food Cakes ❖ Scrumptious Chocolate Cake with Peanut Butter Filling

TO OUTSIDERS, one of the best-loved images of Amish women is that of a group clustered around a quilting frame in their white caps, talking and laughing as they stitch. Quiltings, as the Amish call these gatherings, are still common and reassuring occurrences in these communities, especially in the winter months when the pressing demands of the garden and the preserving of food can be put aside for the more satisfying task of quilting.

However, not all Amish women *like* to quilt. Some of the younger ones would rather work outside with their brothers, even in cold weather. For them, pitching hay, feeding the cattle, and milking cows is preferred to staying inside and doing the meticulous stitching required by the high standards Amish quilters set for themselves, not to mention supervising the tots that have come along with their mothers.

Nonetheless, quilting continues to thrive as the most popular Amish craft, and the domestic architecture of Old Order Amish homes lends itself very well to quilting bees, just as it does to church services. The houses are built for entertaining large groups of people, though the Amish would not consider these events entertaining per se; *fellowship* might be a better word. The kitchen, dining room, and living room are very large, with triple-wide doors that open from room to room. One can generally hear and see everything that is going on in all three rooms at once, which is necessary for church and provides added enjoyment for quilting bees. The furniture, sparse and unadorned, is either removed or pushed back to accommodate the quilting frames.

To the English, the Amish woman has little in her life that would be associated with beauty, but they do appreciate beauty, even though their lives might be considered austere. Their quilts, like their flower gardens, provide them with an avenue for expressing their creative talents. At the same time, the Amish belief in doing a job well allows the quilter to show off her skills in a very acceptable way. She brings together, in an art form, her talent for sewing, coordinating colors, and quilting, as well as a way to express affection to her family, and also for income.

If a woman does quilt as a way to bring in additional income, frequently the whole family gets involved. Katie Lapp, a successful quilt

FROM 'THE BUDGET'

LATE SPRING ISSUE

On the 20th, there was a quilting at Sarah Martin's (widow). The proceeds from the quilts were to go to Country View and Cloverleaf schools. **—LOYAL, WI**

maker in Hubbard, Oregon, says, "My older children will mark patches and snip strips of patches apart at the right places as they are sewn together. The smaller ones keep the needles threaded, and they are all responsible for the noon meal and starting the evening one. The boys do the garden work, the girls do the canning. We have a saying, 'Idle hands lead to the devil.'"

> Thursday P.M. the older women's Sunday School class were at Mary Lois Kauffman's home to cut out a quilt and sew the top together for a festival in May. They had a carry-in dinner. —**DOVER, DE**

Not all of the quilts are made to be sold; when a girl marries, she wants to have at least twelve quilts in her "hope chest." Katie showed me some of her oldest daughter's quilts. "I've made some of them, some she's done herself." This would be a most acceptable dowry in any society! Crib quilts will be made when the babies begin to arrive, and these have real cachet among collectors. These are special, for most crib quilts wear out and are discarded. To discover an old crib quilt in good condition is a real find.

> There was a quilting bee at Ella Yoder's house last week to get the quilts finished up for the Mennonite Relief Sale. This is the 5th year our community has donated quilts to the auction. We had a big evening meal to celebrate and the men joined in. —**BERRYVILLE, AR**

A quilting is a happy social outing for the eight to sixteen women who congregate at one house to stitch and gossip away the day. There are discussions about who is pregnant, who is going to use a midwife instead of a doctor for delivery, and who will be the family's hired girl for the six weeks following the baby's birth, a nice-sounding custom, I must say.

To begin work on each quilt, the pieced and stitched quilt top, batting, and backing are stretched and put in the frame. Women take their places around the quilt and the sewing begins from all four sides at once. Each stitcher quilts the fabric directly in front of her, stitching as far as she can reach toward the center. When she can go no farther, the two long wooden poles to which the quilt has been anchored are released and the completed part is carefully rolled under, bringing an unquilted section to the top. Pulled tightly in the frame, the quilting begins on the new portion, the pattern lightly traced with pencil lines. The women attempt to keep pace with one another so no one must sit idle. The stitches are minuscule, each one reaching through to all three layers of the quilt.

The noon meal at a quilting bee is generous and is also a place for the women to try out new recipes before they serve them to their skeptical menfolk, who mostly prefer the tried and true. It's also an opportunity to serve somewhat daintier fare than what is expected by men who've put in a long day in the fields. We find molded salads, including aspic, or pressed chicken or veal, casseroles of all kinds and combinations, including the meat pies that are so popular among the Amish—probably because they are so economical. Desserts always include a pie, a fancier cookie or two, and even a more elaborate layer cake or upside-down cake. Coffee and tea are served with the meal, but there are no coffee breaks. This quilting day is in earnest.

Pressed Chicken Salad

Serves 12

A DISH SUCH AS THIS would be considered "lady's food" by most Amish men, and so chicken salad and all its variations appear at quilting bees, where they are greeted with pleasure. For the rest of us, this would be a fine dish for summer entertaining, for it is refreshing and elegant. Serve the loaf slices atop Boston lettuce leaves and pass additional mayonnaise if desired, or Creamy Tomato Dressing (page 142).

CHICKEN
- 1 5-pound roasting chicken, rinsed and cut into pieces
- 1 medium onion, quartered
- 2–3 carrots, quartered
- 2–3 celery ribs, quartered
- 12 whole cloves
- 9 whole black peppercorns
- 2 bay leaves

SALAD
- 2 cups Chicken Stock (page 267) or low-fat canned broth
- 2 teaspoons chicken stock concentrate base
- 2 envelopes unflavored gelatin
- 1 tablespoon finely minced fresh tarragon, or ½ teaspoon dried
- ½ teaspoon celery seeds
- ¼ teaspoon ground white pepper
- 1 10-ounce jar Durkee's Famous Sandwich and Salad Sauce (see Note)
- ½ cup finely minced celery
- ⅓ cup mayonnaise
- ⅓ cup finely minced fresh parsley
- 2 tablespoons chopped red bell pepper or red pimiento

■ MAKE THE CHICKEN: In a large stockpot, combine the chicken, onion, carrots, celery, cloves, peppercorns, and bay leaves with enough water to cover by 3 inches. Cover and bring to a boil over high heat. Lower the heat and simmer for 1 hour, or until the chicken is tender. With tongs, remove the pieces to a large pan and allow them to partially cool. Remove the skin and bones and discard. Refrigerate the stock. (See Note.)

■ Transfer the chicken meat to a food processor bowl (in several batches) and chop finely. (There will be 7 to 8 cups of chicken.) Transfer to a large bowl, cover, and refrigerate overnight. The next day, remove all the hard fat that has congealed on top of the stock and discard.

■ MAKE THE SALAD: Coat a 12 × 16-inch loaf pan (3 inches deep) with nonstick cooking spray; set aside. Dip out 2 cups of the broth and transfer to a small saucepan; add the chicken stock base. Sprinkle the 2 envelopes of gelatin over the broth and whisk in. Add the dried tarragon, if using that instead of the fresh, the celery seeds, and the white pepper. Bring the mixture to a full boil, remove from the heat, and cool slightly. Meanwhile, add the Durkee's sauce, celery, mayonnaise, parsley, and bell pepper (as well as the fresh tarragon, if using that) to the chicken and blend lightly. Add the broth mixture and combine. The mixture will be runny. Not to worry.

■ Transfer to the prepared loaf pan, cover with plastic wrap, and refrigerate until firm, about 45 minutes, and preferably at least 24 hours for the flavors to marry. Slice the loaf and serve.

NOTE: The chicken should be simmered at least a day in advance in order to skim the fat off the broth. Any extra broth can be frozen, a wonderful bonus. The chicken is easiest to debone when it is slightly warm. I suggest using a salt-free chicken stock concentrate base (not the cubes) to heighten the chicken flavor in the stock; alas, our carefully raised young chickens need a little help in the stock department, even a roasting hen. Durkee's Sauce is available nationally in the condiment section of your market, but if you can't find it, substitute 1 cup bottled mayonnaise and ¼ cup Dijon mustard.

One woman airs her quilts in an unusual manner, vertically, like a totem. A row of these on her porch was most impressive.

Glazed Ham Balls

Makes 28 balls

"ONE REASON WE LIKE serving a big ham is that we will have leftovers," explains Lucy Miller, who shared this recipe for glazed ham balls with me. The balls are well seasoned, and the glaze, which includes pineapple juice, corn syrup, and cloves, makes this a most appetizing entree.

HAM BALLS
    5 cups (2½ pounds) ground cooked ham
    1¼ cups quick-cooking oats (not instant)
    1 cup milk
    3 eggs, slightly beaten
    ½ teaspoon coarsely ground black pepper

SAUCE
    1 cup plus 2 tablespoons light brown sugar,
        packed
    3 tablespoons cornstarch
    1½ tablespoons prepared mustard
    1¾ cups pineapple juice
    ½ cup light corn syrup
    3 tablespoons cider vinegar
    ½ teaspoon ground cloves

Preheat the oven to 350°F.

MAKE THE HAM BALLS: In a large mixing bowl, combine the ham, oats, milk, eggs, and pepper. Using a 1¾-inch cookie scoop or your hands, shape the mixture into 1½-inch balls and place in a greased 10 × 15-inch baking dish; set aside.

PREPARE THE SAUCE: In a medium saucepan, combine the brown sugar, cornstarch, mustard, pineapple juice, corn syrup, vinegar, and cloves and bring to a boil over medium-high heat, while stirring constantly. Reduce the heat and simmer for 3 minutes.

Pour the sauce over the ham balls and bake for 1 hour. Serve immediately.

Baked Chicken with Pudding on Top

Serves 6

THIS UNUSUAL-SOUNDING chicken dish is baked with a Yorkshire-type pudding topping, and is an extremely tasty dish. I skin the chicken breasts but leave the skin on other parts, for you do want some fat in the bottom of the dish to flavor the pudding. Or so I think.

    ⅓ cup all-purpose flour
    1 tablespoon dried crumbled leaf sage
    1 teaspoon paprika
    1 teaspoon celery salt
    ½ teaspoon coarsely ground black pepper
    1–2 tablespoons vegetable oil
    4–4½ pounds chicken pieces (legs and thighs
        with skin on, breasts skin off)

PUDDING
    1 cup all-purpose flour
    1 teaspoon baking powder
    ½ teaspoon celery salt
    ¼ teaspoon coarsely ground black pepper
    1½ cups milk
    3 eggs, at room temperature
    ¼ cup chopped fresh parsley
    Paprika

Preheat the oven to 400°F. Combine the flour, sage, paprika, celery salt, and pepper in a paper bag. Pour the oil into a 9 × 13-inch baking pan. Toss the chicken in the bag, coating each piece with the flour mixture. Then, using tongs, coat each piece in the oil. When all have been coated, arrange the pieces in the pan skin side down. Bake, uncovered, for 40 minutes.

While the chicken bakes, prepare the pudding: In a mixer bowl, whisk together the flour, baking powder, celery salt, and pepper. Add the milk, eggs, and parsley; blend thoroughly. When the chicken is done, remove from the oven and drain off all but a scant ½ cup of the fat. Immediately pour the batter over the chicken. (It is important that the fat and the juices from baking the chicken be left in the pan to ensure a good pudding.) Sprinkle all with paprika. Return to the oven and bake an additional 30 minutes or until the pudding is puffed up and nicely browned. Serve immediately.

Crusty Salmon Cakes

Serves 6

THE AMISH COOK always keeps canned salmon on hand for a quick and inexpensive meal. The canned red salmon has more flavor than the pink and is worth the extra money it costs. I prepare the cracker crumbs in the food processor, but this can also be done by placing the crackers in a large plastic bag, then crushing them finely with a rolling pin. Serve these salmon cakes with tartar sauce (page 268).

> 1 15-ounce can red salmon, drained
> 1½ tablespoons butter or vegetable oil
> 1 medium onion, finely chopped
> ¼ green bell pepper, finely chopped
> ¾ cup finely crushed saltine crackers
>   (about 20)
> 1 tablespoon finely minced fresh dill
> ½ teaspoon freshly ground black pepper
> 3 shakes of hot red pepper sauce
> 3 tablespoons milk
> 1 tablespoon fresh lemon juice
> 1 egg, beaten
> 1½–2 tablespoons vegetable oil

■ Pick through the salmon and discard the skin and larger bones; set the salmon aside. In a medium saucepan, combine the butter or oil, onion, and bell pepper. Sauté over medium heat for 5 minutes, or until the onion begins to color.

■ Remove the pan from the heat and add the salmon, crackers, dill, black pepper, hot pepper sauce, milk, and lemon juice. Combine lightly, then add the egg and mix lightly again. Pat down the mixture in the pan and cut into 6

wedges. Form into thick patties, about 4 inches in diameter. Heat the oil in a sauté pan or an electric skillet to about 375°F. Sauté the patties about 3 minutes on each side, or until a deep crusty brown. Serve immediately.

Hot Spiced Tea

Makes 4 cups

WHEN THE WOMEN GET TOGETHER, either for a "Sisters Day" or quilting, tea is often served. There are many versions of herbal and spiced teas, and seldom a recipe; the cook uses what she has on hand, or integrates an herb currently growing in the garden.

The addition of rosemary to this tea is inspired. I prefer to start with Earl Grey tea, but the Amish women use a basic black tea bought in bulk at the food co-op.

> 4 cups water
> 4 Earl Grey tea bags
> 4 cinnamon sticks
> 4 whole cloves
> 1 large rosemary sprig
> 2 thin orange slices, halved, for garnish

■ In a large 4-cup measure, heat the water in the microwave to boiling, about 4 minutes on high. Add the tea bags, cinnamon sticks, cloves, and rosemary. Cover the cup with a lid or plate and allow the mixture to steep for 5 minutes.

■ With tongs, remove the sticks, cloves, and rosemary and discard. Pour into cups and garnish each cup with half an orange slice.

QUILT
HISTORY

Though the Amish and Mennonites are now considered among the country's finest quilters, quilting was practiced long before they appeared on the scene. The earliest examples of quilting come from China, India, and Egypt, where the practice was adopted for a practical reason: stitching together three layers of fabric provided good insulation against the cold.

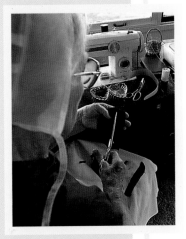

Among all the material I have on quilting, I recently discovered that when the Crusaders encountered the Saracens in the Holy Land, the Saracen foot soldiers were wearing straw-filled quilted canvas shirts in lieu of armor, and the horsemen wore quilted silk undershirts to keep their metal armor from chafing. Our first written record of quilts dates from the twelfth century. The Christian Crusaders brought the technique back to Europe after their wars in the Middle East. Quilting and patchwork remained two separate crafts for at least two centuries, but it is thought that patchwork quilting did evolve first in America. With fabric being so scarce, patches of old clothing were sewed together to make bed coverings. As textiles became more available, both here and abroad, the quilting became more elaborate and decorative.

Like kitchen lore, quilting techniques are taught by example and pass from generation to generation. Geographical differences are easily spotted. The traditional quilts of Pennsylvania may be made of wool and feature wide borders and simple graphic patterns; in Indiana, Ohio, and Iowa, the quilts were and still are made of cotton, with more complex patterns.

Tomato Cheese Bread

Makes 1 loaf

VERA JESS BELONGS to an Old Order Amish community in Arthur, Illinois, and prepares meals for tourists who want to know more about Amish life and food. She gives approximately fifty dinners a year, mostly for busloads of visitors. She also caters banquets for up to one hundred people. She and her fourteen-year-old daughter, Mary, do all the work, rolling out of bed at 2:30 A.M. on the days they have the dinners. She is also a scribe for *The Budget*, the popular Amish and conservative Mennonite weekly newspaper, which is a series of letters from correspondents (scribes) all over the world. (See page 286 for more information on *The Budget*.)

Vera frequently tries new recipes from the *Country Home* and *Taste of Home* magazines, though the foods served at her dinners are traditional recipes, like this flavorful quick bread. It's well seasoned and deep orange in color, and it's unforgettably good.

> 2 1/2 cups all-purpose flour
> 1 1/2 tablespoons sugar
> 2 teaspoons baking powder
> 1 teaspoon salt
> 1 teaspoon ground cumin
> 1/4 teaspoon baking soda
> 1/4 teaspoon freshly ground black pepper
> 1 cup shredded sharp Cheddar cheese
> 1 tablespoon chopped fresh basil,
>   or 1 teaspoon dried
> 2 eggs
> 1 cup fresh tomatoes, peeled, seeded, and finely
>   chopped
> 2 tablespoons tomato paste
> 6 tablespoons melted butter
> 1/8 teaspoon hot red pepper sauce

▨ Preheat the oven to 350°F. Grease a 9 × 5 × 3-inch loaf pan and set aside. In a large mixing bowl, whisk together the flour, sugar, baking powder, salt, cumin, baking soda, and pepper. Stir in the cheese and basil.

▨ In a small mixing bowl, beat the eggs lightly, then add the tomatoes, tomato paste, butter, and hot pepper sauce; mix thoroughly. Make a well in the center of the dry ingredients, pour in the tomato mixture, and stir until the dry ingredients are just moistened; do not overmix. Pour into the prepared pan and smooth the top.

▨ Bake for 55 minutes or until an instant-read thermometer registers 200°F. Let cool in the pan for 10 minutes and then remove and cover with foil and a terry cloth towel. Cool completely, slice, and serve with butter.

Corn and Tomato Pie

Serves 6

WE HAVE SO MUCH corn and tomatoes in our Midwestern gardens that we are always looking for ways to eat them up. This well-seasoned dish is one of those alternate ways. The "pie crust" is of bacon and bread crumbs, and the filling of seasoned tomatoes and corn is quick to assemble. All told, it is a very appetizing combination.

> 8 slices raw turkey or pork bacon, halved
> 2 cups dry bread crumbs
> 1 green bell pepper, seeded and minced
> 2 cups coarsely chopped fresh tomatoes, peeled
>   and seeded
> 3 cups uncooked fresh corn kernels, cut from
>   the cob
> 1 1/2 teaspoons salt
> 1/4 teaspoon ground pepper
> 1 teaspoon brown sugar, packed
> 1/4 cup minced fresh basil (optional)

▨ Preheat the oven to 375°F. Use 4 slices of the bacon to line the bottom of a shallow 2-quart casserole and top with half of the bread crumbs. Layer in the green pepper, tomatoes, and corn, seasoning each layer with a bit of salt, pepper, brown sugar, and basil. Sprinkle the remaining bread crumbs over the top and cover with the remaining bacon. Bake for 1 hour or until the top is lightly browned and the mixture is cooked down. Serve hot.

Strawberry Aspic

Serves 9

BEING FOND OF TOMATO ASPIC, I was intrigued by this version with its hint of strawberry. The tomatoes give the strawberry base real pizzazz—in fact, it's really good. The Amish use cider vinegar, but the balsamic is also very nice. Serve this on Boston lettuce with Creamy Tomato Dressing or a dab of bottled mayonnaise.

Now I want you to understand this is as far as I can go with gelatin salads, even though the Amish and Mennonites serve a lot of them. When serving the Pressed Chicken Salad (page 76), I accompany it with a small molded cup of this aspic; it is a happy combination of flavors and textures.

> 1 28-ounce can stewed tomatoes
> $\frac{1}{2}$ cup vegetable juice, such as V-8
> 2 tablespoons finely minced onion
> 3 tablespoons cider vinegar, or 2 tablespoons balsamic vinegar
> $\frac{1}{8}$ teaspoon hot red pepper sauce
> $\frac{1}{4}$ teaspoon salt
> $\frac{1}{2}$ teaspoon white pepper
> 2 3-ounce boxes strawberry gelatin
> Creamy Tomato Dressing (page 142; optional)

▓ Prepare a 9 × 9-inch square pan or nine $\frac{1}{2}$-cup individual molds with nonstick cooking spray.

▓ In a blender, combine the tomatoes, juice, onion, vinegar, hot pepper sauce, salt, and pepper; puree. The mixture should not be totally smooth. Transfer the mixture to a deep saucepan and bring to a full boil; stir in the gelatin. Remove from the heat and pour into the prepared pan or molds. Chill until completely set.

▓ Serve the chilled aspic with a dollop of Creamy Tomato Dressing.

Baked Pecan Cream Pie

Makes two 9-inch pies; serves 16

THIS IS RATHER LIKE a thick chess pie with pecans, a fine state of affairs if you like chess pie and pecan pie. The filling for this pie can be made three days in advance and refrigerated, though it may be necessary to whisk the mixture lightly to recombine before pouring into the shells. The recipe came to me from an Argos, Indiana, Old Order Mennonite woman, who maintains she really doesn't like to cook—at least not like her mother-in-law, who "lives to see how many people she can fill up at one time."

> Pastry for 2 9-inch single crust pies (page 270)
> $\frac{3}{4}$ cup (1$\frac{1}{2}$ sticks) butter, at room temperature
> 3 cups sugar
> 7 eggs, well beaten
> 1$\frac{1}{2}$ cups milk
> 2 teaspoons vanilla extract
> 3 tablespoons fresh lemon juice
> 1$\frac{1}{2}$ cups very coarsely chopped pecans
> 3 tablespoons all-purpose flour
> 3 tablespoons yellow cornmeal

▓ Preheat the oven to 350° F. Roll out the pie crust on a lightly floured surface and line 2 pie pans; set aside.

▓ In a mixer bowl, whip the butter, then add the sugar gradually and cream thoroughly, about 1 minute. Add the eggs and milk gradually, then the vanilla and lemon juice, and combine, then fold in the nuts. In a small bowl, whisk together the flour and cornmeal, then gradually add to the nut mixture and blend. Pour the filling into the unbaked pie shells and bake for 55 to 60 minutes, or until the top of the pies are golden brown and appear to be set in the center. Cool the pies completely on wire racks before cutting and serving.

Brown-Eyed Susans

Makes 4 dozen cookies

THIS IS A VERY pretty cookie, as its name suggests—a "short" cookie, owing to the confectioners' sugar in the dough. An old, old recipe named after the country wildflower it resembles, these disappear very quickly from the cookie tray. I'm sure you'll be as glad as I was to come across it again.

> 1 cup (2 sticks) butter, at room temperature
> 1/4 cup confectioners' sugar
> 1 teaspoon almond extract
> 1 teaspoon vanilla extract
> 2 cups all-purpose flour
> 1/2 teaspoon salt

FROSTING
> 1 cup confectioners' sugar
> 2 tablespoons cocoa powder
> 2 tablespoons hot water
> 1 teaspoon vanilla extract
>
> 48 whole almonds

■ Preheat the oven to 350°F. In a mixer bowl, cream together the butter and sugar until light and fluffy, about 2 minutes. Blend in the extracts. Add the flour and salt, and mix well.

■ Using a cookie scoop or your hands, lightly shape the dough into 1-inch balls and place on ungreased baking sheets. Flatten slightly with the bottom of a glass. Bake for 12 to 14 minutes or shape the dough into 1-inch balls and place on ungreased baking sheets. Flatten slightly using the bottom of a glass. Bake for 12 to 14 minutes or until the bottoms are lightly browned. Remove to a wire rack and cool the cookies completely before frosting.

■ TO PREPARE THE FROSTING: In a mixing bowl, whisk together the confectioners' sugar and cocoa. Add the hot water and vanilla; mix well. Frost each cookie and top with an almond. Store in an airtight container, using wax paper or plastic wrap between layers. These also freeze very well.

Strawberry Tapioca

Makes 8 generous servings

AMISH AND MENNONITE COOKS use tapioca in a variety of ways: as a thickener for pies, soups, stews, and meat loaves, and also in superb puddings. This most attractive dessert is considered family fare, but all gussied up with whipped cream and mint, it is certainly nice enough for company. Tapioca contains no fat, so this (without the whipped cream) is a fat-free dessert. Not that children will care about that, but they will appreciate its pretty pink color. Any other fruit, except apples, can be substituted for the strawberries.

> 2 cups strawberries, washed and hulled
> 1 cup sugar
> 3 cups boiling water
> 1/2 cup quick-cooking tapioca
> 1/4 teaspoon salt
> 2 teaspoons butter
> 1 teaspoon fresh lemon juice
> 1/4 teaspoon almond extract
> 1/8 teaspoon red food coloring (optional)
> *Whipped cream and fresh mint leaves, for garnish*

■ Puree the strawberries in a food processor bowl with 1/2 cup of the sugar or place the berries and sugar in a bowl and use a potato masher to crush; set aside.

■ In a large saucepan, combine the boiling water, tapioca, and salt; allow the mixture to stand for 10 minutes. Cook, stirring frequently, over medium heat for 15 minutes or until the tapioca is clear. Stir in the remaining sugar and the butter.

■ Remove the pan from the heat and whisk in the lemon juice, almond extract, and food coloring. Then stir in the strawberries, mixing well. Chill for several hours, then serve in individual sauce dishes or compotes, garnished with whipped cream and fresh mint leaves.

The younger women, not yet skilled enough to quilt, prepare the quilters' (and their own) noon meal. The food is served family style in bowls and passed at the table.

Sour Cream Lemon Pie with Never-Fail Meringue

Makes one 9-inch pie; serves 6 to 8

THE ADDITION of sour cream makes this an outstanding lemon pie with a superb texture. Dairy products are used liberally in most Amish and Mennonite kitchens out of tradition and also because many of them maintain herds of Holstein cows, which produce prodigious amounts of rich milk and cream.

Today, most of the cows are milked with electric milking machines run off a generator. As long as the electrical power does not come from an outside source, many individual farms use their own generators, which enables them to still be "separate from the world." This meringue is a tad different from the usual recipe; it does hold up very well.

1 cup plus 2 tablespoons sugar
3 1/2 tablespoons cornstarch
1/8 teaspoon salt
1/2 cup fresh lemon juice (approximately 4 large lemons)
1 tablespoon grated lemon zest
1 cup milk
3 egg yolks
1/4 cup (1/2 stick) butter, at room temperature
1 cup sour cream
Pastry for a 1-crust 9-inch pie (page 270)

MERINGUE
1 tablespoon cornstarch
2 tablespoons cold water
1/2 cup hot water
1 teaspoon vanilla extract
1/8 teaspoon salt
3 egg whites
1/3 cup sugar

■ In a small bowl, whisk together the sugar, cornstarch, and salt. Add the lemon juice and zest, then stir in the milk.

■ In the top of a double boiler, beat the egg yolks and add the sugar-milk mixture gradually, whisking lightly until combined. Place the mixture over simmering water and cook until the custard is thick, about 10 minutes, stirring frequently with a rubber spatula. When thickened, stir in the butter until combined. Remove the top pan from the double boiler and cool slightly. Stir in the sour cream and refrigerate the filling until completely chilled.

■ Preheat the oven to 350° F. Roll out the pastry and line a 9-inch pan. Prick the pastry all over with a fork and bake for 6 to 8 minutes, checking frequently to prick air bubbles and to pat the sides up with a fork if the pastry begins to slip down. Remove from the oven. When cooled completely, pour in the chilled filling.

■ MAKE THE MERINGUE: In a small saucepan, combine the cornstarch and cold water. Add the hot water, vanilla, and salt, then simmer the mixture over medium heat until it is clear and thickened. Set aside until completely cooled; it will be very thick (I speed this cooling process up by placing the pan in the freezer—it cools in about 8 minutes.)

■ When the cornstarch mixture is completely cool, beat the egg whites on high speed until foamy. Lower the speed and gradually add the sugar, a tablespoon at a time, then gradually add the cornstarch mixture. Turn to high speed again and beat a minute longer. Spread the meringue over the top of the cooled lemon pie and bake for 350° F. for 12 to 15 minutes. Cool, then refrigerate until serving time.

Cottage Puffs with Cocoa Sauce

Serves 12

IF YOU LOVE CHOCOLATE, this is your dish. These are really chocolate shortcakes, a fine idea, you'll have to agree. And what an irresistible-sounding dessert name. The tender muffins do resemble puffs—pale, creamy, and a bit like a rich biscuit. If not serving immediately, reheat both the puffs and sauce in the microwave. We like this with a pitcher of milk so we can pour a bit over the top. Serve in "nappies," or dessert dishes.

PUFFS

⅓ cup butter, at room temperature
½ cup sugar
1 egg
1 teaspoon vanilla extract
1½ cups all-purpose flour
1½ tablespoons baking powder
1 teaspoon grated nutmeg
⅓ teaspoon salt
½ cup milk

COCOA SAUCE

½ cup sugar
2 tablespoons cocoa powder
1½ tablespoons cornstarch
½ teaspoon salt
1½ cups water
2 tablespoons butter
1 teaspoon vanilla extract

▧ Preheat the oven to 350°F.

▧ PREPARE THE PUFFS: Spray a 12-cup muffin tin with nonstick cooking spray and set aside. (Do not use muffin papers.)

▧ In a mixer bowl, cream together the butter and sugar until fluffy. Add the egg and vanilla; mix well. In another bowl, whisk together the flour, baking powder, nutmeg, and salt. Add the dry ingredients to the butter mixture alternating with the milk, beginning and ending with the dry ingredients. Do not overmix. Fill the muffin tins equally and bake the puffs for 20 minutes.

▧ PREPARE THE COCOA SAUCE: In a small mixing bowl, whisk together the sugar, cocoa, cornstarch, and salt. In a medium saucepan, heat the water to boiling, then add the butter and vanilla. Whisk in the dry ingredients and cook over medium heat until the sauce thickens, about 3 minutes. Just before serving, ladle the hot sauce over the warm puffs.

Golden Geranium Loaf Cake

Makes one loaf, 10-12 slices

SCENTED GERANIUMS ARE among the houseplants commonly found on Amish and Mennonite windowsills. The leaves release their pungent fragrance when touched or brushed against. The more strongly scented citrus varieties such as lemon rose give cakes an extraordinary flavor. Serve this beautifully textured loaf cake in a puddle of English Pouring Sauce (page 275).

10–12 medium lemon rose geranium leaves
Softened butter, for buttering the pan and leaves
1¾ cups all-purpose flour
1 cup sugar
2 teaspoons baking powder
½ cup (1 stick) butter, at room temperature
1 teaspoon vanilla extract
5 egg yolks, unbeaten
½ cup milk

▧ Wash and dry the geranium leaves. Coat a 9 × 5 × 3-inch pan lavishly with butter, and with a small rubber spatula, coat the backs of the leaves with more butter and "paste" them on the bottom and sides of the pan. They adhere easily.

▧ Preheat the oven to 350°F. In a mixer bowl, whisk together the flour, sugar, and baking powder. Add the butter, vanilla, egg yolks, and milk; beat for 2 minutes. Carefully transfer the cake batter into the prepared pan. (Actually, it's easy—the leaves cling to the sides of the pan just the way they are supposed to.)

▧ Bake the cake for 40 minutes, tent with foil, and bake 20 to 25 minutes longer, or until the top of the cake is brown and the middle springs back when touched with your finger. Remove to a rack and cover with foil and a terry cloth towel for 10 minutes. Remove covering, run a knife around the edges, and slap the cake smartly on the counter. Invert onto a platter and re-cover with the foil and towel. Cool completely, and peel away the leaves just before serving.

ANGEL
FOOD CAKE
HINTS

Angel food cakes have always been popular among the Pennsylvania Dutch, and though the cake's origin is still a mystery, it is recorded in Pennsylvania cookbooks as early as 1870. Of course, it is the best way of all to use up all the egg whites left over from noodle making, and the whites also freeze extremely well.

In these cakes, egg whites are the sole leavening, forming an elastic mesh of trapped air bubbles that expand in the hot oven and cause the cake to rise. A few guidelines will ensure success.

The first rule about angel food cakes is to separate the yolks from the whites when the eggs are cold, and then allow the whites to come to room temperature. Be very careful not to let one speck of yolk get into the whites, or the whites won't whip adequately. Separate each egg over a small bowl to avoid spoiling the whole batch, in case one of those yolks breaks. Be sure the bowl and beater are very clean and grease free; don't use plastic bowls when working with egg whites, for the plastic absorbs grease particles.

It is best to use superfine sugar; it is available in the sugar section and is sometimes called "bar sugar," since it dissolves quickly in cold drinks. However, you can make your own superfine sugar by whizzing regular sugar in the food processor for 5 minutes.

Second, *never* grease an angel food cake pan; the batter needs to cling to the sides of the pan as it rises and bakes.

Finally, bake the cake in the lower third of the oven. After the cake is baked, invert it to cool. Place the upside-down tube of the pan over the neck of a tall narrow bottle to cool completely. With a sharp knife, loosen the cake around the edges of the pan and the inner tube and remove.

Chocolate Glazed Pound Cake

Serves 12 to 16

GOOD CHOCOLATY TEXTURE and the denseness of a pound cake characterize this cake—it's substantial, not fluffy. Since pound cakes are rather firm, this is a good cake for carry-ins or lunch buckets. The creamy chocolate frosting is optional—you could certainly serve the cake with English Pouring Sauce (page 275).

> 1½ cups (3 sticks) butter, at room temperature
> 3 cups sugar
> 2 teaspoons vanilla extract
> 5 eggs, at room temperature
> 2 cups all-purpose flour, sifted
> 1 cup cocoa powder
> 2 tablespoons instant coffee powder
> ½ teaspoon baking powder
> 1 teaspoon salt
> 1 cup buttermilk
> ¼ cup water

FROSTING
> 3 tablespoons butter
> 4 1-ounce squares semisweet chocolate
> 3 tablespoons evaporated milk
> 1 teaspoon vanilla extract
> Pinch of salt
> ⅔–1 cup confectioners' sugar

▓ Preheat the oven to 325°F. Butter and flour a Bundt or tube pan; set aside. In a large mixer bowl, cream the butter until fluffy. Gradually add the sugar and beat for 5 minutes. Add the vanilla and the eggs, one at a time, beating well after each addition. In a large mixing bowl, whisk together the flour, cocoa, coffee powder, baking powder, and salt. Add to the creamed mixture, alternating with the buttermilk and water, beginning and ending with the dry ingredients; blend well. Pour into the prepared pan and bake in the upper third of the oven for 1 hour and 20 minutes, or until a cake tester comes out clean. Remove from the oven and immediately cover with foil and a terry cloth towel, and let stand for 20 minutes; unmold, re-cover, and finish cooling. Frost when completely cooled.

▓ PREPARE THE FROSTING: In the top of a double boiler over medium-high heat, melt the butter with the chocolate and stir until smooth. Remove from the heat and whisk in the milk, vanilla, and salt. Stir in ⅔ cup confectioners' sugar, adding up to ⅓ cup more if the consistency is too thin. Spread the warm frosting over the cooled cake.

Delicate Mini—Angel Food Cakes

Makes 12 mini-cakes or one 10-inch cake

THESE ADORABLE INDIVIDUAL cakes can be frosted and served one per person, or can be split horizontally and topped with fresh sweetened fruit, such as strawberries, then topped with whipped cream. That is a scrumptious shortcake! For the mini-cakes, you will need three pans (each of which makes four cakes), which can be ordered directly from Wilton Enterprises (see page 286). The recipe can also be used for one large 10-inch angel food cake.

> 12 egg whites, at room temperature
> 1½ teaspoons almond extract
> 1½ teaspoons vanilla extract
> 1½ teaspoons cream of tartar
> ¼ teaspoon salt
> 1½ cups sugar, preferably superfine (see box, page 89)
> 1 cup sifted cake flour

▓ Preheat the oven to 350°F. In a large mixer bowl, on medium speed, beat the egg whites, extracts, cream of tartar, and salt together until foamy. Increasing the speed to high, add the sugar 1 tablespoon at a time. When all of the sugar is integrated, the whites will be glossy and stiff.

▓ Remove the bowl from the mixer and sprinkle one-third of the flour over the egg whites. Using a large balloon whisk or large slotted spoon, fold in the flour with 4 to 6 light but deep sweeping strokes. Repeat twice with the remaining flour, folding only enough to evenly incorporate the flour. Don't overmix or you will deflate the egg whites.

■ Transfer the batter to 12 ungreased mini-cake pans, or an ungreased 10-inch angel food cake pan, filling the mini-pans two-thirds full. (If any batter is left over, bake in ungreased glass custard or individual soufflé dishes.) Bake the mini-cakes for 30 minutes, the 10-inch cake for 45 minutes. The top of the cakes will be dry and spring back when touched with your finger. Remove the cakes from the oven and invert in the pans to cool.

■ Cool the cakes completely, then run a sharp thin knife around the edges of the pans and release the cakes from the pans. Frost or fill as desired.

Scrumptious Chocolate Cake with Peanut Butter Filling

Serves 12 to 16

CHOCOLATE AND PEANUT BUTTER is a hard combination to improve on. This cake is moist and finely textured, and the toothsome brown strip of peanut butter filling really enhances the flavor. Topped off with a perfection of chocolate frosting, it's an agreeable version of Reese's famous candy.

2 cups all-purpose flour
2 teaspoons baking soda
1 teaspoon baking powder
$^1/_2$ teaspoon salt
$^3/_4$ cup cocoa powder
2 cups granulated sugar
$^1/_2$ cup vegetable oil
2 eggs
1 cup milk
2 teaspoons vanilla extract
1 cup hot strong coffee

FILLING

1 cup smooth peanut butter
$^1/_4$ cup plus 2 tablespoons confectioners' sugar
1 teaspoon butter, at room temperature
$1^1/_2$ teaspoons vanilla extract
3 tablespoons evaporated milk or heavy cream

Chocolate Fudge Frosting (page 273)

■ Preheat the oven to 350° F. Grease two 9-inch round baking pans and set aside.

■ In a large mixing bowl or large pouring cup, whisk together the flour, baking soda, baking powder, salt, and cocoa. In a mixer bowl, combine the granulated sugar, oil, and eggs and mix thoroughly. Add the milk and vanilla and blend, then pour in the coffee and combine well. (The batter will be thin and runny.) Pour into the prepared pans and bake for 30 to 35 minutes or until the top of the cake springs back when touched with your finger. Remove the cakes from the oven, cover immediately with foil and a terry cloth towel, and allow the layers to stand in the pans for 10 minutes, then turn out onto a rack, re-cover, and cool completely.

■ PREPARE THE FILLING: In a mixer bowl, cream together the peanut butter, confectioners' sugar, and butter on high speed until smooth. Add the vanilla and milk; blend.

■ ASSEMBLE THE CAKE: Place one cake layer on a cake plate and tuck 4 strips of wax paper under the edges of the cake to catch dripping frosting. Top this first layer with all of the filling, smoothing it out to the very edge of the cake. Place the second layer on top of the first. Frost the entire cake with chocolate frosting, doing the sides first, then the top. (If there is any frosting left over, make graham cracker sandwiches with it.)

5
NOON
MEALS

Sausage Potato Soup with Sage ❖ Cream of Cabbage Soup ❖ Succulent Pork Chops with Sauerkraut and Potatoes ❖ Smoked Pork Chops with Cider Glaze ❖ Roast Beef Shortcake ❖ The Very Best Beef Pot Roast ❖ Cheese and Rice Soufflé with Bacon ❖ Creamed Fresh Summer Corn ❖ Roasted Tomatoes ❖ Summer Squash Soufflé with Rosemary ❖ Creamed Red Beets ❖ Spinach Salad with Celery Seed and Bacon Dressing ❖ Five-Vegetable Cole Slaw ❖ Fluffy Mashed Potato Patties ❖ Delicate Butter Muffins ❖ Buttery Spiced Apples ❖ Peachy Baked Apples ❖ Blueberry Rhubarb Pie ❖ Peach Praline Pie ❖ Old-Fashioned Bread Pudding with Hot Caramel Sauce ❖ Old-Fashioned Brown Sugar Cream Pie ❖ Grandma's Rhubarb Meringue Pie

BY JUNE, Amish gardens and fields are planted and the landscape is alive with beauty. The woods' fringe is accented with the foamy green whiteness of black locust trees, its sweet tuberose fragrance scenting the landscape. In the bogs, frogs sing in slow, steady chants and wild roses and small daisies bloom abundantly along the roadsides.

And if one is lucky, they may hear the distinct call of the whippoorwill.

The Amish have their big meal, which they call dinner, at noon, and I arrive at the Lancaster home of the Troyers just in time. All of the family have been up half a day and have accomplished what most of us would consider a full day's hard physical labor, so a substantial meal is in order.

A dinner bell outside the Troyer house is rung by a shy little boy with a bowl haircut. He is dressed in a white shirt and dark blue trousers and heavy black shoes. The bell ringing announces to the Troyer family scattered about the property that the noon meal is ready. Seeing me, the boy runs inside and informs his mother "the recipe lady" has come.

The menu always includes meat, potatoes, and frequently noodles as well as breads and dessert —maybe several. The choices include fresh fruit that's been cut up and sweetened, or canned,

FROM 'THE BUDGET'
SUMMER ISSUE

We finished digging horseradish last week. Want to plant a new crop soon since we use it in canned dill pickles and tomato relish. —BIRD-IN-HAND, PA

brought up from the basement and served with cookies. Pies and puddings are the most popular desserts, and cakes too, generally made as a loaf or sheet cake. Layer cakes are reserved for special occasions or to sell.

I marvel at the amount of food the Amish women prepare, day in and day out. With their large families, it is not unusual for fifteen people to be fed three times a day; some of those meals may be packed lunches, but it is a cooking task, nonetheless. Since most of us would consider fifteen people for one meal either a party or family reunion requiring advance planning, not to mention advance stress, this unremitting culinary responsibility boggles my mind.

However, their kitchens are very large and roomy compared to most, and there are many people to help. The handsome cabinets are custom-made by local Amish woodcrafters; linoleum is the floor covering. There are good-sized, generally uncurtained windows looking out on the barns and garden, and a large table that opens up to seat at least twenty stands in the center of most of the kitchens, doing double duty as an important work space. It is not uncommon to see two stoves, one operating on bottled gas, the other on wood or coal. The light is provided either by gas fixtures or hanging kerosene lanterns. On one wall, there is usually a hutch or china cupboard that contains the treasured unmatched china, collected by the women in the family.

I have never interviewed an Amish woman alone; there were always other female members of the family, either in the kitchen working or passing in and out as they attended to other household duties. It is a supportive, warm, and practical way for Amish women to live. And they never have to hire a baby-sitter.

Other recipes I saw served at noon meals were casseroles that could bake unattended while the women worked outside in the garden, or coped with the never-ending wash, or canned summer crops. Frequently these dishes are misleadingly named; a good example is the almost opulent cheese and rice souf-flé, actually a sturdy combination of well-seasoned rice and cheese, not a soufflé at all. It is an ideal partner to fried chicken or roast meats. One-dish meals, such as pork chops and sauer-kraut, with potatoes or dumplings added late in

> Mrs. Sarah Blosser is canning beans on "shares." The neighbor has the beans and Sarah cans them, keeping two jars and returning one. Most peoples' beans seem to be getting a blight and we are afraid it will shorten the crop. —EPHRATA, PA

> Ammon Millers are moving their house onto the Levi Miller farm to help along with the farming. They finally moved it on Friday. Titus Fox was hauling cement block to use, with four horses hitched to the wagon and had a runaway, ending up breaking the tongue of the buggy, but continued on by getting a tongue at the Melvin Burkholders. —TOMAH, WI

the cooking period, are also popular. All sorts of meat loaves served with roasted potatoes are a staple at noon meals. Overall, chicken is the most popular entree because of its availability. Prepared to ensure the maximum number of servings, chicken might be simmered with noodles and ladled on top of mashed potatoes, or made into what we would call a pot pie. Chicken dressing, or "filling" as it is known, is a puffy well-seasoned baked bread dressing, well laced with poached chicken pieces picked off the bone, that is served topped with gravy, another favorite. Prepared this way, one chicken can easily be stretched to serve twelve people.

The tables are covered in patterned oilcloth, bought at the local fabric or hardware store, and the napkins are paper, never cloth. Knives, forks, and spoons, including soup spoons, are placed together on the right. The table will not have a flower arrangement, though there may be a pitcher or jar of flowers on the windowsill above the sink. After a prayer is given by the male head of the house, the meal is served family style from large serving bowls. However, desserts, such as pies and cakes, are precut and placed in front of each diner on a plate.

Don't attend an Amish dinner and expect to find a container of yogurt. This noon meal is serious, and prepares the diners for a full afternoon's work.

Sausage Potato Soup with Sage

Makes 8 cups

IN YEARS PAST a ninety-acre farm was considered average size, and could comfortably be cultivated by horses. Today, in order to remain self-sufficient, a farmer needs more land, and Amish and Old Order Mennonite families that can afford it are buying farms with more acreage in order to remain working on the land. In these cases, tractor farming is permitted, but only with metal wheels, not rubber-tired tractors.

After a day of plowing, any farmer would be delighted to sit down to a big bowl of this soup.

> 1 pound lean pork sausage with sage
> 2 medium onions, chopped
> 5 cups peeled and thickly sliced potatoes
> 2 cups Chicken Stock (page 267), or
>   1 15-ounce can chicken broth
> 1 teaspoon salt
> ¼ teaspoon celery seeds
> ¼ teaspoon cracked black peppercorns
> 2½ cups milk
> 4 shakes hot red pepper sauce
> 3 tablespoons chopped fresh parsley
> 1 tablespoon minced fresh marjoram, or
>   ½ teaspoon dried (optional)

▓ In a stockpot, brown the sausage over medium heat until the juices are released, about 3 minutes. Add the onions and sauté the mixture until the onions are limp, about 8 minutes. Drain off the fat, and set the sausage aside in a bowl.

▓ Add the potatoes, stock, salt, celery seeds, and pepper to the pot. Bring to a boil, then cover and simmer for 20 minutes or until the potatoes are tender. Slightly mash the potatoes, leaving some in chunks for good texture. Add the reserved sausage, the milk, hot pepper sauce, parsley, and marjoram. Bring to a simmer over medium-low heat, about 10 minutes. Ladle into bowls and serve immediately.

Cream of Cabbage Soup

Makes 14 cups; serves 8 to 10

BECAUSE THEY KEEP SO well, cabbages appear on Amish and Mennonite tables virtually year-round. After the fall harvest, cabbages might be suspended upside down in deep trenches in the garden; the trench is filled in with straw, the cabbages placed stem end up, then more straw piled on top. As the cabbages are needed, the cook goes to the garden and pulls up the head by its stem, then removes the old leaves before she takes it into the house to prepare any number of ways.

This is a distinctive country German soup.

> ½ pound bacon, coarsely chopped
> 12 cups shredded cabbage (about 2½ pounds)
> 1 medium onion, chopped
> 2½ quarts Chicken Stock (page 267), or
>   5 16-ounce cans chicken broth
> 1 cup half-and-half
> 2 teaspoons salt
> ½ teaspoon pepper
>   Grated Swiss cheese

▓ In a large stockpot, fry the bacon until crisp over medium-high heat; remove and set aside. To the drippings in the pan add the cabbage and onion, reduce the heat to medium, and sauté, stirring occasionally, for 10 minutes or until the cabbage is limp. (Do not let it brown.) Add the chicken stock and simmer until the cabbage and onion are tender, 10 to 15 minutes.

▓ Remove from the heat and transfer 3 cups (mainly cabbage) of the soup to a blender and puree. Return to the stockpot and stir in the half-and-half. Season with salt and pepper. Serve garnished with reserved bacon and the cheese.

ABOVE: Amish girls often share responsibility for tending the family's livestock. BELOW: Farm wives usually have their own small kitchen garden close to the house, supplying fresh produce and herbs for the family's meals.

Succulent Pork Chops with Sauerkraut and Potatoes

Serves 6

THIS SURELY HAS TO BE one of the quickest one-dish meals you can make. I really prefer using the smoked pork chops, but if not available, fresh ones are also very good. The potatoes can be omitted and Butter Dumplings (page 266) substituted, adding ½ teaspoon rubbed sage to the dry ingredients. Drop the dumplings on top of the kraut 25 minutes before the baking time is up. Turn up the oven to 425° F. while preparing the dumplings. Or, of course, you can have both potatoes *and* dumplings. This hearty meal is really most appropriately served in cool weather.

> 2 medium onions, coarsely chopped
> 6 ¾-inch-thick fresh or smoked pork chops,
>   well trimmed
>   Coarsely ground black pepper
> 6 small potatoes, peeled, chunked, and precooked
>   (see Note)
> 2 15-ounce cans Bavarian-style sauerkraut,
>   well drained
> 1 quart Chicken Stock (page 267), or
>   2 15-ounce cans low-fat chicken broth
> 9 whole cloves

■ Preheat the oven to 300° F. Coat a large Dutch oven with nonstick cooking spray. Sprinkle half of the onions in the bottom of the pan. Place the pork chops on top; sprinkle with the pepper. Arrange the potatoes around the chops. Top with the sauerkraut, then pour the stock over all. Drop in the whole cloves. Cover and bake for 2 hours. Serve hot in rather deep-lipped plates, adding some stock to each serving.

NOTE: To precook the potatoes, place the peeled chunks in a 9 × 9-inch dish, add 1 cup of water or stock, cover, and microwave on high for 6 to 7 minutes, stirring after 3 minutes. Alternatively, simmer in salted water for 6 to 8 minutes. The potatoes should just be a bit done and will finishing baking in the oven with the meat, kraut, and all those good pan juices.

Smoked Pork Chops with Cider Glaze

Serves 6

"WHEN YOU'VE HAD smoked pork chops, you're spoiled for ham," reports Levi Helmuth as we sit down to a hearty noon meal of chops, mashed potatoes, noodles cooked in chicken stock, green salad, new onions, and radishes.

Levi operates a harness repair shop and has more business than he can handle. The Helmuths moved to Wisconsin from Ohio, after the Cleveland area where they'd lived previously became crowded with "too much car traffic." Though most Amish use reflective red safety emblems on the backs of their buggies, and even 12-volt lights, some of the more conservative Amish, such as those belonging to the Swartzentruber sect, eschew both—much to the dismay of the local police. Nor do the Swartzentruber Amish have small back windows in their buggies, a further indication of their separation from the world.

Now, to smoked pork chops; and I think I am with Levi. I'm now "spoiled for ham."

> ½ cup honey
> 1 cup apple cider or apple juice
> 2 tablespoons horseradish mustard
> 9 whole cloves
> 9 allspice berries
> ¼ teaspoon coarsely ground black pepper
> 6 smoked pork loin chops, cut ½ to ¾ inch
>   thick, trimmed of excess fat and rind

■ In a small saucepan, combine the honey, apple cider, mustard, cloves, allspice, and pepper. Simmer over medium heat until the mixture is reduced by half, 4 to 5 minutes, watching closely so it doesn't reduce too much.

■ Meanwhile, preheat the oven to 300° F. Line a 10 × 12-inch shallow roasting pan with foil. Place the pork chops in a single layer and pour the glaze over them. Bake the chops, uncovered, for 1½ hours, basting occasionally. Serve immediately, with mashed potatoes.

Roast Beef Shortcake

Serves 6 to 8

THIS IS A SUPER WAY to use up leftover beef, especially brisket, as well as turkey or chicken. A crisp biscuit is topped with the savory filling and garnished with a smaller biscuit, a rather fancy interpretation for humble leftovers.

I use a large doughnut cutter to form biscuits, using the doughnut hole for the top layer, but you could just make big 4-inch biscuits and split them to serve as shortcakes.

BISCUITS
> 3 cups all-purpose flour
> 2 tablespoons baking powder
> ¾ teaspoon salt
> ½ teaspoon coarsely ground black pepper
> 1 tablespoon fresh minced thyme, or
>> ½ teaspoon dried (optional)
> ⅓ cup plus 3 tablespoons solid vegetable shortening
> ¾–1 cup milk

MEAT SAUCE
> 3 tablespoons butter
> ⅓ cup plus 3 tablespoons all-purpose flour
> Salt and pepper
> 3 cups milk
> 3 cups leftover beef, turkey, or chicken, cut in bite-size pieces
> 2 tablespoons chopped fresh parsley
> Minced fresh parsley or chervil, for garnish

■ Preheat the oven to 450°F.

■ MAKE THE BISCUITS: In a mixing bowl, whisk together the flour, baking powder, salt, pepper, and thyme. Using a pastry blender or a pastry fork, work in the shortening until the mixture resembles coarse crumbs. Make a well in the center and add ¾ cup milk, stirring vigorously to form a stiff dough; add more milk if needed. Do this quickly and don't overmix—½ minute is about right. Transfer the dough to a floured surface and knead it a bit, 4 or 5 turns, to integrate all the flour, then roll the dough out to a ½-inch thickness. Using a 4-inch round doughnut cutter with a 2-inch hole, or a 4-inch biscuit cutter, cut out the biscuits. Transfer biscuits and holes to a greased baking sheet and bake for 10 minutes or until the biscuits are golden brown.

■ MEANWHILE, PREPARE THE MEAT SAUCE: In a medium saucepan, melt the butter over medium heat. Add the flour and salt and pepper to taste, and cook for 5 minutes. (The mixture will resemble coarse crumbs; keep stirring so the mixture doesn't burn.) Slowly add the milk, stirring and whisking constantly until it is smooth and thickened. Add the meat and parsley and heat thoroughly.

■ When the biscuits are done, place a biscuit on each plate and ladle some meat sauce over it. Top with a biscuit hole. Garnish with more parsley or chervil and serve immediately.

The Very Best Beef Pot Roast

Serves 6

THIS POT ROAST QUALIFIES as the best, not only because of the intense beef flavor but because it's so simple to prepare—no browning! Just place the meat in the oven at a very low temperature and forget it for six hours. Though the recipe calls for no liquid, the roast produces quite a bit of meat juice, which is very nice ladled over mashed potatoes or plain buttered noodles seasoned with a bit of onion.

> 1 3-pound beef chuck roast, all fat removed
> Salt and coarsely ground black pepper
> ½ tablespoon minced fresh thyme, or rounded
>> ½ teaspoon dried (optional)
> 2 crumbled bay leaves
> 1 large onion, sliced

■ Preheat the oven to 275°F. Grease a shallow 9 × 13-inch pan and place the roast in it. Sprinkle the meat with salt and pepper to taste, the thyme, bay leaves, and onion. Cover the dish tightly with heavy-duty foil and bake the roast without lifting the foil, for 6 hours. Let the roast stand for 10 minutes before slicing into serving portions or shredding for sandwiches. Serve hot, though this reheats very well.

Cheese and Rice Soufflé with Bacon

Serves 6 to 8

I THINK THE AMISH rather misnamed this recipe; it is more like a casserole than a puffy soufflé. But it is most appealing and good. As it bakes, it separates into savory layers, with the rice and bacon ending up on top. It is really an ideal dish for buffets. The flavor is nicely subtle and it's a fairly economical dish, too.

4 slices turkey or pork bacon
4 scallions with tops, chopped
6 eggs, separated
1 cup heavy cream
1 cup grated Swiss cheese
2 cups cooked long-grain white rice
1 tablespoon Worcestershire sauce
$1/4$ cup minced fresh parsley
$1/2$ teaspoon salt
$1/4$ teaspoon pepper
Dash of hot red pepper sauce
Paprika

In a medium sauté pan, cook the bacon over medium-high heat until crisp. Drain on paper towels, crumble into small pieces, and set aside. In the remaining fat drippings, sauté the scallions until they are transparent, then remove from the pan and set aside.

Preheat the oven to 350°F. In a mixer bowl, beat the egg whites until stiff; set aside. In a mixing bowl, beat the egg yolks slightly; add the cream, cheese, rice, Worcestershire, parsley, salt, pepper, and hot pepper sauce; mix well. Stir in the bacon and scallions, and then fold in the egg whites. Pour into a greased deep 2-quart baking dish and sprinkle with paprika. Bake for 45 minutes or until set. Serve immediately.

Creamed Fresh Summer Corn

Serves 4 to 5

THIS IS A LUXURIOUS WAY to use up leftover corn-on-the-cob. Cooking the cream and corn together infuses the corn with an intense richness. Yum!

$1/4$ cup ($1/2$ stick) butter
4 cups cooked fresh corn kernels
    (approximately 5 ears)
$1/2$ cup heavy cream
1 teaspoon minced fresh thyme, or $1/4$ teaspoon
    dried (optional)
Pinch of sugar
Salt and pepper
Minced fresh chervil or parsley, for garnish

In a large, heavy saucepan, melt the butter over medium heat. Stir in the corn and sauté for 2 to 3 minutes, then stir in the cream. Reduce the heat to low and cover. Cook for 2 minutes, remove the lid, and cook for 5 minutes longer, or until the liquid is reduced and the mixture is thick and creamy. Season with thyme, sugar, and salt and pepper to taste, and serve immediately, garnished with the minced chervil or parsley.

Spiced Applesauce

Serves 6

THE FIRST SUMMER Green Transparent apples generally find their way into applesauce.

6 to 8 large apples, unpeeled, cored, quartered
$1/4$ cup cider or apple juice
2 tablespoons butter
8 whole cloves
1 bay leaf
$1/2$ to $3/4$ cup sugar, to taste

Combine all the ingredients, except the sugar, in a large saucepan. Simmer until the apples are tender, about 15 minutes. Discard the cloves and bay leaf. Transfer to a food processor and process until smooth. Add sugar to taste and serve warm or cold.

GARDENING BY THE
SIGN OF THE MOON

Many gardeners, not just Amish and Mennonite ones, plant by the sign of the moon. One piece of folklore surrounding this idea is that the "horns" of the moon have a special power. When the horns point up, it creates an upward force, and when the horns point down, there is a downward force. So various beliefs about planting based on these signs have evolved over the years.

One gardener advised me to plant climber beans during the up sign (moon's ascension) so they will climb the poles easily. But onions planted during the up side will not stay in the ground. Similarly, cabbages should be planted when the horns of the moon are up, while potatoes and other root vegetables should be planted when the horns are down, in the moon's descension.

Apples should be picked in the dark of the moon so they won't rot. Trees (and wooden fence posts) should be planted in the ground only when the moon is turned down. Plant peas the day after a new moon, and you will have a better crop.

Roasted Tomatoes

Serves 6

I NEVER SAW TOMATOES cooked this way until I visited Amish communities in Kentucky. This recipe should appeal to cooks who want to use only a few ingredients—the original had just one, the tomatoes—though I've added a couple of others.

Even made with store-bought tomatoes in the off season this dish is still fairly good. But in season, it's to swoon over. The Amish serve the tomatoes as is, but after baking I prefer to cut out the cores and place some brown sugar and butter in each cavity, then transfer them to individual sauce dishes or "nappies." Each person adds salt and pepper to taste.

> 6 large vine-ripened tomatoes, well washed
> Brown sugar (optional)
> Softened butter (optional)
> Salt and pepper

▓ Preheat the oven to 375°F. Place the tomatoes in a greased 9 × 13-inch flat glass dish. They shouldn't be crowded; the heat from the oven should circulate freely around them. Bake until the skins begin to wrinkle; this varies from 30 to 45 minutes.

▓ Transfer the tomatoes to individual bowls, and cut out the core with a pair of scissors or a very sharp knife. Add a bit of brown sugar and softened butter to each cavity, if desired, and sprinkle with salt and pepper. Serve immediately. And you will need a spoon.

Summer Squash Soufflé with Rosemary

Serves 6 to 8

YELLOW CROOKNECK SQUASH, dipped in flour and sautéed in bacon fat, is a popular country side dish. But another way to use this abundant squash is to prepare it as a casserole. This is a sweet-tasting and unusual vegetable dish; if you make it once, you'll make it again and again.

> 9 (approximately $3\frac{1}{4}$ pounds) small yellow squash, unpeeled
> 2 tablespoons water
> 4 eggs, slightly beaten
> 1 cup sugar
> $\frac{3}{4}$ cup ($1\frac{1}{2}$ sticks) butter, at room temperature
> $\frac{1}{2}$ cup chopped onion
> $\frac{1}{4}$ cup minced fresh parsley
> 1 teaspoon fresh rosemary, finely chopped, or $\frac{1}{4}$ teaspoon dried, ground in pestle (optional)
> $\frac{1}{4}$ teaspoon salt
> $\frac{1}{4}$ teaspoon coarsely ground black pepper
> 2 drops hot red pepper sauce
> Paprika

▓ Preheat the oven to 350°F. Coat an 8 × 8-inch casserole with nonstick cooking spray and set aside.

▓ Wash the squash and cut into small cubes. Place in a medium saucepan with the water and bring to a boil. Cook for about 6 minutes or until tender (time will vary); check to make sure the pan doesn't burn dry. Drain and mash the squash with a potato masher. Add the eggs, sugar, butter, onion, parsley, rosemary, salt, pepper, and hot pepper sauce; mix well.

▓ Transfer the squash mixture to the prepared pan, sprinkle paprika liberally over the top, and bake for 1 hour and 15 minutes or until golden brown. Serve hot.

Creamed Red Beets

Serves 6 to 8

IN AMISH HOMES, vegetables such as beets, carrots, potatoes, and cabbages are stored in a root cellar, which generally has an earthen floor. If the floor is not earthen, the root vegetables are packed in huge crocks with a little sand sprinkled around them. Stored by this method, they keep fresh and unwrinkled through spring.

> 6 medium beets
> $^1/_2$ cup plus 1 tablespoon evaporated milk
> 3 tablespoons cider vinegar
> 3 tablespoons light or dark brown sugar, packed
> $^1/_2$ cup coarsely chopped fresh parsley, or chervil or chives
> $^1/_4$ teaspoon salt
> $^1/_4$ teaspoon coarsely ground black pepper

▓ Preheat the oven to 400°F. Wash the beets and trim off all but 1 inch of the tops but leave the root intact. Wrap the beets loosely in foil, place on a foil-lined cookie sheet, and bake until tender, about 1 hour. Open the packet and cool the beets under cold running water. Slip off the skins and discard.

▓ Chop the beets coarsely by hand or shred in a food processor. Transfer the beets to a medium saucepan, and add the evaporated milk, vinegar, sugar, parsley, salt, and pepper. Stir over medium-low heat until heated through. Serve immediately.

Spinach Salad with Celery Seed and Bacon Dressing

Serves 6

SPINACH AND CELERY flourish in the damp fields of Ohio—one reason they are favorite crops of that state's Amish. This is how they typically serve spinach at their own tables. If you do not wish to use the bacon drippings (a pity), you can discard them and substitute olive oil. Placing the heavier ingredients on the bottom of the bowl and adding the greens last ensures that all will be evenly distributed throughout the salad when it is tossed.

Serve this with homemade bread, for it is a hearty salad and more than adequate for an entree.

> 6 slices bacon
> 3 hard-cooked eggs, sliced
> 6 scallions, chopped
> $^3/_4$ pound spinach, washed well

> DRESSING
> $^1/_4$ cup plus 2 tablespoons cider vinegar
> $^1/_2$ cup sugar
> $1^1/_2$ teaspoons horseradish mustard
> $^1/_2$ teaspoon celery seeds
> $^1/_4$ teaspoon freshly ground black pepper

▓ In a medium skillet, sauté the bacon until crisp. Drain on paper towels and when cool, cut into bite-size pieces. Transfer to a deep salad bowl. Top with the hard-cooked eggs and scallions. Remove the stems from the spinach and discard; tear some of the larger pieces into bite-size ones and place on top of the scallions.

▓ PREPARE THE DRESSING: To the bacon drippings (there should be about $^1/_4$ cup) add the vinegar, sugar, mustard, celery seeds, and pepper and whisk until smooth. Bring to a boil to dissolve the sugar (the mixture will be quite foamy), then pour the hot dressing immediately over the spinach and toss. Top with a lid or plate and allow to stand for 5 minutes. Remove the lid and immediately transfer to individual salad plates and serve.

Five-Vegetable Cole Slaw

Serves 6 to 8

I DO NOT LIKE soupy slaw, so when an Amish cook suggested marinating the slaw vegetables by themselves with salt and then draining it, before adding the dressing, that made good sense. This slaw is to be made a day in advance, so plan accordingly. It is a pretty salad with lots of color and flavor. And if you really hate excess moisture in slaw, drain it again before serving.

> 8 cups shredded cabbage (approximately 2 pounds)
> ½ medium onion, thinly sliced
> 2 celery ribs, julienned
> ½ medium red bell pepper, finely julienned
> ½ medium green bell pepper, finely julienned
> 1 large or 2 medium carrots, shredded
> ¼ cup chopped fresh parsley
> 1½ teaspoons salt

DRESSING
> ½ cup fresh lemon juice (approximately 4 large lemons)
> 1½ cups mayonnaise
> ¾ teaspoon salt
> 2 teaspoons black pepper
> ½ cup sugar
> 1 tablespoon celery seeds
> 1 teaspoon mustard seeds
> 1½–2 tablespoons cider vinegar

▤ In a large mixing bowl, combine the vegetables and salt and let stand for 20 to 30 minutes. (Salting the vegetables draws off the liquid in the vegetables so the finished slaw will not be runny.) Drain and set aside.

▤ PREPARE THE DRESSING: In a medium bowl, whisk together the lemon juice, mayonnaise, salt, pepper, sugar, celery seeds, mustard seeds, and vinegar; blend well. Add the dressing to the vegetables and toss gently to combine. Cover and store in the refrigerator overnight.

To beat the rain, the whole family helps with harvesting of the crops. The girls' heads are covered with bandannas, even on the hottest summer day.

Fluffy Mashed Potato Patties

Makes 12 to 14 patties; serves 4 to 6

THIS IS JUST AS GOOD as the original mashed potato dish! Serve the patties with meat loaf of any kind, and you have a delicious dinner. In some communities, tomato gravy or Tomato Sour Cream Gravy (page 246) would be served with these patties.

> 1 egg
> 3 tablespoons all-purpose flour
> 3 tablespoons minced onion
> 2 tablespoons finely minced fresh parsley
> 2 teaspoons baking powder
> 1/8 teaspoon hot red pepper sauce
> 4 cups leftover mashed potatoes
> 2–3 tablespoons peanut oil

■ In a medium mixing bowl, beat the egg slightly, then blend in the flour, onion, parsley, baking powder, and hot red pepper sauce. Stir in the mashed potatoes and blend.

■ In an electric skillet, heat 1 tablespoon of the oil to 375°F. or heat in a sauté pan over medium-high heat. Preheat the oven to 180°F. Using a 1/4-cup scoop, drop the mixture into the hot fat, using 1/4 cup of the batter per patty. Flatten out the patty with the back of the scoop a bit at the same time as you add it to the fat. Sauté the patties 4 to 5 minutes, turn, and sauté 4 to 5 minutes longer, until golden brown and puffy. Remove the patties to a heated platter and place in the oven. Repeat with the remaining ingredients. Serve while hot.

Delicate Butter Muffins

Makes 1 dozen

WHEN TRAVELING in Pennsylvania Dutch country, you will notice the hex signs—brightly colored geometric designs painted on the barns. Folklore has suggested the signs keep lightning away, or even the devil. But the custom of a hex on barns is a fairly recent phenomenon. In 1850 an eight-pointed star was used as a fire mark by the Insurance Company of North America, and they and other insurance companies required insured farmers to mount a pointed star or "sun mark" on their barns. This may have inaugurated the tradition of painted hex signs on barns.

Mull all this over with a cup of tea and one of these nutmeg-scented muffins guaranteed to ward off the blahs.

> 2 cups all-purpose flour
> 1/2 cup sugar
> 1 tablespoon baking powder
> 1/2 teaspoon grated nutmeg
> 3/4 teaspoon salt
> 1 egg
> 3/4 cup milk
> 2 teaspoons vanilla extract
> 1/2 cup melted butter

■ Preheat the oven to 375°F. Prepare the muffin cups by coating lightly with nonstick cooking spray or lining with muffin papers and spraying them.

■ In a mixing bowl, whisk together the flour, sugar, baking powder, nutmeg, and salt. In another small bowl, beat the egg with the milk, and then stir in the vanilla. Add the egg mixture to the dry ingredients and stir with a fork until just combined. Stir in the melted butter.

■ Place 1/4 cup batter in each muffin cup and bake for 25 minutes, or until the muffins are golden brown and firm to the touch. Serve hot with butter and jam.

Buttery Spiced Apples

Serves 6 to 8

AT AN AMISH GROCERY in St. Mary's, Ontario, it was fascinating to observe all of the items available in bulk: poppy seeds, fennel seeds, dried marjoram and savory, ground coriander, anise seeds, curry powder, dried soup blends, and more. Amish women buy in large amounts for their large families; thanks to dishes such as this one, they can use up a pound of cinnamon within a month, so their spices and herbs never become stale.

This recipe, which can be made at the last minute from ingredients in your pantry, yields lots of sauce, so a scoop of ice cream is really an ideal accompaniment. It reheats well in the microwave.

> 8 small cooking apples, such as Gala or Yellow
>   Delicious
> ⅔ cup butter
> ¾ cup granulated sugar
> ¾ cup dark brown sugar, packed
> ¼ cup cornstarch
> 3 cups cider or apple juice
> ½ teaspoon grated nutmeg
> ½ teaspoon ground cinnamon
> ⅛ teaspoon salt

▦ Peel, core, and halve the apples; set aside. In an 11-inch sauté pan, melt the butter over medium heat. In a small bowl, whisk together the sugars and cornstarch, then stir into the melted butter and blend. Add the cider, nutmeg, cinnamon, and salt; mix well.

▦ Add the apples to the skillet, cover, and cook over medium heat for 8 minutes. Uncover and spoon the sauce over the apples. Re-cover and cook another 12 minutes, uncovering the pan for the last 4 to 5 minutes to reduce the sauce. The apples should be fork-tender and the sauce thickened. Transfer to individual dessert dishes and serve with ice cream or cream.

Peachy Baked Apples

Serves 6

BAKED APPLES ARE a quick and popular dessert for Amish and Mennonite dinners. This version, with peach preserves and spices, is a nice re-interpretation of an old favorite. Topped with some leftover Bushel Oatmeal Church Cookies (page 191) or store-bought oatmeal ones, it's a most pleasing dish.

Most Amish families store fall-maturing apples all winter long. Summer apples, such as Green Transparents and Lodis, do not store well and are eaten immediately or canned as applesauce or pie filling. For storage, the apples must be blemish free and ideally kept at 32°F. in a spot with rather high humidity. The traditional container is an old metal milk can, with the apples wrapped individually in newspaper. Some families store apples on the back porch or in unheated bedrooms.

> 6 small cooking apples, such as Rome, Empire,
>   or Yellow Delicious, halved and cored but
>   not peeled
> 1 cup light brown sugar, packed
> ¼ cup peach preserves
> ¼ teaspoon ground cinnamon
> ¼ teaspoon grated nutmeg
> ¼ cup apple cider or juice
> 2 tablespoons melted butter
> 1 cup crumbled chewy oatmeal cookies

▦ Preheat the oven to 350°F. Place the 12 apple halves cut side up in a 9 × 13-inch baking pan. It doesn't matter if they are a bit crowded, for they shrink as they bake.

▦ In a small mixing bowl, combine the brown sugar, preserves, cinnamon, nutmeg, cider, and butter. Drizzle this over the apples and cover the pan tightly with foil. Bake for 30 minutes or until the apples are just tender.

▦ Remove from the oven and sprinkle the crumbs over the tops, then spoon the juice in the bottom of the pan over each apple. Return to the oven and bake, uncovered, for 5 minutes longer. Serve warm or cold.

Blueberry Rhubarb Pie

Makes one 9-inch pie; serves 6 to 8

THE BLUEBERRIES THAT GROW in Amish country are generally the larger, cultivated ones, and they flourish on bushes that reach about ten feet tall. Picking blueberries is considered one of the happier picking chores, since it can be done standing up. Attaching a small pail to a belt around one's waist leaves both hands free for picking. You can also make this pie with frozen berries.

This combination of blueberries and rhubarb in a pie is unique and always well received.

> 1 1/2 cups granulated sugar
> 1/4 cup light brown sugar, packed
> 1/4 teaspoon grated nutmeg
> 1/4 teaspoon salt
> 3 tablespoons quick-cooking tapioca
> 2 cups fresh or unthawed frozen rhubarb, cut into 1/2-inch pieces
> 2 cups fresh or unthawed frozen blueberries
> Pastry for 2-crust 9-inch pie (page 270)
> 1 tablespoon butter, cut into small pieces

▨ Preheat the oven to 425°F. In a large mixing bowl, combine the sugars, nutmeg, salt, tapioca, rhubarb, and blueberries; mix well. Allow to stand for 10 minutes.

▨ Roll out half the pastry on a floured surface and line a 9-inch pan, patting it in firmly. Pour in the filling and dot with the butter. Roll out a top crust, place on top of the filling, and seal the edges; slash the top to allow steam to escape. Bake for 10 minutes, then lower the temperature to 400°F. and bake for 30 minutes more or until the crust is brown and the juices are bubbling up in the pie. Remove from the oven, transfer to a wire rack, and allow to cool completely before serving.

NOTE: If using fresh fruit, increase the baking time until juices appear on top of the pie, 10 to 15 minutes more. Tent with foil if the crust begins to get too brown.

Big berries like these fill up the bucket quickly. The women occasionally sing in unison as they pick.

Peach Praline Pie

Makes one 9-inch pie; serves 6

THIS IS AN UNBEATABLE peach pie, a real treat when succulent peaches are in season—or anytime, made with frozen fruit.

> Pastry for a 1-crust 9-inch pie (page 270)
> 3/4 cup granulated sugar
> 3 tablespoons quick-cooking tapioca
> 4 cups peeled and sliced fresh peaches, or 5 cups partially thawed and still crisp frozen peaches
> 1 1/2 teaspoons fresh lemon juice
> 1/4 teaspoon almond extract
> 1/4 teaspoon grated lemon zest

PRALINE TOPPING
> 1/3 cup light or dark brown sugar, packed
> 1/4 cup all-purpose flour
> 1/2 cup chopped pecans
> 1/2 teaspoon grated nutmeg
> 1/4 teaspoon salt
> 3 tablespoons cold butter

▨ Preheat the oven to 350°F. Line a 9-inch pie pan with the pastry and set aside.

▨ In a large mixing bowl, combine the granulated sugar and tapioca. Add the peaches, lemon juice, extract, and lemon zest and let the mixture stand for 10 minutes.

▨ Meanwhile, make the topping: In a small bowl, combine the brown sugar, flour, pecans, nutmeg, and salt. With a pastry blender or fork, cut in the butter until the mixture becomes crumbly. Sprinkle one-third of the topping into the pastry shell and cover with the peach mixture. Sprinkle with the remaining topping. Bake for 1 hour or until the juices in the middle of the pie begin to bubble. Cool completely on a rack before cutting.

Old-Fashioned Bread Pudding with Hot Caramel Sauce

Serves 12

BREAD PUDDING HAS ALWAYS been a favorite among the Amish and Mennonites because it is so economical. And it remains an all-time favorite with the rest of us, too. It is nice to see it appearing on elegant restaurant menus all over the country. This version, with its own hot caramel sauce, is so easy; the bread does not have to be dried first, nor is the pudding baked in a hot water bath. It's a quick and utterly beguiling dessert.

> 7 cups fresh or stale white bread, crusts
>   removed, cut into 1-inch cubes
> 1/2 cup golden raisins
> 1/2 cup melted butter
> 4 eggs
> 1 cup granulated sugar
> 1/4 cup light brown sugar, packed
> 1 teaspoon grated nutmeg
> 2 teaspoons vanilla extract
> 2 cups half-and-half
> 2 cups whole milk
>   Grated nutmeg

> CARAMEL SAUCE
> 1/2 cup (1 stick) butter
> 1 cup light brown sugar, packed
> 1/4 teaspoon salt
> 1 teaspoon vanilla extract
> 1/2 cup evaporated milk

■ Place the bread in a greased 9 × 13-inch glass baking dish. Sprinkle the raisins over the bread, then drizzle on the melted butter but do not mix; set aside.

■ In a large mixer bowl, beat the eggs until broken up, then blend in the sugars, nutmeg, and vanilla. Add the half-and-half and milk, but do not overbeat—bubbles are not necessary here. Pour the milk mixture over the bread cubes and let it soak for 15 minutes, gently patting the bread down into the milk mixture now and then

with the back of a spoon. Sprinkle the top generously with nutmeg.

■ Preheat the oven to 350°F. Bake the pudding for 55 minutes, checking after 40 minutes that the top is not becoming too brown. If it is, cover lightly with foil. Bake 15 minutes longer until the pudding is puffy all over and golden brown. Remove to a rack to cool.

■ MEANWHILE, MAKE THE SAUCE: In a small saucepan, over medium heat, melt the butter and brown sugar together, whisking vigorously as the mixture cooks. Bring to a boil, remove from the heat, and whisk in the salt, vanilla, and evaporated milk. (This sauce can be made ahead of time and reheated in the microwave.)

■ Cut the cooled pudding into squares and top each serving with some of the hot sauce.

Old-Fashioned Brown Sugar Cream Pie

Makes one 9-inch pie; serves 6 to 8

PENNSYLVANIA GERMAN COOKS used to have a reputation for serving pie at morning, noon, and night meals, and then for a midnight snack as well. Sounds like a delightful tradition to me, and one I plan to embrace, when I am, say, eighty years old.

The pies found today in Pennsylvania Dutch, Amish, and Mennonite country had their origin in England, where they were originally called *coffins*. That word went out of style, thank goodness. Sugar pies such as this were called "poor man's pie," for they were made when no fruit was available and money was scarce.

> Pastry for a 1-crust 9-inch pie (page 270)
> 1 cup light brown sugar, lightly packed
> 4 1/2 tablespoons all-purpose flour
> 1/4 teaspoon salt
> 1 cup half-and-half
> 1 cup Milnot (see page 7)
> 1 teaspoon vanilla extract
>   Ground cinnamon

Roll out the pastry and line a 9-inch pie pan. Chill in the refrigerator for at least 1 hour. Preheat the oven to 350°F.

In a mixing bowl, whisk together the brown sugar, flour, and salt. Stir in the half-and-half and let stand for 15 minutes to dissolve the brown sugar, then stir in the Milnot and vanilla; mix well. Pour into the pastry shell and drift cinnamon lightly across the top. Bake for 55 minutes or until the top bubbles up a bit. If the crust is getting too brown, cover the pie lightly with a piece of foil. The pie will be shaky when you remove it from the oven but will set up as it cools.

Cool completely on a rack, cut into wedges, and serve.

NOTE: By chilling the pie crust before the filling is poured in, you reduce the likelihood of the crust puffing up in the bottom of the pie as it bakes. Milnot is a canned skim milk product; the butterfat has been replaced by vegetable oil.

Grandma's Rhubarb Meringue Pie

Makes one 9-inch pie; serves 6 to 8

THE TEN OLD ORDER Mennonite families in Argos, Indiana, scouted for two years to find enough land at the right price. It was important to them to have farms large enough so that they could live and work on the land without having to work even part-time for the English.

"The farm is a good place to raise children," John Martin tells me. "Many kids grow up not knowing anything and get into trouble. I'm afraid the next generation will find land so expensive they won't be able to live on farms."

The Martin farm is a dairy farm, with 120 Holstein cows, milked electrically. The whole family gets up at 4:15 A.M. every day to do the work, and that includes all six children. They have a large garden, which is bordered by a big rhubarb patch, so pies like this one are often on spring menus. Mrs. Martin also freezes rhubarb for winter use.

Pastry for a 1-crust 9-inch pie (page 270)
4 cups chopped fresh rhubarb, or frozen
    rhubarb thawed just enough to measure
1 1/2 cups sugar
2 tablespoons quick-cooking tapioca
1/2 teaspoon ground cinnamon
3 egg yolks

MERINGUE
3 egg whites, at room temperature
1/4 teaspoon salt
1/4 teaspoon cream of tartar
6 tablespoons sugar
1 1/2 teaspoons cornstarch

Preheat the oven to 375°F. Roll out the pastry and line a 9-inch pie pan with the pastry. Set aside.

In a large mixing bowl, combine the rhubarb, sugar, tapioca, cinnamon, and egg yolks. Mix well and let stand for 10 minutes. Transfer to the pie shell and bake for 45 minutes or until the rhubarb is tender and bubbling up in the center. (You may need to cover the pie with foil during baking if the crust begins to over-brown.)

While the pie is baking, prepare the meringue: In a large mixer bowl, beat the egg whites, salt, and cream of tartar until soft peaks form. Gradually add the sugar, a tablespoon at a time, and continue beating until stiff peaks form and the mixture is glossy. Just before the beating is completed, sprinkle in the cornstarch. The peaks should not topple over when the beating is completed.

Spread the meringue on the hot filling, clear over the edge of the crust with a knife, and swoop the meringue into attractive peaks. Lower the oven temperature to 325°F. and bake for 15 to 18 minutes, or until the peaks are golden brown. Cool the pie on a rack completely (there should be no warmth left in the meringue at all), and then refrigerate until serving time.

6
AUCTION
DAY

Shredded Beef Sandwiches with Broth Dip ❖ Old-Fashioned Spicy Lemonade ❖ Amish Auction Beef Barbecue ❖ Onion Fritters ❖ Beef Kraut Balls ❖ Sweet and Hot Kraut Piccalilli ❖ Grilled Chicken with Garlic ❖ Grandmother Yoder's Potato Salad with Sweet and Sour Boiled Dressing ❖ Maple Baked Beans ❖ Relief Sale Doughnuts ❖ Chocolate Fudge Pie ❖ Tears-on-Your-Pillow Pie ❖ Pear Cranberry Pie ❖ Boiled Cider Pie ❖ Sour Cream Raisin Pie ❖ Apple Squares with Lemon Sauce ❖ Pecan Sandies ❖ Overnight Butterscotch Cookies

MIDSUMMER IS THE PEAK season for auctions in most Amish communities. This is a good time to be driving about the countryside, for July and August are mellow generous months. The mornings are misty blue and timeless in feeling. The hay is mowed and raked into windrows, and bright blue chicory, black-eyed Susans, and orange butterflyweed accent the landscape; raspberries, gooseberries, and green Transparent apples appear at roadside stands and the auctions.

If you are headed to an Amish auction, you can expect to share the road with buggies and vans full of Amish daytrippers. Not only are auctions a most acceptable social outing for the Amish, but they also provide these thrifty folk with a chance to pursue good buys. There are many local horse and livestock auctions in every large Amish community, generally held on a weekly basis. And it's not just Amish and Mennonite farmers who come to bid on everything from colts to lambs; so do other astute farmers who prefer to skip the middleman, buying directly from other farmers.

The horse auctions are fascinating, for the Amish take a great deal of interest in their horses. I don't want to say "pride," for that is forbidden, but I suspect that, as far as horses

FROM 'THE BUDGET'

SUMMER ISSUE

Last week, LeRoy Zooks, Harry Lemhans, and Andy Bontragers went to Indiana by van for the Topeka horse sale, to see doctors and also to visit relatives they hadn't seen for awhile. They bought a new team of horses, which will be trucked in next week. **—ARTHUR, IL**

go, the men wrestle with those worldly emotions. Some horses are bought to pull buggies; others, such as Percherons, are for work in the fields. Because of their abhorrence of anything that appears to be associated with the military, the Amish do not ride horses; this attitude can be traced to seventeenth-century Europe, when only the soldiers rode on horseback. (This same reasoning may explain why the men wear clothes without buttons, since buttons and epaulets are also associated with soldiers.)

One of the most poignant horse auctions I ever attended was at Topeka, Indiana, when a pair of perfectly matched female white Welsh ponies came into the ring, their manes tied with colored yarn, ready for show. They were sisters and had been together fourteen years. Fortunately, they were sold as a pair and bought by an older couple for their grandchildren. I can only hope they were able to last out their lives in tandem, the way they always had lived.

One auction that attracts collectors from all over the world is the Carriage Auction in Topeka, Indiana, held during June and October (see page 280 for more information). Frequently, one can find beautifully made antique sleighs, and certainly more recently handcrafted sleighs, for they are still used by the Amish during snowy winters. Made of wood and sometimes fiberglass, and often lined with wool plush, they are especially prized by young people.

The popular Shipshewana Auction and Flea Market is held every Tuesday and Wednesday, May through October. It is the granddaddy of all country auctions. The Shipshe Auction, as it is affectionately known, began as a livestock auction. Then came the antiques, then the flea market, which encompasses a huge neighboring field next door. You can still pick up a good buy or two, but go early, for on Tuesdays and Wednesdays this little town of 600 people swells to 30,000 eager buyers and tourists.

Sales on a much smaller scale, such as Amish household auctions, are sometimes open to the public, but frequently are not. The Amish handle the passing down of family heirlooms this way: everything goes to auction on a certain day and everything is for sale. "If you want your grandmother's Majolica plate or your grandfather's hoe, it is best you've saved your money, for it will be sold to the highest bidder. No hard feelings this way, like when the family divides it up among themselves," explains auctioneer Kevin Lambright, who owns and manages the Shipshe Auction.

However, once in a while, a family auction will be open to the public, and it is country theater at its best. The Amish families arrive in buggies and spend the day. It is a place to meet friends and catch up on the gossip, and where children meet other children from different communities. Of course, there is food to eat; this is prepared by the family holding the auction and is sold all day long. The amount of food is prodigious—huge roasters of barbecue and hot dogs, sometimes baked beans and potato salad, replenished at regular intervals throughout the day since there are no refrigerators. There are pies of all sorts—peach pie, shoofly pie, tears-on-your-pillow pie . . . and cookies. Crispy peanut butter cookies, soft cakelike molasses cookies, and the white cakelike Amish church sugar cookies, dusted with sugar and topped with raisins, are wrapped individually for the nosher, or by the dozen. If it is really an enterprising family and the auction is open to the public, angel food cakes, whole pies, noodles, breads, and jams or conserves will also be sold. So even if you are not successful in bidding on an antique quilt, you can still go home with a purchase.

> A van load left from Marlette, MI for Gladwin, MI last Saturday for an auction sale, returning the same day. They didn't buy much, but Alta Kay Yoder sold 4 of her quilts so it wasn't a totally wasted day. —BRONSON, MI

> Noah Martins had a lovely day, weatherwise, on Saturday for their farm auction, prior to their move to Aroda, VA. The Levi Shenks returned to their Iowa home after being here a week to help out. Martins' household things were loaded on Tuesday and the truck and trailer left the same evening. The cows were loaded on Wednesday evening after being milked and left for their new home that night. Noah traveled with the cattle truck. —FRYBURG, OH

Shredded Beef Sandwiches with Broth Dip

Serves 8 to 10

THIS IS A VERSION of the French dip sandwich; I have no idea where or how the Amish found it (nor do they call it a French dip), but this recipe is showing up in quite a few Amish cookbooks and is served in quite a few households. The *jus* is very well seasoned. Serve this with Five-Vegetable Cole Slaw (page 105) on the side.

1 3-pound bone-in beef chuck roast, well trimmed
1 large onion, coarsely chopped
1/3 cup cider vinegar
2 bay leaves
1 tablespoon chili powder
2 teaspoons ground cumin
1/2 teaspoon salt
1/4 teaspoon coarsely ground black pepper
1/4 teaspoon ground cloves
1 garlic clove, crushed
1/2 cup Beef Stock (page 267) or canned broth
8–10 Kaiser buns, split1

▨ The day before serving, place the roast and onion in a large resealable plastic bag. In a small bowl, mix the vinegar, bay leaves, chili powder, cumin, salt, pepper, ground cloves, and garlic. Pour over the roast and seal the bag tightly. Place in a 10 × 7-inch dish and marinate in the refrigerator for at least 24 hours, turning occasionally.

▨ The next day, place the meat with its marinade plus the stock in a slow cooker. Cover and set on low, and cook 10 to 12 hours or until the meat is very tender. Or you can slow-cook in a 200° F. oven; place the meat, marinade, and stock in an ovenproof pan or Dutch oven, cover, and bake for 8 hours or until tender.

▨ To serve, remove the meat to a platter and using forks, shred the beef into bite-size pieces. Discard the fat and bone. Defat the juices, then strain into a gravy boat. Fill the hard rolls with slices of roast beef. Serve with some of the juices (I use small ramekins) for dipping, if desired.

Old-Fashioned Spicy Lemonade

Makes a scant quart syrup; approximately 32 glasses

LEMONADE IS A FAVORITE beverage in Amish and Mennonite communities, not just in the summer but year-round. Lemons were at one time considered a great luxury and if a housewife had six lemons a year, she considered herself very lucky. When refrigeration was not available, lemons were stored, buried in sand, in crocks.

This version starts with a spicy lemon syrup base that can be kept on hand in the refrigerator; it is very convenient and most refreshing after a hot summer day of antiquing.

3 tablespoons lemon zest
4 cups sugar
4 cups water
2 cinnamon sticks
Juice of 6 lemons
Additional lemon slices studded with whole cloves, or fresh mint

▨ In a deep saucepan, combine the lemon zest, sugar, water, and cinnamon sticks. Bring the mixture to a rolling boil. Boil gently, uncovered, over medium heat for 5 minutes. Remove from the heat and cool. Strain the mixture through a fine wire sieve or cheesecloth. Add the strained lemon juice to the sugar syrup. Transfer to a glass container and refrigerate until needed.

▨ To make the lemonade, mix 4 tablespoons of the lemon syrup with 1 cup of cold water. Fill 2 water glasses with ice and pour in the lemonade; this is enough for 2 average-size water glasses. Garnish and serve.

Those attending an auction are reflected in a mirror that is for sale. A mirror this size in an Amish house is most unusual and probably would be partially draped for modesty.

Amish Auction
Beef Barbecue

Makes 10 to 12 hearty, plump sandwiches

BEEF ON A BUN is quintessential auction fare. Most of what is served at these events is stand-up food, as seating is rarely provided.

> 1 3-pound bone-in chuck roast, well trimmed
> 1 large onion, coarsely chopped
> 2 celery ribs, coarsely chopped
> 1 bay leaf
> 6 whole peppercorns
> 2½ cups Beef Stock (page 267), or
> 2 10-ounce cans beef broth

> BARBECUE SAUCE
> ¾ cup ketchup or chili sauce
> ¼ cup brown sugar, packed
> 2 tablespoons cider vinegar
> 1 tablespoon Worcestershire sauce
> 2 teaspoons prepared mustard
> 1 teaspoon chili powder
> ½ teaspoon paprika
> ⅛ teaspoon hot red pepper sauce

> Sandwich buns

■ In a large slow cooker, combine the meat, seasonings, and stock. Cover and cook on low for 10 to 12 hours, or until the meat is very tender. Alternatively, preheat the oven to 200° F. Place the meat, seasonings, and stock in an oven-proof dish or Dutch oven, cover, and bake for 8 hours or until tender.

■ Remove the meat with a slotted spoon and metal spatula to a platter; pour the liquid into a degreasing pitcher and skim off the fat.

■ PREPARE THE BARBECUE SAUCE: Combine all of the sauce ingredients plus 1½ cups of the beef liquid. Shred the meat with 2 forks, leaving it in quite large pieces, then add to the barbecue sauce. Reheat the mixture on high in the slow cooker or on top of the stove for about 20 minutes. Serve the meat and sauce on buns.

Onion Fritters

Makes 2 dozen

SOME AMISH AND Mennonite cooks call these onion patties; call them what you will, they are a very special vegetable treat—crispy like an onion ring and full of flavor. Though devised to be part of a meal, I can recommend them as a cocktail accompaniment as well. Make a double recipe; these evaporate into thin air as soon as they appear.

Allow enough cooking oil so the fritters can cook without crowding. My deep-fryer uses three (24-ounce) bottles of peanut oil. An electric skillet or sauté pan can be used, which will require less oil.

> Peanut oil, for deep-frying
> ¾ cup all-purpose flour
> 1 tablespoon yellow cornmeal
> 1 tablespoon sugar
> 2 teaspoons baking powder
> ½ teaspoon salt
> ¼ teaspoon black pepper
> Dash of grated nutmeg
> ½ cup cold milk
> Dash of hot red pepper sauce
> 2½ cups finely chopped onions

■ Heat the peanut oil to 375° F. in a deep-fryer or deep, straight-sided pan. Meanwhile, in a large mixing bowl, whisk together the flour, cornmeal, sugar, baking powder, salt, pepper, and nutmeg. Stir in the milk to make a thick batter, smoothing out the lumps. Add the pepper sauce and onions; mix well.

■ Drop several heaping teaspoonfuls of batter into the hot oil and begin turning the first fritter over as soon as you finish dropping in the last teaspoonful of batter. Fry until golden brown on both sides, then remove with a slotted spoon to a paper towel to drain. Serve immediately! And you won't regret the double recipe!

Beef Kraut Balls

Makes 5 dozen

YOU'LL FIND THIS FAVORITE snack treat at county fairs and auctions, such as the Mennonite Relief Quilt Auctions (see page 279). They are also served in the Midwest with cocktails as a hot hors d'oeuvre. Like potato chips, you can't eat just one.

> 14 Rye-Crisp crackers
> 3 cups (1-pound 11-ounce can) sauerkraut, drained lightly (see Note)
> 1 12-ounce can corned beef
> 1 egg, slightly beaten
> 1 tablespoon sugar
> 1 cup all-purpose flour
> At least 5 cups peanut oil, for deep-frying

■ In a food processor bowl, process the crackers until finely ground. Set aside. To the processor bowl, add the sauerkraut and corned beef; process until well combined. Add the egg, sugar, flour, and cracker crumbs; process again until just mixed. Using a 1-inch cookie scoop or a tablespoon, shape the mixture into 1-inch balls and set aside.

■ Meanwhile, in a deep-fryer, heat the oil to 375°F. Place a few balls at a time in the hot oil and fry for about 1 minute, or until browned. Remove with a slotted spoon and drain on paper towels. Repeat until all the balls are fried. These fried balls may be frozen, then thawed and re-heated in a 400°F. oven for 15 minutes.

NOTE: The sauerkraut should have some juice still included for flavor, but the mixture should not be soppy.

Sweet and Hot Kraut Piccalilli

Makes 2½ cups

GRILLING OUTSIDE in the summer is as appealing to the Amish as it is to English cooks, since their kitchens are not air-conditioned. Chicken, hamburgers, brats, and hot dogs are all popular entrees. You will also find large grills made of metal barrel halves set up at auctions, where all of the above foods are big sellers. Dressed up with a heaping spoonful of kraut piccalilli, a hot dog or brat tastes especially good after a few hours of seeking out and bidding on bargains. The Amish would probably use homemade sweet Hungarian pepper relish; you can order a first-rate version of it from Ralph Sechler and Sons (see page 287); it is outstanding, as are all their products.

> 1 cup sauerkraut, drained and with juice reserved
> ½ cup mild Hungarian sweet pepper relish or sweet pickle relish
> 3 tablespoons chopped onion
> ¼ teaspoon celery seeds
> 1 teaspoon caraway seeds

■ In a small bowl, combine the drained kraut, sweet pepper relish, and onion. In a small saucepan, combine the reserved kraut juice, celery seeds, and caraway seeds. Heat to boiling and simmer for 2 to 3 minutes. Pour over the kraut mixture and toss. Set aside to cool, then transfer to a covered container and store in the refrigerator until ready to use. Bring to room temperature and serve with grilled brats or hot dogs.

HAYSTACK SUPPERS

The famous Amish "haystack suppers" have become a popular fund-raiser in many communities across the country. Though by no means *haute cuisine,* the dinners are always well attended and happy events. The money raised goes to local Amish families who have high medical bills, and sometimes even to Amish families in other communities who have experienced natural disasters, such as flooding and tornado damage.

All of the ingredients for the "haystack," a sort of taco salad, are lined up as a buffet; the diners, who pay from $50 to several hundred dollars per family, pass along the double-sided buffet line with paper plates to construct their "stack." The bottom layer is corn chips or rice, followed by a layer of browned hamburger. Stacked on top of this are layers of kidney beans, chopped tomatoes, lettuce, and grated cheese, all topped with salsa or heated spaghetti sauce. The ingredients are donated and prepared by various families, and transported by buggies or wagons to a neighborhood center, where hundreds will come to eat and to enjoy the fellowship with one another.

Grilled Chicken with Garlic

Serves 12

GRILLING CHICKEN OUTSIDE in the summer is an easy way to feed hungry auction goers as well as large farm families. Frequently the grill is made from a halved metal barrel, topped with "found" electric oven shelves. The marinade assures the chicken will be succulent and moist. The marinade keeps indefinitely; the full recipe is enough for 24 pieces of chicken, but I have given instructions for dividing the recipe in half as well. Any leftover chicken is very good cold, served with mayonnaise. The salt sounds excessive, but is necessary.

An English way to shorten the chicken's cooking time, and also to assure completely cooked chicken, is to microwave the uncooked marinated chicken on high for 4 to 5 minutes, arranging the chicken in the microwave with the thicker parts to the outside, and the bony parts toward the center. Transfer the chicken to the grill, brush with sauce, and finish cooking.

> 4 cups cider vinegar
> 5 cups water
> $1/2$ cup corn oil
> $1/3$ cup salt
> 6 garlic cloves, crushed
> 4 tablespoons Worcestershire sauce
> 2 teaspoons coarsely ground black pepper
> 24 chicken pieces, such as legs, thighs, and breast halves, skin on

■ Combine all the ingredients, except the chicken, in a large saucepan and bring to a boil. Immediately remove from the heat, cool, transfer to a covered container, and refrigerate until ready to use.

■ To prepare grilled chicken for 6 servings, place 12 chicken pieces in a 2-gallon food storage bag. Heat 4 cups of the marinade in the microwave, and pour over the chicken. Close the bag tightly, place in a 3-quart flat glass dish, and refrigerate for 24 hours, turning once or twice.

■ Remove the chicken from the refrigerator and bring to room temperature. Grill the chicken pieces 12 to 15 minutes on each side (time will vary) or until browned and the juices run clear when pierced with a knife. Serve hot or cold.

■ For 24 pieces of chicken, use all the marinade.

NOTE: A quick way to peel garlic is to place the cloves on a paper plate or towel and heat in the microwave for about 10 seconds. The heat loosens the skin. Holding one end, gently press the clove against the counter—the garlic pops right out. You can do several cloves at a time, but increase the time in the microwave by about 2 seconds for each additional clove

Grandmother Yoder's Potato Salad with Sweet and Sour Boiled Dressing

Serves 6

MEMORIES OF FAMILY REUNIONS flew back to my consciousness when I tasted this sprightly potato salad with its vibrantly flavored boiled dressing. Homemade dressing does indeed beat the bottled stuff; it feels a bit grainy to the tongue when tasted by itself, but this is not noticeable when combined with the other elements of this super potato salad.

Adding vinegar to the potato cooking water keeps the potatoes firm, which is just what is wanted for potato salad.

> DRESSING
> 3 eggs
> $1/4$ cup sugar
> $1/4$ cup cider vinegar
> $3/4$ teaspoon salt
> 1 teaspoon coarsely ground black pepper, or more to taste
> $1 1/2$ teaspoons prepared mustard
> $1/3$ cup coarsely chopped sweet pickles or sweet pickle relish
> $3/4$ cup mayonnaise

SALAD
- 4–5 medium potatoes, peeled and halved
- 2 teaspoons cider vinegar
- 1/2 cup chopped celery
- 1/2 cup chopped fresh parsley
- 1/4 cup minced onion
- 1/2 teaspoon celery seeds
- 2 hard-cooked eggs, chopped

▨ MAKE THE DRESSING: In a medium, heavy saucepan, beat the eggs, then whisk in the sugar, vinegar, salt, and pepper. Heat and whisk over medium-low heat (it will burn easily so watch it carefully) until thick, 2 or 3 minutes. The mixture will resemble a roux; remove from the heat and cool for 10 minutes. Stir in the mustard, sweet pickles, and mayonnaise. Cool, cover, and refrigerate until needed. (This makes a liberal cup of dressing.)

▨ MAKE THE SALAD: Combine the potatoes and vinegar in a saucepan with water to cover, about 2 inches. Bring to a boil, cover, then simmer until tender, 20 to 25 minutes. Drain, cool, and cut into 3/4-inch cubes and transfer to a large mixing bowl. Add the rest of the salad ingredients and toss. Stir in the dressing gently, adjust the seasonings, and serve immediately, or refrigerate until serving time.

Maple Baked Beans

Serves 4 to 6

MELLOW IS THE WORD to describe the flavor of these baked beans. I used to think nothing could improve the traditional recipe using molasses, but I am prone to think this version is even better. It might seem like an extravagant use of maple syrup, but since many Amish have their own sugar bushes, the syrup is quite casually used in many ways. You needn't use the very best quality syrup, but do not substitute commercial pancake syrup. Start the recipe the night before by soaking the beans.

- 1 pound (2 cups) dried white navy or pea beans
  - Liberal pinch of baking soda
- 1 cup maple syrup
- 2 teaspoons ground mustard
- 1/4 teaspoon coarsely ground black pepper
- 2 tablespoons molasses
- 1/2 cup coarsely chopped onion
- 1/4–1/3 pound salt pork, scored

▨ Rinse the beans in a colander under running water; transfer to a large stockpot and add water to cover by 4 inches. Soak overnight.

▨ The next morning, drain the beans and cover with fresh water. Bring to a boil, skimming off the foam regularly. Add the baking soda and continue skimming. Simmer the beans, partially covered, for 30 minutes to an hour or until tender—this time will vary depending on the age and type of bean. The skins of the beans should split when you blow on them. Don't overcook the beans, or they will get mushy. Drain the beans, reserving the liquid.

▨ Preheat the oven to 300°F. Transfer the beans to a greased 3-quart bean pot or a heavy, deep casserole. Add the syrup, mustard, pepper, molasses, and onion and combine lightly. Place the salt pork on top of the beans and press it down into the beans. Add enough of the reserved bean water to cover the mixture. Cover and bake for 6 to 8 hours, or until the beans are tender and the mixture is a deep brown. Keep adding more bean water so the liquid always covers the top of the beans. Serve the beans immediately, or cool to lukewarm.

Relief Sale Doughnuts

Makes 5 dozen doughnuts and 60 doughnut holes

WHENEVER THERE is a Mennonite relief sale, and these generally center on hundreds of marvelous handmade quilts, food is also sold. And lots of it. You will always find a booth where someone is frying doughnuts, and there will be long lines of people waiting to buy them. Some are shaken in bags of granulated sugar and others, like these, get a glaze. This version is dipped immediately into a sugar syrup made with orange juice, and they are tender and cakelike, even though they are made with yeast.

These do require two risings, so plan accordingly—they are worth it. And prepare the syrup before frying the doughnuts so you can dip them while they are hot.

1 package active dry yeast
1 cup warm water
1 cup milk
1 cup unseasoned mashed potatoes, at room temperature
1 cup solid vegetable shortening
$^1/_2$ cup sugar
2 eggs
1 tablespoon vanilla extract
1 tablespoon grated orange zest
1 teaspoon ground cinnamon
1 teaspoon ground mace
1 teaspoon grated nutmeg
$^1/_2$ teaspoon salt
6 cups all-purpose flour
Peanut oil, for deep-frying (for deep-fryer, use 3 24-ounce bottles)

GLAZE
1 pound confectioners' sugar
$^1/_2$ cup orange juice
$^1/_8$ teaspoon salt

■ Sprinkle the yeast over the cup of warm water, stir, and allow to stand for 10 minutes or until the mixture foams. Scald the milk in the microwave or in a saucepan until bubbles just form around the edge of the pan; set aside.

■ In a large mixing bowl, combine the yeast, scalded milk, potatoes, shortening, sugar, eggs, vanilla, orange zest, cinnamon, mace, nutmeg, and salt and mix well. Slowly begin working in the flour, 2 cups at a time, until the dough is stiff and does not stick to your fingers. Place the dough in a mixing bowl sprayed with nonstick cooking spray and cover with plastic wrap or a tea towel. Let the dough rise in a warm place until doubled in size, 1 to 1$^1/_2$ hours.

■ On a floured surface, roll out the dough to a $^1/_2$-inch thickness and cut with a 2$^1/_2$-inch doughnut cutter. Transfer the doughnuts and their holes to baking sheets that have been dusted with flour. Cover with plastic wrap or terry cloth towels, and let rise again in a warm place until the doughnuts and holes are doubled in size, approximately 1 hour.

■ In a deep-fryer, heat the oil to 375°F.

■ MAKE THE GLAZE: In a mixing bowl, whisk together the confectioners' sugar, orange juice, and salt.

■ When the oil is hot, fry each doughnut approximately 1 minute and 45 seconds on each side or until golden brown, using tongs to turn. Drain on paper toweling. Fry the doughnut holes several at a time, holding them down with a fork until they begin to brown, turn, and brown remaining side, remove to paper toweling.

■ Using tongs, dip each hot doughnut in the glaze, let drain, and place on a metal rack to dry. Repeat for all doughnuts.

■ Store the doughnuts and doughnut holes in an airtight container, separating the layers with wax paper or plastic wrap between the layers.

FASSNACHT KUCHE
(GERMAN DOUGHNUTS)

Shrove Tuesday, the day before Ash Wednesday, is the start of Lent. Among the Pennsylvania Germans, one of their religious Easter traditions is the preparation of the *fassnacht* or *fastnacht*. This custom is also still observed in parts of Germany, where the doughnut is thought to be closely related to the cakes that were baked and eaten in pre-Christian times. Using mashed potatoes in the batter assures a tender, moist doughnut. The dough is prepared on the day before Shrove Tuesday, then deep-fried on Tuesday

morning as soon as the cook rolls out of bed. Very similar to yeast doughnuts, but formed in rectangles with a cross-cut in the center instead of a hole, the fried golden-brown pastry is then glazed with honey or dusted with granulated sugar. The *fassnachts* are served with cups of hot black coffee. Some Pennsylvania farmer's markets still make them year-round. Shrove Tuesday is also called Fat Tuesday in New Orleans; could these *fassnachts* have anything to do with that?

Chocolate Fudge Pie

Makes one 9-inch pie; serves 8

ARGOS, INDIANA, a small rural farm town in the north of the state close to Culver Military Academy, is seeing an influx of Old Order Mennonites in their area.

"Good people, these Old Order Mennonites" said the local banker, whom I interviewed. "Couldn't ask for better farmers. And they pay their bills on time." He took me later to a local café, where at his insistence we tried this chocolate fudge pie. Why should anyone yearn for the city when they can have pie like this in a small town? It is excellent and so rich you should cut it into small pieces—at least 8 servings.

> Pastry for 1-crust 9-inch pie (page 270)
> ½ cup (1 stick) butter
> 3 1-ounce squares unsweetened chocolate
> 4 eggs
> 3 tablespoons light corn syrup
> 1½ cups sugar
> ¼ teaspoon salt
> 1 teaspoon vanilla extract

▦ Preheat the oven to 325°F. Roll out the pastry and line a 9-inch pie pan; set aside.

▦ In the top of a double boiler, heat the butter and chocolate together over barely simmering water, stirring until melted and well blended. Remove the pan from the water and cool the chocolate mixture for 3 minutes. In the meantime, in a mixer bowl, lightly beat the eggs until just broken up. Stir in the corn syrup, sugar, salt, and vanilla; mix until just blended. (Don't overbeat or bubbles will form, causing an unpleasant crusty top on the pie.) Add the cooled chocolate, blending well. Pour into the pie shell and bake for 45 minutes or until the pie is almost but not quite firm when shaken.

▦ Remove the pie from the oven, cool completely on a rack, cut into wedges, and serve, either plain or with a bit of Whipped Cream Topping (page 271) or English Pouring Sauce (page 275).

Tears-on-Your-Pillow Pie

Makes one 8-inch pie; serves 6

WHAT I WOULDN'T GIVE to know the story behind the name of this pie! The Ohio Amish lady who passed the recipe along had no idea how the name originated. I have to speculate that this is the kind of pie you might want to eat after you've had a spat with your significant other. It is a brown sugar chess pie, a trifle more coarse than a white sugar chess pie. And it is a most admirable pie. This does make a thin, small pie; however, I don't think you'll complain, for one piece is very satisfying, thin as it is.

> Pastry for a 1-crust 8-inch pie (page 270)
> 2 eggs
> 1½ cups dark brown sugar, packed
> 1 tablespoon all-purpose flour
> ⅓ cup melted butter
> ½ cup evaporated milk
> 1 teaspoon vanilla extract
> Salt
> Grated nutmeg
> Whipped cream (optional)

▦ Preheat the oven to 350°F. Roll out the pastry and line an 8-inch pie pan. The scant filling will not be enough for a standard 9-inch pie pan, so do use the smaller one.

▦ In a mixer bowl, beat the eggs until broken up. In a small bowl, whisk the brown sugar and flour together and gradually add to the eggs. Gradually add the butter, milk, vanilla, and a pinch of salt. Do not overbeat. Pour the filling into the pie shell. Sift nutmeg liberally over the top. Bake the pie for 30 minutes, then without opening the door, turn the oven off and leave the pie in the oven for another 45 minutes. Remove to a rack to cool. Cut into small wedges and serve with whipped cream, if desired.

Pear Cranberry Pie

Makes one 9-inch pie; serves 6

THIS IS SUCH a captivating combination of flavors, with the sweet mellowness of the pears and the tartness of the cranberries melding together to form a beautiful pink filling. When cranberries are in season, buy extra and freeze them for year-long use. No preparation is needed; just toss the bags in the freezer.

And don't forget to write where the cranberries are stored on an inventory sheet taped to the front of the freezer. This will save you precious minutes of looking around in the wrong area, believe me. I also keep a flashlight on top of the freezer so I can peer more easily into the back corners; it is surprising what delicious tidbit might be lurking back there—pesto, toffee, and the like.

Pastry for a 2-crust 9-inch pie (page 270)
$1/2$ cup light brown sugar, packed
$1/2$ cup granulated sugar
3 tablespoons quick-cooking tapioca
$1/2$ teaspoon ground ginger
$1/2$ teaspoon ground allspice
$1/8$ teaspoon salt
6 cups peeled, cored, and sliced pears
$1/2$ cup fresh or frozen cranberries
1 tablespoon fresh lemon juice
2 teaspoons grated lemon zest
1 tablespoon butter, in small pieces

▓ Preheat the oven to 425°F. Roll out half the pastry thinly on a floured surface and line a 9-inch pan, patting it in firmly.

▓ In a large mixing bowl, combine the sugars, tapioca, ginger, allspice, and salt. Add the pears, cranberries, lemon juice, and zest; toss lightly and allow the mixture to stand for 10 minutes. Transfer the filling to the pastry shell and dot with the butter.

▓ Roll out the top crust, roll onto the top of the fruit, and crimp the edges to seal. Slash the top to let the steam escape. Bake for 55 to 60 minutes, or until the crust is browned and the juices are bubbly. Transfer the pie to a rack and cool completely before cutting into wedges.

Boiled Cider Pie

Makes one 9-inch deep-dish pie; serves 6 to 8

THIS LOOKS LIKE a pumpkin pie, but tastes like a tart, silky applesauce pie. It is most unusual and delicious, and I like to serve it with Foamy Sauce (page 275) or Whipped Cream Topping (page 271).

Boiled cider is cider that has been reduced to a syruplike thickness. It makes a very good liquid sweetener—I like it in Boston Baked Beans instead of molasses. If boiled cider is not available in your area, write or call the Cider Press (page 287).

Pastry for a 1-crust 9-inch pie (page 270)
4 eggs
$1/3$ cup sugar
$1/2$ teaspoon salt
1 cup boiled cider
$1 1/2$ cups whole milk
2 teaspoons vanilla extract
Grated nutmeg

▓ Preheat the oven to 400°F. Roll out the pie crust and line a 9-inch pie pan with the pastry; set aside.

▓ In a large bowl, combine the eggs, sugar, and salt and beat thoroughly. Stir in the boiled cider, milk, and vanilla and combine. Pour into the pastry shell; drift nutmeg over the top.

▓ Bake the pie for 10 minutes, then reduce the oven temperature to 350°F. and bake for 55 to 60 minutes, or until a knife inserted in the center of the pie comes out clean. Cool the pie on a wire rack, cover lightly, and refrigerate. To serve, cut into wedges and top with your favorite topping.

MENNONITE CENTRAL COMMITTEE QUILTS AND SALES

Mennonite Church groups meet in their churches for monthly or weekly sewing circles. These gatherings are held to make quilts for relief projects abroad or for the annual Mennonite Central Committee Quilt Auctions, for which the Amish also provide quilts. (For a partial list of these auctions, see page 279.) These auctions are a splendid place to see and buy stunning and carefully sewn quilts. They are held indoors or in large tents and the quilts are hung by the hundreds on long lines, a veritable forest of quilts. Amish and Mennonite women alike wander up and down the rows, observing patterns and stitchery. The auction lasts all day, and a nearby food tent or building offers Amish and Mennonite specialties, such as *fass-nachts* (rectangular doughnuts), homemade breads, chicken filling (dressing), superb pies, and other culinary enticements, to an appreciative audience.

The Mennonite Central Committee, which organizes the auctions, is a worldwide relief organization that sends food, clothing, and personnel all over the world. The monies raised by the donated quilts at auction is a gift from the women; the quilts are seldom signed and are given in the name of the church or the community.

Sour Cream Raisin Pie

Makes one 10-inch pie; serves 8 to 10

THIS TWO-LAYER GOLDEN vanilla custard pie is subtly sweetened with maple syrup and boasts a layer of raisins on the bottom. I first ate it at the Mennonite Relief Auction in Goshen, Indiana, and was not content until I'd found the recipe. It is a lighter version of the raisin pie served at Amish funerals, a tradition that dates back to the times when raisins were very costly and the raisin pies were offered to mourners as a sign of respect to the deceased.

> Pastry for a 1-crust 10-inch pie
> (page 270)
> 1 cup golden raisins
> 3 extra-large egg yolks
> 1 extra-large egg
> 2 cups sour cream
> $\frac{1}{2}$ cup maple syrup
> 2 tablespoons sugar
> 1 teaspoon grated nutmeg
> 1 teaspoon vanilla extract
> 1 tablespoon all-purpose flour
> Grated nutmeg, for garnish

■ Preheat the oven to 375° F. Roll out the pie dough and line a 10-inch pie pan. Evenly sprinkle the raisins over the pie crust, and set aside.

■ In a mixer bowl, combine the egg yolks, egg, sour cream, syrup, sugar, nutmeg, vanilla, and flour. Mix just until blended—you don't want too many bubbles to form. Pour over the raisins and sprinkle the top of the pie with nutmeg.

■ Bake the pie for 30 to 35 minutes or until a knife inserted in the middle comes out clean. Remove to a rack to cool, then refrigerate. It really is best if this pie is eaten the same day it is made—that is generally never a problem!

ABOVE: The men talk about their crops, the women peruse the stalls for bits of antique china or good buys on Tupperware. BELOW: Auctioneering is a profitable business, and the auctioneers (both men and women) attend a school to develop the jargon and skill.

Apple Squares with Lemon Sauce

Serves 9

APPLES ARE AN IMPORTANT ingredient in Amish and Mennonite cookery; not only used in pies, cakes, cookies, and dumplings, they appear in a variety of other unusual ways. In a Missouri community where apples grow exceptionally well, it is also an autumn Sunday after-church dish. Depending on the size of the congregation, on the Wednesday before, a bushel or two of apples are peeled and quartered, then placed in 5-gallon pails, layered with 2 cups of light brown sugar per layer, plus spices such as nutmeg and cinnamon. The pail is covered tightly and transferred to the cool milk house or cellar, and by Sunday, the apples have softened and are suspended in a well-spiced juice. Served in sauce dishes, this is a quick and easy fruit compote—and sometimes, they call it that. This is a more conventional recipe, a soft fragrant cake topped with a citrus, bright sauce.

> $^1/_2$ cup solid vegetable shortening
> 1 cup sugar
> 1 egg
> $^1/_4$ cup milk
> 1 teaspoon vanilla extract
> 1 cup all-purpose flour
> 1 teaspoon baking powder
> $^1/_2$ teaspoon salt
> $^1/_2$ teaspoon grated nutmeg
> 2 medium apples, peeled, cored, and finely chopped
>
> LEMON SAUCE
> 2 tablespoons cornstarch
> $^1/_2$ cup water
> $^1/_2$ cup light corn syrup
> 2 tablespoons ($^1/_4$ stick) butter
>   Grated zest and juice of 1 lemon
> $^1/_8$ teaspoon salt

■ Preheat the oven to 350°F. In a mixer bowl, cream together the shortening and sugar until light. Add the egg, milk, and vanilla and blend. In a small mixing bowl, whisk together the flour, baking powder, salt, and nutmeg; add to the creamed ingredients, combining well. Stir in the apples. Spread into a greased 9-inch square baking pan and bake for 30 to 35 minutes, or until the top of the cake is brown and springs back when touched with your fingertip. Cool in the pan.

■ MEANWHILE, MAKE THE LEMON SAUCE: In a saucepan, whisk together the cornstarch and water over medium heat. Add the corn syrup and cook until the mixture comes to a full boil. Simmer for 5 minutes, then remove from the heat. Add the butter, lemon zest, juice, and salt; mix until the butter is melted. Cut the cooled cake into 9 squares and serve with the warm lemon sauce.

Pecan Sandies

Makes about 4 dozen cookies

ONE THING WE NOTICED about Kentucky's Amish community was that the houses and outbuildings were designed precisely like those in Ohio, from whence the people came. The difference was the mountainous seclusion of the farms. In the spring, the hillsides glow pink with redbud trees.

I have always adored store-bought pecan sandies, and was delighted to find a recipe for this wonderfully crisp, buttery, and not overly sweet cookie in one of the Kentucky Amish country cookbooks.

> 1 cup (2 sticks) butter, at room temperature
> $^1/_2$ cup granulated sugar
> 2 teaspoons vanilla extract
> 2 teaspoons water
> 2 cups all-purpose flour
> 1 teaspoon salt
> 1 cup finely chopped pecans
> 1 cup confectioners' sugar

In a mixer bowl, cream together the butter and granulated sugar until fluffy. Add the vanilla and water and blend. In a mixing bowl, whisk together the flour and salt; add to the butter mixture and blend. Add the nuts, mixing until combined. Cover the cookie dough and chill for several hours or overnight.

Preheat the oven to 350°F. These cookies can be made by one of two methods: Roll the dough into 1-inch balls and bake on ungreased baking sheets for 20 minutes. While they are still hot, shake in a bag with the confectioners' sugar, then transfer to wire racks to cool. Alternatively, divide the dough in half, forming 2 logs each about 8 inches long. Slice into ¼-inch-thick patties and bake on ungreased baking sheets for 15 minutes. Transfer to wire racks and immediately sift confectioners' sugar over the top of the warm cookies. Cool completely and store in airtight containers.

Overnight Butterscotch Cookies

Makes 5 dozen cookies

MY MOTHER AND BOTH grandmothers made an overnight cookie that I remember with special fondness; it was a favorite snack cookie—substantial, crisp, just perfect with a glass of cold milk or hot chocolate before bed.

And somehow the recipe got lost. The Amish and Mennonites also make versions of this cookie, and I tried several of the recipes, but they just weren't as I remembered them. Then one day, when I finally found a few moments to go through some old recipe files of my mother's, I came across an old printed recipe with a check beside it. I tried it, and hallelujah, it was the recipe I'd been seeking.

I love the way the cookies were originally described in the printed version: "They can be made at night and can lie long, as the older they get the better they are."

½ cup butter, at room temperature
½ cup lard, at room temperature (*see Note*)
1 tablespoon vanilla extract
3½ cups dark brown sugar, packed
4 eggs
5 cups all-purpose flour
1 teaspoon baking soda
1 teaspoon cream of tartar
1½ teaspoons salt
1 cup coarsely chopped pecans or black walnuts

In a large mixer bowl, cream the butter, lard, and vanilla to combine, then gradually add the brown sugar and beat well, about 2 minutes. Add the eggs one at a time, blending well after each addition.

In a large mixing bowl, whisk together the flour, baking soda, cream of tartar, and salt. Gradually add the flour mixture to the creamed ingredients; combine well, then mix in the nuts.

Divide the dough in half. Shape each half into a roll about 2½ inches in diameter and 10 inches long. Cover with plastic wrap and refrigerate overnight.

Preheat the oven to 350°F. Cut each roll into ¼-inch-thick slices and arrange approximately 2 inches apart on an ungreased baking sheet. Bake for 8 minutes, then remove the trays from the oven, loosen each cookie with a metal spatula, and allow to cool on the baking sheet. Transfer to airtight containers or freeze.

NOTE: All butter can be used, though the flavor isn't quite the same.

7
ROADSIDE
STAND

Sautéed Zucchini and Corn ❖ Delicate Asparagus Pie ❖ Baked Acorn Squash with Marvelous Orange Glaze ❖ Orange Glazed Beets ❖ Buttered Brussels Sprouts with Bacon ❖ New String Beans with Red-Skinned Potatoes and Bacon ❖ Salad Greens with Homemade Thousand Island Dressing ❖ Creamy Tomato Dressing ❖ Sweet and Sour Bacon Dressing ❖ Special Summer Suet for Special Birds ❖ Apple Cookies with Caramel Frosting ❖ Fudge Nut Bars ❖ Crispy Cornmeal Sugar Cookies ❖ Lemon Drop Pie ❖ Simply Wonderful Peanut Butter Chocolate Sauce ❖ Mennonite Butter Tarts ❖ Chocolate Caramel Bars ❖ Soft Orange Frosted Cookies

AMISH MARRIAGES are very much a partnership, and the wife and husband may share a joint checking account at the local bank. However, most married women do strive to earn a modest income of their own by baking, selling quilts and potholders, making preserves,

handpainting eggs or bits of wood, crocheting, tatting, or weaving rag rugs. Some of these articles are sold directly from their homes; others are taken to the local Amish grocery or hardware, where they are placed on consignment. In the summer, just driving through an Amish community, you will find many roadside stands where the women sell produce from their garden as well as crafts and handiwork. Bouquets of annual flowers are arranged in tin cans of water, and they gladden the eyes and the heart. If one arrives early in the morning, there will be pies, breads, and muffins still warm from the oven. The family that owns maple groves will sell its spring syrup, and there are always eggs, fresh from the chicken coop.

In Arthur, Illinois, awesomely flat prairie country with big skies, we stop at the Bontragers' stand. There are the usual paper plates of cookies tightly wrapped in clear plastic, a variety of seasonal vegetables, and potholders, but also an astonishing array of birdhouses, some made of

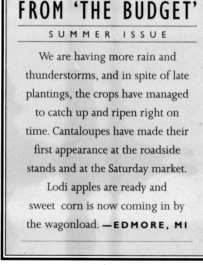

FROM 'THE BUDGET'
SUMMER ISSUE

We are having more rain and thunderstorms, and in spite of late plantings, the crops have managed to catch up and ripen right on time. Cantaloupes have made their first appearance at the roadside stands and at the Saturday market. Lodi apples are ready and sweet corn is now coming in by the wagonload. **—EDMORE, MI**

wood in intricate designs, others from dried gourds. "My granddaddy makes those," offers the white-bonneted slim girl in a dark lavender dress, nodding toward the birdhouses. "They sell real good." I browse among the cookies.

From underneath the counter, the girl, whose name is Bess, brings out a shallow basket of cookies covered with a tatted linen napkin and offers us some samples. The intensely flavored orange cookies are soft and cakelike, totally irresistible. And this is the first time I taste Amish boiled cookies, which are made in most communities, but have different names—I didn't expect them to be good, but I find them wonderful. When I ask who is responsible for the tatting, she takes me to the house to meet her mother.

"She has some things inside I could show you," she tells me. "We don't keep them out here 'cause they get dirty from the dust from the road." I am happy to follow her inside.

Rachel Bontrager sits in a wheelchair in the living room by a big window, where she can see the marten house, road, and farm stand. The nearby table is stacked with pieces of white fabric, cut in various-sized pieces.

Rachel talks candidly and with acceptance about her multiple sclerosis. Like all Amish, her family has no health insurance, and any income she can bring in with her handiwork helps pay her medical bills. "I learned how to tat from an English lady that I worked for before I got married. We Amish don't use tatting ourselves, but the English like tatted napkins and handkerchiefs. So when I got sick, I started tatting, partly because I was bored, partly because I did think maybe I could sell some of it. I've never been able to stop," she laughed.

Her husband, Amos, comes in from the garden with a bushel basket of green beans, the first of the season. The beans will be picked over, weighed, and transferred to plastic bags for selling at the stand. The Bontragers also can at least 100 quarts of green beans for themselves. They don't sell the canned beans at the stand, for they will eat all they preserve over the course of the winter.

Amos, in addition to farming, makes chairs with hand-woven caned seats. Like his wife's tatting, most of his chairs are special-ordered. When business is slow, he repairs furniture brought in by the English.

> There are 20 swarms of bees on the way, so we are busy getting hives ready for those, which we need to pollinate the new orchard. It seems the wild geese like our flock of tame ones. They fly low and some stop. They don't stay long or mix though. **—HAVEN, KS**

> We hung out a new suet cake in the cage the other day and it was completely gone the next morning. We think a raccoon or possum got it. The cage was still there so we got a new suet cake and put it on a more flimsy branch. So far, it is still there and the downy woodpecker, that really likes the suet, is back. **—DELTA, CO**

Amos takes me out to see the vegetable garden. The Bontrager half-acre garden is a beautiful thing—not a single weed and the rows laid out with flawless precision. Amos plants by the signs of the moon. There were many rows of cabbages—an inordinate amount, it seemed to me, though Amos assured me it is not too much. "Lots of heads will be sold at the stand and we use cabbage for slaw all summer." Those remaining in the garden until autumn will be made into kraut and kept in crocks on the unheated back porch.

Small Kirby cucumbers, grown for pickles and "sauce," peek out from under their sheltering leaves. The Bontragers have been growing chili peppers for several years; they like Mexican food themselves, and can and sell salsa at the stand. They raise several kinds of chilies, including the all-purpose jalapeño, glossy poblanos, and fiery slender cayennes, which the girls dry and grind up for their own use in tomato sauces and pizza toppings, and to sell. Herbs have become popular items at the stand, and so there are several varieties of basil, plus thyme, marjoram, and long rows of dill. Though grown mostly for the English trade, the Amish communities have begun to use herbs in their own dishes, generally an enhancement to their otherwise simple recipes. So change comes to these people, just as it does to the rest of us.

Sautéed Zucchini and Corn

Serves 6

As Dick and I traveled about from community to community, we soon observed that there was a great variety among the white organdy caps or *kops* the women wear. It is not uncommon for each order to have a different style of cap—some are plain and attached to a headband, others are intricately and finely pleated, and some, such as those in the Lancaster area, are heart-shaped. Whether the caps are tied under the chin or the ties allowed to fall free also depends on the community. As do most of their customs, this one derives from a passage in the Bible that the Amish use as their guide: "But every woman that prayeth . . . with her head uncovered dishonoroth her head," I Corinthians: 11.5.

Back to the recipes. This is a real good way to use up the ubiquitous zucchini, as well as leftover corn-on-the-cob. The combination of vegetables is most attractive.

> 1 tablespoon butter
> 1 tablespoon corn oil
> 6 small zucchini, trimmed and cut into
> ¼-inch slices
> 3 large ears corn, cooked and cut from cob
> 1 tablespoon minced fresh marjoram, or
> ½ teaspoon dried (optional)
> 1 teaspoon sugar
> Salt and pepper

■ In a large sauté pan, over medium-high heat, melt the butter with the corn oil until very hot, being careful not to let the butter burn. Add the zucchini and sauté until golden brown, 5 to 6 minutes. Add the corn, marjoram, sugar, and salt and pepper to taste and cook until heated through, 2 to 3 minutes. Serve immediately.

ABOVE: The blackboard gives you the message. Most people opt to pick for themselves. BELOW: Softly colored homemade dresses dry in the shade so the sun will not fade them.

RACHEL'S ADVICE ON CARING FOR LINENS

Rachel Bontrager pre-washes any material she is going to make up into tablecloths and napkins. She uses only linen thread, which she thinks holds up better than cotton. The completed napkins and clothes can be washed by hand, or for just a few minutes on a gentle cycle in an electric

machine. "The tatting is strong stuff," she says. For washing, she uses L.O.C., an Amway liquid organic product. This can also be used for long-term soaking of yellowed antique linens to improve their color. Any stains should be pretreated.

The cloths and napkins are dried outside on the clothesline, and if any stains remain, the wet linen pieces are spread out on shrubs or thick grass to bleach in the sun.

To preserve old linens, she recommends not ironing, but drenching the clean items in water, then patting them out firmly and tightly, dripping wet, on a clean hard surface, and allowing them to dry. They dry without a wrinkle. Napkins are a breeze to do this way; unfortunately, few of us have the space to do large tablecloths. But it is a good technique and since learning about it, I seldom iron napkins anymore.

Rachel suggests wrapping white linen tablecloths and napkins in blue tissue paper for storage, and placing rolls of blue paper between layers of the tablecloth before folding.

Delicate Asparagus Pie

Makes one 9-inch pie; serves 6

I DON'T WANT TO CLAIM positively absolutely that the Mennonites in America were making quiche lorraine long before the rest of us, but they do have a recipe for an onion cheese pie called *tourte*, or onion tart, that is very, very similar. This version, with its addition of asparagus, is a nice lunch dish. It is an attractive golden brown, with definite layers of cheese and asparagus.

> Pastry for 1-crust 9-inch pie (page 270)
> 8 slices bacon
> 1½ pounds fresh or 1 10-ounce box frozen chopped asparagus
> 10 ounces grated Swiss cheese
> 2 tablespoons all-purpose flour
> 2 eggs, at room temperature
> ¾ cup half-and-half, at room temperature
> 3 shakes of hot red pepper sauce
> Salt and pepper
> Paprika

■ Preheat the oven to 400°F. Roll out the pastry and line a 9-inch pie pan. Bake the pastry shell for 10 minutes, checking it regularly. Prick any bubbles with a fork. Set aside to cool.

■ Meanwhile, in a sauté pan, fry the bacon until crisp. Remove and drain on paper towels and then crumble into small pieces. Sprinkle on the bottom of the prebaked pastry shell; set aside.

■ In a vegetable steamer, over boiling water, steam the fresh asparagus for 3 minutes. If using frozen, cook according to package directions. Drain on paper towels and cool.

■ In a small mixing bowl, combine the cheese and flour; set aside. In another mixing bowl, whisk together the eggs, half-and-half, pepper sauce, and salt and pepper to taste; stir in the cheese. Arrange the asparagus pieces in a layer on top of the crumbled bacon and pour the eggs on top. Do not combine. Sprinkle the pie with paprika and bake for 25 minutes or until a knife inserted in the center comes out clean and the pie is a deep golden brown. Cool on a rack for 10 minutes, then cut into wedges and serve.

Baked Acorn Squash with Marvelous Orange Glaze

Serves 8

HARD-SHELLED SQUASH, such as acorn and butternut, are popular among the Amish and Mennonites, since they are easy to raise and store well over the winter. Sometimes acorn squash is halved and stuffed with a meat-loaf-type mixture or baked with maple syrup. However, among all their squash recipes, I like this one the most.

The highly flavored orange sauce makes this dish just plain elegant. Prepare the sauce several days in advance and keep refrigerated. You might want to consider this for your Thanksgiving dinner. And any leftover sauce is great on ice cream or angel food cake, or folded into a mixture of assorted fresh fruits for a compote.

> 4 small acorn squash, washed and cut in half lengthwise
> 1 6-ounce can frozen orange juice concentrate, thawed
> 2 cups fresh orange juice
> ½ teaspoon grated orange zest
> 2 cups sugar
> ¼ cup (½ stick) butter
> ½ teaspoon salt
> ½ teaspoon grated nutmeg
> ¼ teaspoon black pepper

■ Preheat the oven to 450°F. With a teaspoon, remove the seeds and membranes from the squash and discard. Place the squash, cut side down, in a foil-lined 12 × 16-inch baking pan. Add 1 inch of hot water to the pan, cover tightly with foil, and bake for 40 minutes.

■ In a medium saucepan, combine the remaining ingredients. Bring to a boil, then reduce the heat and simmer, uncovered, for 30 minutes, stirring now and then. The sauce will be syrupy and a light orange-butterscotch color.

■ Remove the squash from the oven and drain off the cooking water; the squash should be nearly, or completely tender. Turn the squash cut side up and pour 1 to 2 tablespoons of orange sauce into each squash half. Return the pan to the oven and bake, uncovered, for 20 minutes longer, occasionally basting the squash with the orange sauce. Add more sauce, if you like. When the squash is browned and completely tender, serve immediately, basting again with the sauce.

Orange Glazed Beets

Serves 6 to 8 liberally

PIQUANT WITH CIDER and frozen orange juice concentrate, this superb country dish gets an extra bit of dash from minced fresh dill. In the winter, if the Amish cook has not stored her own garden-raised beets in the root cellar, she will use three 13-ounce cans of small beets as a substitute for fresh ones. And canned beets are a very acceptable substitution.

> 32 very small beets (approximately 2 pounds, untrimmed)
> $^3/_4$ cup dark brown sugar, packed
> $^1/_2$ cup cider vinegar
> 1 tablespoon butter
> 2 tablespoons finely minced fresh dill
> $^1/_4$ teaspoon salt
> $^1/_4$ teaspoon freshly ground black pepper
> 2 tablespoons cornstarch
> $^1/_4$ cup frozen orange juice concentrate, thawed

■ Preheat the oven to 400° F. Remove the beet greens, leaving 1 inch of the stem and roots intact so the beets don't bleed during baking. Arrange the beets on a foil-lined baking sheet or a 12 × 17-inch pan and cover tightly with additional foil. Bake for 35 to 45 minutes, or until the beets are tender when pierced with a fork. Remove from the oven, remove the foil, and allow the beets to cool about 30 minutes. Peel away the skins, roots, and stems and discard. Depending on their size, slice the beets thinly or leave whole and set aside.

■ In a large saucepan, combine the brown sugar, vinegar, butter, dill, salt, and pepper and bring to a boil. Meanwhile, in a measuring cup, combine the cornstarch and orange juice concentrate until the mixture is smooth. Gradually add to the vinegar mixture and cook and whisk until the liquid is thickened and smooth. Add the beets, lower the heat, and simmer until the beets are heated through, about 5 minutes. Serve immediately.

NOTE: I freeze dill in the summer, snipping the fragrant thin leaves into a wide-mouthed plastic quart container. Frozen dill is so much better than dried dill. Adding it to cottage cheese, cabbage dishes, fish recipes (including tuna salad), and creamy vegetables really enhances your winter cookery.

Buttered Brussels Sprouts with Bacon

Serves 6

LOOKING FOR A DIFFERENT fall and winter vegetable dish? This is so good! And it is a good seasonal recipe for Thanksgiving dinner. Cooking them uncovered keeps the sprouts brightly colored.

> $1^1/_2$ pints fresh Brussels sprouts (about 18)
> 1 teaspoon salt
> 2 tablespoons butter
> 9 strips bacon, cooked until crisp and chopped
> Coarsely ground black pepper

■ Wash the Brussels sprouts under cold running water and remove any damaged outer leaves. Trim off the stems and cut an × in the bottom of each sprout.

■ In a large saucepan, bring about 4 quarts of water to a rolling boil over high heat. Add the Brussels sprouts and salt, lower the heat to medium, and cook, uncovered, for about 12 minutes or until tender-crisp. Drain well.

■ Melt the butter in a sauté pan, add the cooked bacon and sprouts, and gently toss together until heated through. Season to taste with pepper and transfer to a serving dish. Serve immediately.

New String Beans with Red-Skinned Potatoes and Bacon

Serves 8

THIS IS CONSIDERED a side dish in the country, but most of us would think it hearty enough for an entree. It is a perfect way to showcase new red potatoes and slender green beans. Sometimes this dish is made with smoked pork hocks, but bacon is easier, believe me.

$^1/_2$ pound bacon, diced
2 pounds very young green beans, washed and trimmed, left whole
4 new red-skinned potatoes, unpeeled, cut into $^1/_2$-inch cubes
2 small onions, diced
$^1/_2$ teaspoon salt
$^1/_4$ teaspoon coarsely ground black pepper
1 tablespoon chopped fresh summer savory, or $^1/_2$ teaspoon dried (optional)
1$^1/_2$ cups Chicken Stock (page 267) or canned broth

▨ In a large saucepan, over medium-high heat, brown the bacon until crisp and pour off the fat. Add the beans, potatoes, onions, salt, pepper, savory, and stock; stir. Simmer for 15 to 20 minutes or until the beans and potatoes are tender. Serve immediately.

CLOCKWISE FROM TOP LEFT: Yellow beans in a bucket resemble an abstract painting. A handcrafted weather vane atop a barn plainly tells the farmer about the weather. The image of the family farm is a reality, not a memory, in Amish country. Old work shoes provide whimsical containers for houseplants. This is recycling!

Salad Greens with Homemade Thousand Island Dressing

Makes 2 cups dressing; serves 8

FOR A COOK, there is nothing quite like the delight of being able to step out into one's garden and pick fresh salad greens. Making staggered plantings, however, all spring, early summer, and again in the fall is a good idea for consistent crops. Tossed with homemade Thousand Island dressing (and add some sliced hard-cooked eggs), this is a real treat. Though I use Boston or Bibb here, a bit of iceberg lettuce is all right too, for the dressing is heavy enough to compete with the firm and chewy iceberg.

> $1\frac{1}{2}$ cups mayonnaise
> $\frac{1}{2}$ cup chili sauce
> $\frac{1}{4}$ cup sweet pickle relish (I prefer Sechler's Hungarian Pepper Relish, page 287)
> 2 tablespoons finely minced onion
> $\frac{1}{4}$ teaspoon celery seeds
> $\frac{1}{4}$ teaspoon coarsely ground black pepper
> $\frac{1}{2}$ head Boston or Bibb lettuce, halved
>   Assorted green leaves, shredded
>   Hard-cooked egg or scallions, coarsely chopped, for garnish

■ In a 3-cup plastic container or bowl, combine the mayonnaise, chili sauce, relish, onion, celery seeds, and pepper, blending well. Cover and refrigerate until needed.

■ To serve, arrange the lettuce wedges and greens on individual salad plates, top with the dressing, and garnish with sliced eggs or scallions.

Creamy Tomato Dressing

Makes 2½ to 3 cups; serves 10 to 12

THE ROADSIDE STANDS feature fresh greens most of the summer, including red-leaved and curly varieties, and even mesclun. The greens are picked early in the morning while still dewy and are packed lightly into plastic bags.

This dressing is excellent over tender greens. It resembles a light mayonnaise, but there are no eggs in it, and it is very well seasoned. It is good on all greens, and I also drizzle it over Strawberry Aspic (page 83), which is a delightful and unexpected taste sensation.

> $\frac{1}{2}$ cup canned stewed tomatoes, drained
> $\frac{1}{2}$ cup chopped fresh parsley
> $\frac{1}{4}$ cup chopped fresh basil
> 1 garlic clove, minced
> $\frac{1}{2}$ cup cider vinegar
> $\frac{1}{2}$ cup mayonnaise
> 2 tablespoons horseradish mustard
> 2 teaspoons sugar
> $\frac{1}{4}$ teaspoon salt
> $\frac{1}{4}$ teaspoon coarsely ground black pepper
> 1 cup olive oil

■ In a food processor, blend the tomatoes, parsley, basil, and garlic until well combined. Add the vinegar, mayonnaise, mustard, sugar, salt, and pepper and process until mixture is integrated. With the processor running, slowly drizzle in the oil and continue processing until the mixture resembles mayonnaise and is very smooth. Transfer to a covered container and keep refrigerated until needed.

Sweet and Sour Bacon Dressing

Makes 3 cups; serves 16

GREEN SALADS ARE POPULAR with the Amish, especially in the spring when the tender new lettuces are harvested. Deer Tongue, Ruby, and Great Lakes are all favored varieties, and are planted every week during the spring season and again in September for staggered ongoing crops.

Creamy bacon dressing is a country favorite, and this rendition is especially easy, as it can be made ahead and served at room temperature. And it makes a large amount, which is fine, for it keeps indefinitely in the refrigerator.

1 pound lean bacon, chopped
1 cup water
1 cup sugar
1 cup cider vinegar
3 eggs
Salt
Freshly ground black pepper

▇ In a medium sauté pan, fry the bacon until crisp over medium-high heat. Drain the bacon on paper toweling; set aside. Pour the bacon grease through a sieve into a glass measuring cup and let stand for a few minutes until slightly cooled.

▇ Measure out 5 tablespoons of the clear bacon grease and return it to the sauté pan. Whisk in the water, sugar, and vinegar and bring to a boil over medium-high heat, about 4 minutes. Strain through a fine mesh sieve or cheesecloth. Remove $1/2$ cup of the strained mixture and allow to cool to room temperature.

▇ In a medium mixing bowl, beat the eggs and then whisk in the reserved $1/2$ cup cooled vinegar mixture; add the remaining vinegar mixture and season to taste with salt and pepper. Pour all into a clean medium saucepan and cook, stirring frequently, over medium-low heat until the mixture thickens, about 10 minutes. Add salt if necessary, and the pepper. Cool to room temperature and serve over salad greens, topped with the reserved bacon.

Special Summer Suet for Special Birds

Makes 5 cups, or 6 squares

THE AMISH SO APPRECIATE the birds in their yards that they have devised any number of ways to entice these feathered friends to their feeders. This recipe for summer suet (suet is actually trimmed hard beef fat; lard is rendered pork fat) is a good example. It can also be used in the winter, but the advantage of it is that it doesn't turn rancid or melt in the heat of summer. It's a good use for any odds and ends of nuts left over from baking. Such mixtures are sold at Amish markets and roadside stands.

We find this blend brings many unusual birds, including woodpeckers, and it has been our observation that if we feed the woodpeckers, they leave our house alone.

1 cup crunchy peanut butter
1 cup lard, at room temperature
2 cups quick-cooking oats (not instant)
2 cups cornmeal
1 cup all-purpose flour
$1/3$ cup sugar
Leftover nuts of any kind

▇ In a sauté pan, melt the peanut butter and lard together over medium heat. Stir in the remaining ingredients. Pour into an 8 × 8-inch pan. The mixture should be about 1 inch thick. Cool completely and cut into squares that will fit in a suet cage. Wrap extra squares in plastic wrap and store in a cool place until needed.

WEATHER
LORE

Like many farmers, the Amish and Mennonites are rightfully concerned with weather conditions; it is important to their lifestyle, and when reading the newspaper, *The Budget*, one notes that most of the scribes begin each piece with an account of weather conditions in their area. Many natural phenomena are considered harbingers of weather. A thick husk on the corn in the fields means a long, cold, hard winter; if the ears protrude from the husk, the winter will be short and mild.

And corn is not the only weather forecaster. If woolly caterpillars have a broader brown band than usual, this also presages a cold winter. When a rooster crows at 10 P.M., it will rain before morning. If it rains before 7 A.M., the sun will shine before eleven. If the hair on the dog becomes heavy during the fall, a long winter will follow. The first frost will be six months after the first spring thunderstorm. And there will be no killing frosts after the last full moon in May, so to be safe, don't set out tender plants before then. That is one rule I always observe!

Temperature affects the way a black cricket chirps. As the temperature rises, the cricket chirps more rapidly. If you count the number of chirps the cricket makes in fourteen seconds and add that number to 40, you will have the temperature in Fahrenheit to within one or two degrees.

Air pressure drops before a storm and continues to fall until the storm has passed. Animals can feel this (and so do some people, claim those with arthritis). "Frogs croak before a rain, but in the sun stay quiet again" is an old Amish saying, as well as "When the donkey blows his horn, 'Tis time to house your corn."

Apple Cookies with Caramel Frosting

Makes 4 dozen

DICK AND I WERE DRIVING about in the Sugar Creek, Millersburg, Ohio, area on a windy April day. The farmers were in their fields, many with four or six horses pulling stone-weighted plows through the rich earth. Flowering dogwoods were white clouds in the fencerows, and occasionally yellow daffodils bloomed by the mail boxes, a rather uncommon sight in most conservative communities. Passing one Amish farmhouse, we noticed that the yard was filled with baskets and there was a card table on the porch heaped with baked goods.

As we were prowling among the baskets, a woman emerged from the house accompanied by five small children. She said she had spent the winter weaving the baskets, which is not a traditional Amish craft, but these were beauties. I picked a handled one, a version of an Amish trug, to carry my gardening tools around, and Dick settled on a plate of these soft apple cookies with caramel frosting.

$^1/_2$ cup solid vegetable shortening
$1^1/_3$ cups light brown sugar, packed
1 egg
2 cups all-purpose flour
1 teaspoon baking soda
$^1/_2$ teaspoon salt
$^1/_2$ teaspoon grated nutmeg
$^1/_2$ teaspoon ground cloves
$^3/_4$ teaspoon ground cinnamon
$^1/_4$ cup apple juice
1 cup finely chopped peeled and cored apple
1 cup chopped English walnuts
1 cup dark raisins, plumped (page 270)

FROSTING
$^1/_3$ cup butter
$^3/_4$ cup dark brown sugar, packed
3 tablespoons milk
$^1/_4$ teaspoon salt
$^3/_4$ teaspoon vanilla extract
$1^1/_2$–2 cups confectioners' sugar

▓ Preheat the oven to 400° F. In a large mixer bowl, cream the shortening and then add the brown sugar and beat until light and fluffy. Add the egg and mix well. In a large mixing bowl, whisk together the flour, baking soda, salt, nutmeg, cloves, and cinnamon. Add to the sugar mixture alternating with the apple juice, combining well after each addition. Stir in the apple, walnuts, and raisins.

▓ Using a $1^1/_2$-inch cookie scoop or a heaping tablespoon, drop the dough onto parchment-lined or greased baking sheets and bake for 11 to 14 minutes or until brown. Transfer to a rack to cool.

▓ PREPARE THE FROSTING: Melt the butter in a small saucepan. Stir in the brown sugar and bring the mixture to a boil over high heat. Reduce the heat and simmer for 2 minutes, stirring constantly. Add the milk and bring back to a boil, stirring constantly. Remove from the heat and pour into a mixer bowl; cool. Add the salt and vanilla, and gradually beat in the confectioners' sugar until the frosting is creamy and the right consistency for spreading.

▓ Frost the cooled cookies liberally and allow them to stand until the frosting becomes firm. Store in a tight container, using sheets of wax paper between layers.

Fudge Nut Bars

Makes 4 dozen 2-inch bars

VERA JESS, an Amish woman who serves meals at her house in Arthur, Illinois, passed along this gem. It is a most satisfying chocolate cookie. The crust is crispy with an interesting texture and the chocolate layer is substantial but not messy.

1 cup (2 sticks) butter, at room temperature
2 cups light brown sugar, packed
2 eggs
2 teaspoons vanilla extract
3 cups quick-cooking oats (not instant)
2 cups all-purpose flour
1 teaspoon baking soda
1 teaspoon salt

FILLING
7 ounces sweetened condensed milk
1 cup milk chocolate chips
1 tablespoon butter
$^1/_4$ teaspoon salt
1 teaspoon vanilla extract
$^1/_2$ cup chopped English walnuts

▨ Preheat the oven to 350°F. In a mixer bowl, cream together the butter and brown sugar. Add the eggs and vanilla; mix well. In a large mixing bowl, whisk together the oats, flour, baking soda, and salt. Add to the butter mixture, blending well. Spread only three-fourths of the dough on an ungreased 11 × 17-inch jelly-roll pan and set aside.

▨ PREPARE THE FILLING: In a medium saucepan, over low heat, mix the condensed milk, chocolate chips, and butter. Whisk until melted and smooth. Blend in the vanilla, salt, and nuts and spread evenly over the dough.

▨ Roll the remaining one-fourth of dough between 2 sheets of wax paper into a thin layer. Cut it into odd-size pieces with a sharp knife. Using a spatula, lay the dough pieces on top of the chocolate layer. Bake for 25 to 30 minutes. Remove from the oven and allow to stand for 10 minutes. Loosen from the sides of the pan and cut into squares while still warm. Cool, cover tightly, and store.

Crispy Cornmeal Sugar Cookies

Makes 30 cookies

THIS IS A GREAT COOKIE—crisp, sugary, and elegantly simple. It's quite perfect with fruit or ice cream desserts, or for a private afternoon treat. I have only found this cookie in Mennonite communities, and it is a treasure.

1 cup (2 sticks) butter, at room temperature
1 cup sugar
2 egg yolks
1 teaspoon vanilla extract
1 teaspoon grated lemon zest
$1^1/_2$ cups all-purpose flour
1 cup yellow cornmeal
$^1/_2$ teaspoon salt
Sugar and grated nutmeg, for topping

▨ In a mixer bowl, combine the butter and sugar and beat until light and fluffy, about 2 minutes. Add the egg yolks, vanilla, and zest and mix well. Stir in the flour, cornmeal, and salt and combine thoroughly. Refrigerate the dough (see Note) for 3 to 4 hours, until firm.

▨ Preheat the oven to 350°F. On a floured surface, roll the dough out to a $^1/_4$-inch thickness. Cut into shapes using a $2^1/_2$-inch cutter. Transfer to an ungreased baking sheet and sprinkle the cookies liberally with sugar and nutmeg. Bake for 8 to 10 minutes or until the edges are browned. Remove to a rack to cool, then store in an airtight container.

NOTE: The dough may also be rolled into a 2-inch cylinder before chilling and cut into rounds about $^1/_4$ inch thick before baking.

Lemon Drop Pie

Makes one 9-inch pie; serves 8

YOU MUST NOT FAIL to try this pie! It is unusual and wonderful. I have only seen or eaten this recipe near Wooster, Ohio, where it is sometimes called lemon gravel pie or Montgomery County pie.

This is a rich lemon cream pie with a touch of mace. Just before it is baked, little dollops of cake batter are dropped on top, which will run together to form a deep golden brown layer. It is a most alluring dessert. Use your deepest pie pan.

> Pastry for a 1-crust deep-dish 9-inch pie (page 270)
> 1 cup sugar
> 3 tablespoons all-purpose flour
> 1/4 teaspoon mace
> 1/8 teaspoon salt
> 2 eggs
> 1/4 cup fresh lemon juice
> 1 tablespoon plus 1 teaspoon grated lemon zest
> 2 cups whole milk
>
> TOPPING
> 1/4 cup (1/2 stick) butter, at room temperature
> 1/2 cup sugar
> 1 teaspoon vanilla extract
> 1/2 cup plus 2 tablespoons all-purpose flour
> 1/2 teaspoon baking soda
> 1/8 teaspoon salt
> 1/4 cup whole milk
> Mace

■ Roll out the pastry until thin and use it to line a 9-inch, deep-dish pie pan. Set aside.

■ Fill the bottom of a double boiler half full of hot water and bring to a simmer. Meanwhile, whisk together the sugar, flour, mace, and salt; set aside. In the top of the double boiler, beat the eggs thoroughly. Gradually whisk in the lemon juice and zest. Blend in the flour mixture gradually, until the mixture is smooth, then gradually add the milk. Place the double boiler atop the simmering water. Cover and cook over low heat for 25 minutes, stirring now and then with a rubber spatula. The pudding will thicken and be puffy-looking when done. Remove from the heat and allow to cool for 10 minutes. Preheat the oven to 425°F.

■ MEANWHILE, MAKE THE TOPPING: In a mixer bowl, beat the butter, then gradually add the sugar and vanilla, and continue beating until the mixture is fluffy, about 1 minute. In a measuring cup, combine the flour, baking soda, and salt. Add the flour mixture to the butter-sugar mixture alternately with the milk, beginning and ending with the flour. (This can be made ahead and refrigerated until needed.)

■ Transfer the partially cooled filling to the unbaked shell. Using a 1 1/2-inch cookie scoop or a heaping tablespoon, evenly drop 16 dollops of the topping on the pie, about 1 inch apart. Sprinkle a bit more mace on the top. Bake the pie for 10 minutes, then lower the heat to 350° and continue baking the pie for 30 minutes longer, or until the top of the pie is a deep golden brown and a bit puffy. Remove from the oven to a rack and cool thoroughly before cutting into wedges.

Simply Wonderful Peanut Butter Chocolate Sauce

Makes 2 cups; serves 8

LEAVE IT TO THE AMISH cook to come up with a recipe like this—two ingredients and fantastic flavor and texture. And as an ice cream topping, it is out of this world. This is also a nice bread-and-butter gift, if you can possibly get it out of the house before someone scarfs it down.

> 1 cup smooth or crunchy peanut butter
> 1 cup chocolate syrup

■ In a small bowl, using an electric hand mixer, combine the peanut butter and syrup. Transfer to a pint jar, cover tightly, and store at room temperature. Serve over ice cream or angel food cake slices.

Peanuts are a good cash root crop for this Mennonite farmer and others who farm in the South.

Mennonite Butter Tarts

Makes 12 large tarts

I FIRST SAMPLED THESE in a Stratford, Ontario, bakery; there is a large Mennonite and Amish settlement nearby, and some of the English bakeries make their specialties. I was so impressed, for this is a delightful confection, similar to a mini–chess pie with texture. It took a lot of looking to find the recipe, and even more experimenting to get it right.

The filling in the tarts puffs up during baking, then slumps a bit. These are perfect for picnics or pickup desserts. If you are serving at home, the tarts could be topped with a bit of Whipped Cream Topping (page 271) or crème fraîche.

> Pastry for 1-crust 9-inch pie (page 270)
> ¼ cup (½ stick) butter, at room temperature
> ½ cup dark brown sugar, packed
> 1 tablespoon all-purpose flour
> ½ cup light corn syrup
> 1 egg, lightly beaten
> 1 rounded ¼ teaspoon mace
> ¼ teaspoon salt
> 1 teaspoon vanilla extract
> ½ cup golden raisins, plumped (page 270) and drained
> ¼ cup finely chopped pecans

■ Roll out the pastry as thin as possible. Cut into rounds with a 4½-inch cutter and fit the rounds into a 12-cup muffin tin. The pastry will come evenly to the top of the cup. Set aside.

■ Preheat the oven to 375°F. In a mixer bowl, cream the butter for 10 seconds, then gradually add the brown sugar and flour; cream for 30 seconds or until the mixture is combined. By hand, blend in the corn syrup, egg, mace, salt, and vanilla; mix until just integrated. Fold in the drained raisins and the nuts.

■ Using a 2-inch cookie scoop or 2 tablespoonfuls of batter, half-fill the pastry-lined tins. Place the tarts in the oven and immediately reduce the temperature to 350°. Bake the tarts for 20 minutes or until the pastry is golden and the filling brown. Remove to a rack, and allow to cool for 10 minutes. With a knife, loosen the edges of the tarts so any filling that might have spilled over will not stick to the pans. Cool completely in the pans, then remove gently with a small rubber spatula, and let them cool completely on a wire rack. Store in tightly covered containers, separated by wax paper.

NOTE: These tarts freeze very well.

Chocolate Caramel Bars

Makes 36 1½-inch bars

ORDINARILY, AMISH women do not buy English magazines, but one of the women who prepares meals for tourists did show me her issues of *Good Housekeeping* and *Country Woman*, which she subscribes to because she is on the lookout for new recipes. This person was also a reader, in spite of getting up at 4:30 A.M. most mornings to get ready for her noon dinner guests. She likes "Christian books, which are acceptable clean reading," and has read all the Louisa May Alcott books, as well as Gene Stratton Porter's books. "I sure would like to see her house sometime," she said wistfully. Porter (1868–1924) wrote sentimental romances alternately with distinguished nature books, and her work is still in print. Her house in northern Indiana is open to the public and worth the trip (page 280). Even in a buggy.

This is one of the recipes served at this woman's noon meals. Quick and easy to assemble, the cookies will be moister if you use a metal pan.

CRUST
> 1 cup all-purpose flour
> ½ cup (1 stick) butter, at room temperature
> ⅓ cup granulated sugar

FILLING
> 2 eggs
> ½ cup granulated sugar
> ½ cup light corn syrup
> ¼ cup crunchy regular peanut butter
> ½ teaspoon vanilla extract
> ¼ teaspoon salt

½ cup sweetened flaked coconut
½ cup milk chocolate chips

■ Preheat the oven to 350°F.

■ PREPARE THE CRUST: In a mixer bowl, on low speed, combine the flour, butter, and granulated sugar until crumbly. Press evenly onto the bottom of a 9- or 10-inch square baking pan. Bake for 12 to 17 minutes or until the edges are slightly browned.

■ MEANWHILE, PREPARE THE FILLING: In a mixer bowl, beat the eggs and granulated sugar together until combined. Add the corn syrup, peanut butter, vanilla, and salt; mix well. Fold in by hand the coconut and chocolate chips. Spread evenly over the prepared crust, return to the oven, and bake for 15 to 20 minutes or until the filling is set and golden brown. Remove from the oven and cut the cookies while still a bit warm. Allow the cookies to cool completely and store in an airtight container or freeze.

Soft Orange Frosted Cookies

Makes about 75 cookies

VISITING A KENTUCKY AMISH community is a treat since they are so private and rural. Since some of this group deliberately moved to Kentucky to escape the hurly-burly of the encroaching English world, they have not encouraged tourism in any way. There are no signs in their yards advertising quilts for sale, nor are there roadside stands. This exemplifies the dissimilarities that are allowed, even encouraged, among a people whom we tend to think of as a homogenous group.

Now to cookies. This is a superb cookie—soft, cakelike, and definitely orange! The frosting is really good. When these are sold at a roadside stand, customers flock to buy them.

1 6-ounce can orange juice concentrate, thawed
1½ cups granulated sugar
1 cup (2 sticks) butter, at room temperature
1 cup sour cream, at room temperature
2 eggs
4 cups all-purpose flour
1 teaspoon baking powder
1 teaspoon baking soda
½ teaspoon salt
2 tablespoons grated orange zest

ORANGE FROSTING
1 3-ounce package cream cheese, at room temperature
1 tablespoon butter, at room temperature
2 cups confectioners' sugar
2 tablespoons orange juice concentrate
2 tablespoons milk

■ Preheat the oven to 350°F. Remove 2 tablespoons of juice concentrate for the frosting and set aside.

■ In a large mixer bowl, cream the granulated sugar and butter together for about 2 minutes, then add the sour cream, eggs, and remaining juice concentrate; mix well. In another mixing bowl, whisk together the flour, baking powder, baking soda, and salt. Add the flour mixture and zest to the sugar-butter mixture and beat thoroughly. Using a 1-inch cookie scoop or a tablespoon of dough, drop the cookies onto a nonstick baking sheet or a parchment-lined one, and bake for 10 minutes or until the bottoms are lightly browned. Do not overbake. Remove the cookies to a rack to cool.

■ MAKE THE FROSTING: In a mixer bowl, beat the cream cheese and butter until blended. Add 1 cup of the confectioners' sugar, then the 2 tablespoons of orange juice concentrate and the milk. Add the remaining sugar and beat until smooth.

■ Frost the top of each cookie, allow the frosting to firm up, then transfer to tightly covered tins or plastic containers, placing wax paper between the layers.

8

THE HARVEST
CELLAR

Curried Mustard Pickles ❖ Spicy Refrigerator Pickles ❖ Cinnamon Tomato Preserves ❖ Three-Pepper Relish with Cumin ❖ Pear and Raisin Chutney with Candied Ginger ❖ Candied Ginger ❖ Old-Fashioned Peach Butter ❖ Pear Marmalade ❖ Delicate Pear Mincemeat ❖ Spicy Country Chili Sauce ❖ Onion Confetti Relish ❖ Mexican Hot Salsa ❖ Zesty Tomato Barbecue Sauce ❖ Tomato Lemon Chutney ❖ Cranberry Pear Jam ❖ The Easiest Strawberry Jam Ever ❖ Silky Pumpkin Butter ❖ Triple-Berry Jam with Rosemary ❖ Homemade Grape Juice

THE PRUDENT habits of the Amish women and the care they devote to their family's well-being are never more obvious than during canning season. Preserving the riches of the garden and orchard takes most of the summer and fall; the peak canning season is August and

September. By this time, morning mists rise like steam from the ponds and lakes, and one hears the occasional *skronk* of a heron as it elegantly searches for fish. Cicadas sing in the elderberry bushes, bent low with purple fruits. Roadside stands and gardens are still lifes of abundance, and the work never seems to stop.

"We can about 600 jars of food every summer—vegetables, fruits, soups, and poultry, including turkey and guineas. A guinea bird fits perfectly in a wide-mouthed jar," explains Erma Struzman. "We hardly buy anything at the grocery." Meats such as beef and pork are canned or cured at butchering time, generally right after Christmas. Many houses have special summer kitchens, either attached or separate, close to the regular kitchen where all the canning takes place. Frequently, this is also the washhouse, and there will be an enormous deep pot that is imbedded in its own stove. This is used on wash day, as well as for making apple butter, head cheese, and mincemeat, and for rendering lard when butchering is done; how-

FROM 'THE BUDGET'

AUTUMN ISSUE

The Aden Sees had their children in to help pick their peach orchard clean. They all stayed and made peach butter, and had a picnic in the orchard. Later the men went fishing. **—NAPPANEE, IN**

ever, as more communities accept natural gas as a cooking fuel, these pots are becoming relics.

The canning jars and lids are bought at local hardware stores and the jars kept from year to year. Most Amish have a few fruit trees of their own, and there are always large orchards nearby to supply more than enough applesauce and pie filling. Jams, jellies, and conserves are preserved all summer long, some for selling at roadside stands, others for personal use.

The men, too, are finding ways to supplement their small farm incomes, and they are developing businesses that are still home centered and family oriented. In the Guthrie, Kentucky, area, we visited an Amish hydroponic tomato-growing operation, certainly high-tech agriculture of the highest order. A large greenhouse was filled with eight-foot-high tomato plants, all state-of-the-art specimens loaded with ripening fruit. Elton Hostetler, the owner, begins with three-inch peat cubes with young eight-inch plants in long rows of Perlite encased in flat plastic tubes. The young plants are watered and fed by automatic timers four or five times a day, and when mature, are watered and fed every hour. These are some tomatoes!

Elton uses propane gas to generate heat and electricity for this operation, which produces over 45,000 pounds of tomatoes a season. His wife, Erma, assists him, removing the side suckers from the plants, tying up the plants, and then helping with the picking three times a week. The fruit is packed in cardboard boxes and shipped to a wholesaler.

When tomatoes are in season, bushel after bushel of the fragrant, robust globes are preserved in a variety of ways. "Sometimes I don't think we'll ever be done with the tomatoes," sighs Erma. "We can them, make chili sauce, homemade ketchup, juice, and now, lots of salsa."

After Christmas, life in an Amish household is quieter. The menfolk spend their time repairing machinery and the barns, while quilting is an enjoyable activity for the women. One pleasure that spouses enjoy together is the perusal of the gardening catalogs that arrive in the mail in profusion. Both the husband and wife take interest in these brightly illustrated catalogs and fantasize, as all gardeners do, about the treasures they will grow this summer.

Most of the seeds ordered are the usual, sensible ones: green beans, lima beans, beets, cucumbers for pickling, cabbage for salad and kraut, chard, peas, rutabagas, melons, sweet corn (planted when the oak leaves are as big as squirrels' ears), popcorn, pumpkins, squash of all kinds, and assorted lettuces, bell peppers, and radishes.

Tomato plants and onion sets will be bought at the local hardware or Farm Bureau when it is planting time.

The housewife, whose responsibility the garden is, waits until all the vegetable seeds are ordered before adding her modest list of annuals—unless she grows flowers to sell at a roadside stand; then she allows herself to be more extravagant. Mennonite women may plant perennial borders of flowers, but the Amish women think that too worldly and generally have just annuals, though occasionally I do see some daffodils in an Amish yard in the spring and a solitary chrysanthemum in the fall. But not often.

The vegetable gardens are splendid; there is no other word for it. The soil is rich and friable, and plantings are staggered so there is provender all season long. The gardens extend to the very edge of the road, utilizing every inch of soil. They are bordered by strongly colored annuals: enormous zinnias, feathery celosia, tall nodding cosmos, and ornamental kale. One Amish woman I know raises calla lilies. From these flowers, the women derive both visual pleasure and ideas for their quilt designs.

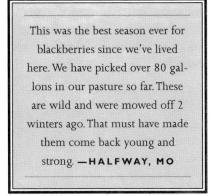

It was cloudy and cool most of the week. That made it very nice for all the "corn days." The gas corn cookers were in use nearly every day at one place or another. This was a good year for corn in this area. Plans are to put corn up today at the Arthur Kropfs and Willard Millers and that should about finish everyone up for this season. —**HORSE CAVE, KY**

This was the best season ever for blackberries since we've lived here. We have picked over 80 gallons in our pasture so far. These are wild and were mowed off 2 winters ago. That must have made them come back young and strong. —**HALFWAY, MO**

Curried Mustard Pickles

Makes 5 pints

MUSTARD PICKLES ARE a good accompaniment to any sandwich, and at family dinners, they are presented in long cut-glass pickle dishes. Jars are brought to barn raisings and funerals, where they are served right out of the containers. And sometimes pickles of this type are served after church with a light meal. Be sure to use pickling salt—iodized salt will soften the pickles.

> 10 cups peeled and sliced Kirby cucumbers (approximately 14)
> 4 cups sliced onions (approximately 2 large)
> 2 tablespoons pickling or kosher salt
> 2 cups light brown sugar, packed
> 2 tablespoons mustard seeds
> $1\frac{1}{2}$ teaspoons curry powder
> $\frac{1}{2}$ teaspoon turmeric
> 1 heaping tablespoon all-purpose flour
> 2 cups cider vinegar

▪ See the basic canning instructions on page 168 and prepare 5 pint jars for canning. Place the sliced cucumbers and onions in a very large, nonreactive mixing bowl, layering and sprinkling each layer with the salt. Cover and refrigerate overnight.

▪ The next day, in a large saucepan, whisk together the brown sugar, mustard seeds, curry, turmeric, and flour. Gradually whisk in the vinegar and bring the mixture to a boil. Meanwhile, drain the pickles and onions thoroughly.

▪ Pour the hot liquid over the cucumbers and onions; mix well. pack into the prepared jar and pour the remaining liquid into each jar, leaving a $\frac{1}{4}$-inch headspace. Wipe the rims of the jars clean, place a warm lid on top, and screw on the bands firmly. Process in a boiling water bath for 20 minutes. Remove to a towel-lined wire rack and let the jars cool completely. Store in a dark, cool place and refrigerate after opening.

Spicy Refrigerator Pickles

Makes 3 pints

THIS IS SUCH AN easy and fresh-tasting sweet pickle. Note that you don't have to process it; the pickles are stored in the refrigerator or the freezer. It's a popular pickle to send in the Amish children's lunch buckets in small jars.

> 7 cups unpeeled and thinly sliced cucumbers (small ones such as Kirby)
> $\frac{1}{2}$ cup chopped onion
> 2 tablespoons pickling or kosher salt (not iodized)
> $1\frac{1}{2}$ cups sugar
> 1 cup distilled white vinegar
> 1 teaspoon celery seeds
> $\frac{1}{4}$ teaspoon coarsely ground black pepper
> $\frac{1}{4}$ teaspoon hot red pepper flakes
> 9 whole cloves
> 3 cinnamon sticks

▪ In a large bowl, mix the cucumbers, onion, and salt; cover and refrigerate overnight. The next day, drain off the liquid and discard; set the cucumbers aside.

▪ In a small saucepan, combine the sugar, vinegar, celery seeds, pepper, red pepper flakes, cloves, and cinnamon sticks. Bring to a boil and cook for 1 minute, then set aside to cool. When cooled, remove the cinnamon sticks and reserve. Pour the liquid over the cucumbers and onion. Transfer to sterilized jars and add a cinnamon stick to each jar. Add enough of the remaining liquid to fill each jar. Cover and refrigerate or freeze until ready to use.

This gentle-faced tot clutches a pet duck to her chest. Her cap is black, instead of white, indicating her family belongs to a conservative group.

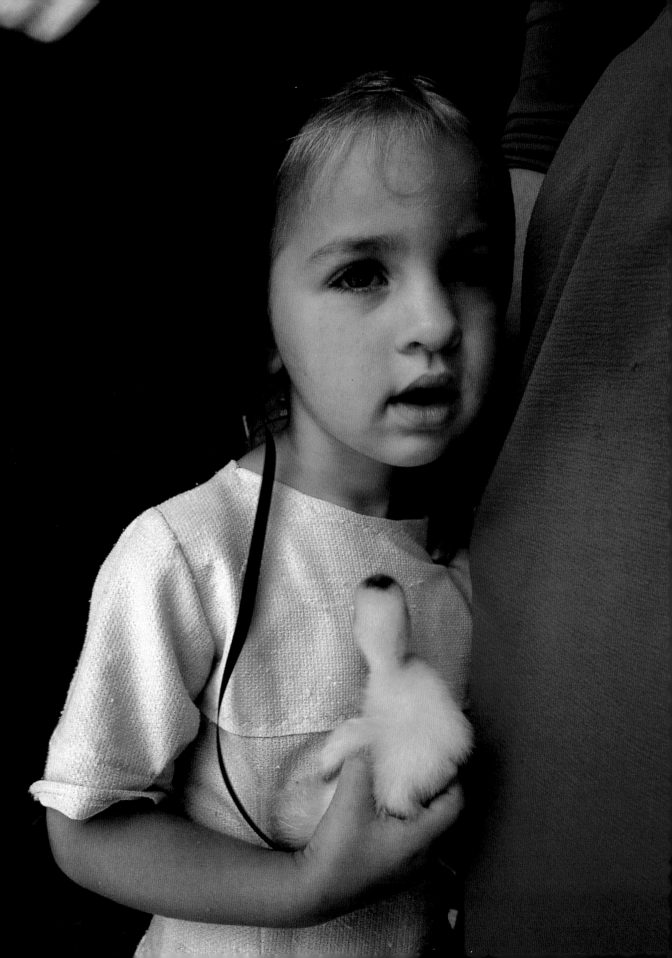

Cinnamon Tomato Preserves

Makes five 8-ounce jars

THIS IS A SPLENDID WAY to use up those extra tomatoes from your garden. And this is a splendid-tasting preserve recipe. I not only use it on toast but as a sauce for pork and lamb roasts. Need I mention, it is a great gift.

As in all preserving recipes, follow the measurements to the letter. The proportions are very important.

> 2 1/2 pounds fully ripe tomatoes
> 4 1/2 cups sugar
> 1 1/2 teaspoons grated lemon zest
> 1/4 cup fresh lemon juice
> 1/2 teaspoon ground allspice
> 1/2 teaspoon ground cinnamon
> 1/2 teaspoon kosher or canning salt
> 1/4 teaspoon ground cloves
> 2 bay leaves
> 1 box fruit pectin
> 1/2 teaspoon butter or margarine
> 6 cinnamon sticks

▧ Prepare your jars and rings (see Note).

▧ Peel and chop the tomatoes and place in a saucepan. Bring to a boil over high heat, reduce the heat, cover, and simmer for 10 minutes, stirring occasionally.

▧ Measure the sugar into a separate bowl; set aside. Measure out 3 cups of the cooked tomatoes and place in a 6- or 8-quart saucepan. (Reserve any remaining tomatoes for another use.) Stir in the lemon zest, juice, allspice, cinnamon, salt, cloves, and bay leaves. Stir in the fruit pectin and butter and, over high heat, bring to a full rolling boil. Quickly stir in all the sugar. Return to a full rolling boil and boil for exactly 1 minute, stirring constantly. Remove from the heat, discard the bay leaves, and skim off any foam with a metal spoon.

▧ Ladle quickly into clean, hot jars, adding a cinnamon stick to each jar, and filling to within 1/8 inch of the tops. Wipe the jar rims and threads with a clean cloth and cover with a lid and screw band. Invert the jars for 5 minutes, then turn upright. After the jars are cooled completely, check the seals. Label, date, and store in a dark, cool place.

NOTE: Prepare the jars and rings first by washing thoroughly and then placing in a large stockpot filled with hot water. Place the lids in a pan of hot water also. Let all stand in hot water until ready to fill, then drain well. Instead of inverting the jars to seal, you may also use the Basic Boiling Water Bath Canning Instructions (page 168).

Three-Pepper Relish with Cumin

Makes six 8-ounce jars

EVEN THOUGH THE RECIPE calls for jalapeños, this is not a mouth-searing relish. It is a most attractive one, though, and so good on hot dogs, hamburgers, and brats, as well as for glazing chicken and pork. Be sure to follow the measurements carefully, not adding more or less than the recipe calls for, or the relish will not "set up" properly.

> 5 cups sugar
> 3 medium red bell peppers
> 2 medium green bell peppers
> 10 jalapeño peppers, approximately 3 inches long
> 1 cup cider vinegar
> 2 tablespoons ground cumin
> 2 teaspoons celery seeds
> 1 teaspoon kosher or canning salt
> 1 box fruit pectin
> 1/2 teaspoon butter or margarine

▧ Prepare your jars and rings (see Note above).

▧ Measure the sugar into a bowl; set aside.

▧ Stem and halve all the peppers, discarding the seeds. Chop the green and red bell peppers in a food processor or by hand into 1/4- or 1/2-inch pieces and transfer to a 6- or 8-quart saucepan. Stem, halve, and seed the jalapeños, then chop finely and add to the saucepan. Stir in the vinegar, ground cumin, celery seeds, and salt.

Stir in the fruit pectin and butter and bring to a full rolling boil over high heat, stirring constantly. Quickly stir in all of the sugar and return to a full rolling boil and boil for exactly 1 minute, stirring constantly. Remove from the heat and, using a metal spoon, skim off the foam.

Ladle quickly into clean, hot jars, filling to within $1/8$ inch of the tops. Wipe the jar rims and threads with a clean cloth and cover with a lid and screw band. Invert the jars for 5 minutes, then turn upright. Cool for 1 to $1\frac{1}{2}$ hours, then shake the jars gently to distribute the peppers evenly throughout the relish. After the jars are cooled completely, check the seals. Label, date, and store in a dark, cool place.

Pear and Raisin Chutney with Candied Ginger

Makes approximately 6 pints

CHUTNEY IS ONE of my favorite condiments, and I think this one just might be my *favorite* favorite. The sweet and sour ratio is just right. Chutneys are quite common in Amish and Mennonite areas where the early settlers came from England. Though East Indian in origin, chutney was adopted with relish when sea captains brought it back to England, along with saris, curry powders, and tea.

> $4\frac{1}{2}$ *pounds peeled, cored, and chopped pears*
> *(approximately $1/2$ peck)*
> 1 *pound raisins, light or dark*
> 3 *large green bell peppers, chopped*
> 6 *cups sugar*
> $1/2$ *teaspoon salt*
> 2 *cups cider vinegar*
> 1 *tablespoon whole cloves, 2 cinnamon sticks,*
> *and 8 peppercorns tied in a cheesecloth bag*
> $1\frac{1}{2}$ *cups finely chopped candied ginger*

See basic canning instructions on page 168 and prepare 6 pint jars for canning.

Combine all of the ingredients in a deep, heavy pan, such as a stockpot. Bring the mixture to a boil, reduce the heat to low, and cook,

uncovered, for 1 to $1\frac{1}{2}$ hours or until the mixture is very thick. Stir frequently to prevent sticking.

Transfer the hot mixture to the hot sterilized pint jars, leaving about $1/4$ inch headspace. Adjust the lids and rings. Process 10 minutes in a boiling hot water bath, counting the time after the water returns to a full rolling boil. Remove from the water bath and place on a towel-lined wire rack. Cool completely, check the seals, and store the chutney in a dark, cool place.

Candied Ginger

Makes 2 cups

WHILE STORE-BOUGHT preserved ginger can be pricey, frugal Amish housewives can buy it cheaply at bulk food stores. However, it is simple (and even less costly) to make your own.

> $1/2$ *pound fresh ginger root*
> 2 *cups water*
> 2 *cups sugar*
> *Additional sugar, for rolling*

Peel the ginger and cut into $1/8$-inch thick julienne strips. Place the ginger in a saucepan with the water and sugar and bring to a boil; reduce the heat to medium to medium-low and simmer for 15 minutes, or until the ginger appears translucent.

Drain the ginger well and spread out on a layer of paper towels to partially dry for about 3 minutes. Roll each piece in sugar and place back on the paper toweling in a single layer to continue drying completely, about 24 hours (the time may vary, depending on the humidity). When dried, store in an airtight container in the refrigerator or freezer.

ZODIAC BELIEFS

Some farmers believe that at planting time it is important to consider the sign of the zodiac the moon is passing through. Corn planted under Gemini is said to yield the largest ears. Tomatoes planted under Libra will be large and heavy. Anything planted when the moon is in the sign of Gemini will be abundant. Pisces is not a good time to make sauerkraut; it goes soft. Cider should be drawn off for vinegar only during the sign of Leo. And when chickens are hatched under the sign of Aries, they will be more patient and quieter in the coops. And the hens should be set on an odd number of eggs under the sign of Virgo.

Old-Fashioned Peach Butter

Makes 6 half-pints or 6 cups

PEACH BUTTER IS SUBTLE, and the honey flavor is quite discernible in this country spread. The length of time needed to cook the butter depends a bit on your peaches and the rainfall received during the growing season. To test whether the butter is the right consistency after twenty-five minutes, remove the pot from the stove, dip a tablespoon of the butter onto a small plate, and place in the freezer for ten to fifteen minutes; when cooled the texture should be similar to apple butter. If it is too runny, return the pan to the stove and cook the butter a bit longer.

For absolute protection against scorching, you might want to invest in a Flame Tamer—a perforated disc that is placed between the burner and the pot to moderate the heat. It does slow down cooking time, so plan accordingly.

¼ cup water

2 tablespoons ascorbic acid, such as Fruit-
   Fresh

18 medium peaches, peeled, pitted, and coarsely
   chopped

   Orange juice, if needed

1 cup honey

1 cup granulated sugar

1¾ cups dark brown sugar, packed

½ teaspoon ground cloves

½ teaspoon ground ginger

½ teaspoon ground allspice

½ teaspoon grated nutmeg

■ In a large, heavy saucepan, combine the water and ascorbic acid. Add the peaches and cook, uncovered, over medium heat for 20 minutes, stirring occasionally, until soft. Cool slightly. Transfer to a blender or food processor and puree until smooth. Measure out 8 cups and return the puree to the pan. (If more liquid is needed to make 8 cups, add orange juice. If you have more than 8 cups, serve the extra over ice cream.) Stir in the honey, sugars, cloves, ginger, allspice, and nutmeg. Cook slowly over low heat, still uncovered, stirring frequently to prevent sticking, for 30 minutes or until thickened.

■ Ladle the hot mixture into hot sterilized half-pint jars, leaving about ¼ inch headspace. Adjust the lids and rings. Process 10 minutes in a boiling water bath, counting the time after the water returns to a full rolling boil. Remove from the water bath and place on a towel-lined wire rack. Cool completely, check the seals, and store in a dark, cool place. (See page 168 for basic canning instructions.)

The quiet back and forth, back and forth movement of the team and the thrasher creates a pattern of harmony and oneness with the land.

Pear Marmalade

Makes 4 pints

MY IMMEDIATE-REACTION note on the testing sheet for this recipe reads "FAB!" This recipe is sometimes called pear honey, but it has a more beautiful yellow color than honey. You should double the recipe if you have room for storage, for it disappears very fast. Not only is it good on toast, it is ideal on ice cream.

Pears grow well in the Midwest, and some later varieties are stored in root cellars, along with apples. During the winter, apples and pears are watched carefully for rot, for one bad one can ruin a whole bushel.

> 4 pounds firm, ripe pears
> 1 large orange
> 1 large lemon
> 6 cups sugar
> 4 cinnamon sticks
> 16 whole cloves

■ Wash, peel, and core the pears. Cut each into quarters, then in half crosswise. Wash the orange and lemon and cut each into 8 chunks; discard the seeds. Chop all the fruit in a food processor, being careful to keep it chunky.

■ Transfer the fruit and sugar to a large, deep saucepan and bring the mixture to a boil. Reduce the heat to low and add the cinnamon sticks and cloves. Simmer, uncovered, stirring frequently, for 1 hour or until thickened—the pears will be transparent. Remove from the heat. To test whether the marmalade is the right consistency, dip out a tablespoon of the marmalade on a small plate and place in the freezer for 10 to 15 minutes. It should not freeze, but be totally cooled and the texture should be like jam. If the mixture is too runny, return the pan to the stove and cook the marmalade a bit longer. With tongs, remove the cinnamon and cloves; cover and allow the marmalade to stand overnight at room temperature. Ladle into pint containers and freeze, or can according to Basic Boiling Water Bath Canning Instructions (page 168).

Delicate Pear Mincemeat

Makes 3 quarts or filling for three 9-inch pies

IF YOU THINK MINCEMEAT PIE is too heavy a dessert, this one is for you. It's very light and spicy, and candied pineapple and cherries make it so good even purists won't miss the traditional beef. I add sherry, which is very non-Amish, but nice. Substitute apple juice, cider, or pineapple juice if you don't use the sherry.

Though mincemeat has early English antecedents, country folk have always appreciated it as a way to use up small amounts of leftover meat. Generally, mincemeat was made at butchering time for just that reason. The mincemeat was packed in crocks or made into pies and left outside on the back porch to freeze for use all winter.

> 5 pounds firm pears, peeled and cored
> 1 orange, unpeeled, cut into chunks and seeded
> 1 1/2 pounds dark seedless raisins
> 1 cup candied red cherries, chopped
> 3 rings candied pineapple, chopped
> 4 cups sugar
> 3/4 cup cider vinegar
> 1 tablespoon ground cinnamon
> 1 tablespoon grated nutmeg
> 1 tablespoon ground allspice
> 2 teaspoons ground cloves
> 1/2 cup sweet sherry
> 1/2 cup light corn syrup

■ In a food processor, coarsely chop the pears; transfer to a heavy stockpot. Place the orange in the food processor and chop finer than the pears. Transfer to the pot with the pears. Add the raisins, cherries, pineapple, sugar, vinegar, cinnamon, nutmeg, allspice, cloves, sherry, and corn syrup; stir well and bring to a boil. Reduce the heat and simmer, uncovered, for about 2 hours or until thick, stirring occasionally. Cool, transfer to quart containers, and freeze until needed.

Spicy Country Chili Sauce

Makes 4 pints

THIS IS NOT TOO SWEET and nicely tart. The dark brown sugar and spices make it a deep red sauce, quite wonderful with roast pork, with sausages, or in salad dressings. You surely should make a double recipe.

The cooking time varies, depending on the type of tomato used and the rainfall of the season. If there has been a lot of rain, the tomatoes will have a higher water content and the chili sauce will take longer to cook down. Sorry to be so imprecise, but there it is. Just don't worry about it.

> 9 large red-ripe tomatoes, peeled, cored, and chopped
> 1 cup finely chopped onion
> 1 cup finely chopped green or red bell pepper
> 1 cup dark brown sugar, packed
> 1 tablespoon celery seeds
> 1 tablespoon ground ginger
> 1 tablespoon ground cinnamon
> $\frac{1}{2}$ tablespoon ground allspice
> 1 tablespoon salt
> 1 teaspoon ground black pepper
> 1 cup cider vinegar

▦ See page 168 for complete basic canning instructions and prepare 4 pint jars for canning.

▦ In a large stockpot, combine all the ingredients and bring to a boil. Lower the heat and simmer, stirring frequently, until the chili sauce is as thick as you want, 1 to 2 hours. Pour the hot sauce into the hot jars, leaving $\frac{1}{4}$ inch headspace. Wipe the rims clean, place a warm lid on top, and screw on the bands firmly. Process in a boiling water bath for 15 minutes. Remove to a towel-lined wire rack and let the jars cool completely. Store in a dark, cool place.

Onion Confetti Relish

Makes 2 cups

THE AMISH CALL THIS RELISH, but it is really more of a marinated onion salad. It adds real style to a cookout because it is so attractive. At big Amish gatherings, this relish is always served right out of a canning jar. It keeps indefinitely in the refrigerator.

This type of relish is occasionally sold at roadside stands. The profits these small businesses bring in cannot be underestimated. "I don't think we should complain about so many shops and the advertising that goes on," muses one of the owners of an Amish roadside stand. "If we didn't have tourists, who would buy our things, especially the quilts? The only bad thing about tourists is that their cars are a hazard to our buggies on the road."

> 3 cups thinly sliced sweet Spanish or Vidalia onions
> 1 small green bell pepper, diced
> 2 tablespoons diced red bell pepper
> $\frac{3}{4}$ cup cider vinegar
> $\frac{1}{2}$ cup water
> $\frac{1}{3}$ cup sugar
> 2 teaspoons pickling spices
> $\frac{1}{2}$ teaspoon salt
> $\frac{1}{4}$ teaspoon or more coarsely ground black pepper

▦ Separate the onions into rings and place in a medium mixing bowl. Add the diced peppers; set aside. In a small saucepan, over medium-high heat, combine the vinegar, water, sugar, pickling spices, salt, and pepper. Bring to a boil, lower the heat, and simmer for 5 minutes. Pour hot over the onions and peppers. Cool, cover, and refrigerate for several hours before serving.

Mexican Hot Salsa

Makes 2 pints

MEXICAN FOOD HAS BECOME popular with the Amish and Mennonite communities, and all the smaller town markets now stock chips, corn and flour tortillas, taco sauce, and refried beans. Since salsa is so easily prepared from tomatoes, onions, and chilies, it is not uncommon for an average Amish family to process sixty-five pints of very good quality salsa. Some cooks add a pint of salsa to a couple pounds of hamburger, a couple eggs, and some saltine cracker crumbs for a quick meat loaf.

This all-purpose condiment is so irresistible that a recipe for 2 pints will probably never get canned but will be eaten up immediately. I suggest quadrupling this recipe, using 16 pounds of tomatoes, 4 cans of vegetable juice, and so on, which will yield approximately 11 pints of salsa. Even after canning, the salsa has lots of flavor, pizzazz, and color.

> 4 pounds fresh tomatoes, peeled, seeded, and
>   coarsely chopped (about 5 cups)
> 1 6-ounce can vegetable juice, such as V-8
> 1 small green bell pepper, finely chopped
> 1 medium onion, finely chopped
> 6 serrano chilies, seeds and membranes
>   removed, finely chopped
> 1 teaspoon salt
> 1 teaspoon ground black pepper
> $\frac{1}{2}$ teaspoon ground red pepper, or to taste
> $\frac{1}{2}$ cup chopped fresh cilantro
>   Sugar (optional)

■ See page 168 for complete canning instructions and prepare 2 pint jars for canning.

■ In a large saucepan, combine the tomatoes, vegetable juice, green pepper, onion, and chilies. Simmer, uncovered, over medium heat for 10 minutes. Add the salt, black and red peppers, and cilantro. Taste, and add a bit of sugar if needed.

■ Transfer the hot mixture to the hot jars, leaving $\frac{1}{4}$ inch headspace. Adjust the caps. Process in a hot water bath for 40 minutes, counting the time after the water returns to a rolling boil. Remove from the water and place on a towel-lined rack to cool. Store in a dark, cool cupboard.

Zesty Tomato Barbecue Sauce

Makes 2 quarts

TRY BRUSHING THIS SASSY, thick barbecue sauce on chicken, ribs, or hamburgers just before taking them off the grill. Some cooks also add this to sautéed ground beef or turkey to make a sloppy joe sandwich. And it can also be poured over chuck roast that is covered and baked in a slow oven for a long time to create an easy, well-seasoned entree. In short, it is a versatile sauce to have on hand.

> 1 quart water
> 2 12-ounce cans tomato paste
> 2 lemons, seeded and cut into eighths
> 2 garlic cloves, minced
> 1 medium onion, finely chopped
> 6 large bay leaves
> 1 teaspoon celery salt
> 1 teaspoon ground allspice
> 1 teaspoon coarsely ground black pepper
> $1\frac{1}{2}$ teaspoons ground red pepper
> 2 teaspoons salt
> $1\frac{1}{2}$ cups dark brown sugar, packed
> $1\frac{1}{2}$ cups cider vinegar

■ Combine all the ingredients in a large stockpot and bring to a boil over medium-high heat. Reduce the heat and simmer, uncovered, for 45 minutes. Remove the lemon and bay leaves and discard. Cool somewhat, then transfer the sauce to jars that can be well sealed and refrigerate. This mixture keeps well indefinitely.

PRECEDING PAGES: A large selection of used horse harnesses and bridles will be sold at auction. The leather cannot be decorated with any special trim.

Tomato Lemon Chutney

Makes 2 cups

I HAVE MADE THIS in the winter, but it is much better with tomatoes fresh from the August garden. And I always double the recipe. It is especially good with grilled meats or poultry, or with a ploughman's lunch of bread and cheese. Serve this in individual ramekins right on the plate with the entree.

    1 tablespoon vegetable oil
    2 fresh jalapeño peppers, seeds and membranes
        removed, finely chopped
    ³/₄ teaspoon cumin seeds
    ¹/₂ teaspoon mustard seeds
    ¹/₂ teaspoon grated nutmeg
    1¹/₂ pounds ripe tomatoes, peeled, cored, seeded,
        and very thinly sliced
    ¹/₂ lemon, very thinly sliced and seeded
    ¹/₂ cup sugar
    ¹/₃ cup dried currants
    ¹/₂ teaspoon salt
    ¹/₄ teaspoon freshly ground black pepper

In a large sauté pan, heat the oil over medium-high heat. Add the peppers, cumin and mustard seeds, and nutmeg; stir to combine. When the seeds begin to "jump" in the hot oil, stir in the tomatoes and arrange the lemon slices, cut side down, on top of the tomatoes. Reduce the heat, cover, and simmer slowly for 15 minutes, stirring occasionally to keep the mixture from scorching (or use a Flame Tamer). Blend in the sugar, currants, salt, and pepper. Bring to a boil, reduce the heat, and boil gently, uncovered, for 25 to 35 minutes, until thickened. Stir frequently.

With a slotted spoon, remove the lemon slices and discard. Transfer the chutney to a non-reactive container, cover, and store in the refrigerator, though this can be canned, processing for 10 minutes; see page 168 for basic canning instructions.

Cranberry Pear Jam

Makes 9 half-pint jars

THIS IS NOT A PROCESSED JAM; it is made to be frozen. It has an unusual, pretty color and zesty flavor. I like to use the attractive, fancy jelly jars by Ball, and then present jars of this jam as a bread-and-butter gift. Try it on toast, English muffins, or biscuits.

    1 cup cranberries
    ¹/₂ cup water
    6¹/₂ cups sugar
    1¹/₂–2 pounds pears, cored, peeled, and finely
        chopped (3 cups)
    9 cinnamon sticks
    ³/₄ cup finely chopped English walnuts or
        pecans
    2 teaspoons finely shredded lemon zest
    ¹/₃ cup fresh lemon juice
    1 6-ounce package liquid pectin (2 foil
        pouches)

In a 4-quart saucepan, combine the cranberries and water, cover, and cook over medium-high heat for 6 minutes, or until almost all the cranberries have "popped." Add the sugar, pears, and cinnamon sticks; combine and bring to a boil. Cover, reduce the heat to medium low, and cook for 40 minutes or until the mixture is cooked down and the pears are tender.

Remove the saucepan from the heat, and with tongs, remove the cinnamon sticks and place one in each of 9 half-pint jars or containers. Add the nuts, lemon zest, and lemon juice, and return the pear mixture to the heat. Stir in the liquid pectin, bring the mixture again to a boil, and simmer 1 minute. Ladle into clean containers leaving ¹/₂ inch headspace. Seal and cool to room temperature, then freeze or refrigerate. Store up to 3 weeks in the refrigerator or 1 year in the freezer.

BASIC BOILING WATER BATH CANNING INSTRUCTIONS

For complete canning information, the *Ball Blue Book* is enormously helpful. It can be ordered by mail; see page 286.

You will need the following special equipment

❖ Boiling water bath canner with a rack and lid, or a stockpot 2 to 3 inches taller than your jars with a lid, and a trivet or rack in the bottom—old screw band lids work well laid side by side.

❖ Jar lifter

❖ Canning jars. Use only glass canning jars made specifically for home canning. Discard any jars with chips or cracks. Don't use old mayonnaise jars for canning.

❖ Vacuum lids. Use new ones each time.

❖ Screw band jar lids. If not new, check for dents, rust, etc., and discard any that do not appear to be in pristine condition.

❖ Standard kitchen equipment such as slotted spoons, tongs, scales, timers, funnels, and rubber spatulas.

Wash the jars, bands, and lids in hot, soapy water and rinse well. If you have a dishwasher, wash them and leave in the machine until they are ready to be filled and sealed. New lids should be simmered in hot water (180° F.) for 3 minutes, then left in the water until ready to use.

Fill the canner three-quarters full of water and bring to a boil. Cover and reduce the heat to keep the water hot until filled with jars. Lift jars out of hot water with jar lifter as needed.

Pack or pour the food into each jar and leave headspace as recommended in the recipe. Slide in a rubber or nonmetallic spatula between the food and the jar to release any trapped air bubbles. Wipe the tops and threads of the jar with a clean dampened cloth, and then, using tongs, remove one lid from the hot water and place on the jar. Add a screw band and tighten firmly. As you fill each jar, place it in the canner on the rack. After the canner is filled, make sure that the jars are covered with 1 to 2 inches of water (add more boiling water if needed). Cover the canner and bring the water to a boil. Start counting the processing time after the water returns to a boil.

When the required time has elapsed, remove the jars and set on a towel-covered rack several inches apart in a draft-free area and allow to cool for 12 hours. (Do not disturb the jars or tighten the screw bands.)

At that time, test each seal by pressing the center of the lid. If the dome is down or stays down when pressed, the jar is sealed. If the dome pops up and down, the jar did not seal and you should use that food immediately or remove the seal and screw band and reprocess. All metal screw bands should be removed and each jar should be washed in hot, soapy water, and rinsed to remove any food residue clinging along the seal and rim or on sides of jar. Store jars in a dry, dark, cool place.

The Easiest Strawberry Jam Ever

Makes five 8-ounce plastic containers

THIS IS THE QUICKEST WAY to make jam I know. The finished mixture is to be frozen, not processed, and this makes the strawberries taste like they were just brought in from the patch. This is a superb jam to use for strawberry trifle, too.

> 4 cups sugar
> 2 cups crushed strawberries (about 1 quart fully ripe strawberries)
> 1 box fruit pectin
> ¾ cup water

▨ Place the sugar and crushed strawberries in a large bowl and mix well. Set aside for 10 minutes, stirring occasionally.

▨ In a small saucepan, stir the fruit pectin and water together and bring to a boil over high heat, stirring constantly. Boil and stir for one minute, then remove from the heat and stir into the fruit mixture. Stir constantly until the sugar is completely dissolved and no longer grainy, about 3 minutes.

▨ Pour the jam into clean refrigerator or freezer containers to within ½ inch of the tops and cover. Let stand at room temperature for 24 hours then refrigerate or freeze until ready to serve. Let frozen jam thaw in the refrigerator before using.

Silky Pumpkin Butter

Makes 3 cups

PUMPKIN BUTTER is a surprise to most people, for the texture and intense orange color is very different from jams. It is an interesting addition to the holiday table, and guests can spread it on biscuits or freshly baked dinner rolls. My niece, Mary Ellen, who helps me test recipes, gives it as Christmas gifts—it's that good!

In Ohio, the Amish raise a buff-colored flat pumpkin (appropriately called an Amish pumpkin) that they store in straw stacks in the barnyard all winter long. How they find them I do not know—maybe they are all kept on the north side of the stack, three feet up from the ground and three feet in? The frugal Amish would make this butter from pumpkins they raise, but using canned pumpkin is much, much easier and just as good.

> 2 cups sugar
> 1½ cups solid pack pumpkin
> ¼ cup water
> ¼ cup fresh lemon juice
> 1 teaspoon grated lemon zest
> ½ teaspoon grated nutmeg
> ¼ teaspoon ground cinnamon
> ¼ teaspoon mace
> 1 3-ounce package liquid pectin

▨ In a large saucepan, over medium-high heat, combine the sugar, pumpkin, water, lemon juice, lemon zest, nutmeg, cinnamon, and mace; mix well. Bring to a rolling boil, stirring constantly. Reduce the heat to low and continue to simmer for 20 minutes, stirring occasionally. Stir in the pectin, raise the heat to medium high, and boil for 1 minute. Cool and store in the refrigerator or freeze.

Triple-Berry Jam with Rosemary

Makes eight 8-ounce jars

THE BLENDING of the three fruits with a touch of rosemary yields a most provocative jam. Since rosemary is a woody herb, it is necessary to "bruise" the leaves to release the oils. Ordinarily this is done with a mortar and pestle, but for this recipe, do it in a glass measure. As with all preserving, follow the measurements exactly so the jam will "set up" properly.

> 7 cups sugar
> 3 pints ripe strawberries
> 1 1/2 pints ripe red raspberries
> 1 cup ripe blueberries (or a 12-ounce bag, barely thawed)
> 1/4 cup fresh rosemary leaves
> 1 box fruit pectin
> 1/2 teaspoon butter or margarine

▦ Prepare your jars and rings (see Note, page 158).

▦ Measure the sugar into a separate bowl and set aside.

▦ Wash and stem the strawberries and place in a mixing bowl. Using a potato masher or pastry fork, crush the berries and measure out 2 1/2 cups and place in a 6- or 8-quart saucepan. Repeat with the raspberries, measuring 1 1/2 cups into the saucepan. Repeat with the blueberries and measure 1 cup into the saucepan. Any remaining crushed fruit can be served over ice cream or shortcakes.

▦ Remove 1/2 cup juice from the fruit mixture and place in a 2-cup glass measure. Add the rosemary and with a pestle or wooden spoon, firmly press the rosemary leaves against the sides of the cup to release the oils. Microwave the rosemary mixture on high for 4 minutes. Pour the juice through a strainer back into the saucepan with the fruit; discard the rosemary.

▦ Stir the fruit pectin and butter into the fruit and, over high heat, bring to a full rolling boil, stirring constantly. Quickly stir in all of the sugar and return to a full rolling boil and boil for exactly 1 minute, stirring constantly. Remove from the heat and, using a metal spoon, skim off any foam.

▦ Ladle quickly into clean, hot jars, filling to within 1/8 inch of the tops. Wipe the jar rims and threads with a clean cloth and cover with a lid and screw band. Invert the jars for 5 minutes, then turn upright. After the jars are cooled completely, check the seals. Label, date, and store in a dark, cool place.

Homemade Grape Juice

Makes 10 quarts

WHAT AN EASY WAY to make juice and use up the generous yield of the grape arbor! This method of preparing it is simplicity itself. Grape juice, like lemonade, is a popular drink among the Amish, and it is served at all times of the day. Combined in a bowl with ice cubes, thinly sliced lemons, and fresh mint, it is also a very pleasant punch.

> 10 cups firm, ripe grapes
> 3–4 cups sugar
> Approximately 9 quarts hot boiling water

▦ Wash and stem the grapes. Put 1 cup grapes into a hot quart jar. Add 1/4 cup sugar (more if the grapes are not real sweet that season) and slowly fill with boiling water leaving 1/4 inch headspace at the top. Adjust the caps and process 15 minutes in a boiling water bath. See Basic Boiling Water Bath Canning Instructions on page 168. Store canned juice in a dark, cool place and serve chilled.

SUPPER TIME

[NACHTESSE]

❖

AS THE SUN sets in Quilt Country, the slow rhythm of the windmill, barely turning in the dying breeze, casts long shadows across the garden. Wood warblers, nocturnal birds, congregate in the copse of elderberries, nattering toward night. The martens swoop and dive for mosquitos in the fading light of the farmyard. The night sky flickers a bit and there is a rumble of thunder in the distance, tantalizing the farmer with the possibility of rain. An occasional show of heat lightning reinforces his hopes. The lemony blooms of the evening primrose open by the porch swing. The return of the men and the sound of their creaking buggy wheels on the gravel roads signal their day is over, but for the women still busy in the kitchen there remains one final meal to get on the table.

9
CASSEROLES
AND
CARRY-INS

Spicy Oven-Fried Chicken ❖ Mexican Baked Chicken ❖ Amish Filling with Chicken ❖ Savory Pork Pie ❖ Candied Ham Loaf ❖ Creamy Noodle and Ground Beef Casserole ❖ Creamy Escalloped Potatoes and Ham ❖ Creamy Kidney Bean Salad ❖ Green Beans with Mustard Sauce ❖ Sweet Baked Sauerkraut with Tomatoes ❖ Escalloped Cheese and Rice ❖ Country Peach Cobbler ❖ Bushel Oatmeal Church Cookies ❖ Gingersnap Rhubarb Crisp ❖ Mincemeat Tea Bread ❖ Date Pudding Trifle ❖ Date Treasures

FOR THE AMISH and conservative Mennonites, social life revolves around the church and the home. Living in a society where much of the work is done without electricity, the tradition of coming together to share the workload has evolved very naturally. It was always a

necessity in the earlier centuries, and it remains so today for the Amish.

Wisely, these projects are treated as happy gatherings, and are called "frolics." The semantics are clever; the word doesn't necessarily denote frivolity, but rather, means "work party." Frolics can vary from candy making by a group of women to raising monies for financially stressed families to the ultimate frolic, which is a barn raising. All frolics are looked forward to as a time of fellowship, and as a visible means of support within a self-sufficient community.

When Amish or Old Order Mennonites move to a new site, they tend to move as a group, so as to create a new community. Old Order Amish live by the maxim that "The family who works together stays together," and they extend this to the religious district. They believe working together on a given task is one of the best ways to build a cohesive community. Their efforts show concern for each other, while certainly their limited use of technology underscores this need.

FROM 'THE BUDGET'

LATE FALL ISSUE

There were two building frolics yesterday. One was at Jacob Shetlers and one at Ivan Shetlers, both for an addition to their houses, badly needed after some twins arrived in both families! That must be some sort of record. **—GLASGOW, KY**

Middle-of-the-week singings or frolics for the young people are another important means of social interaction organized by Amish families. But participation is by no means restricted to youngsters. Lydia Beachy is looking forward to an apple butter frolic at her house; she has invited her sisters and neighbors to come in and help. It's late fall; drooping bittersweet vines on the fences have opened their little orange spheres, and green knobby hedge apples lie in the road, begging to be picked up. Wild geese rise up unexpectedly from the ponds with a great rushing of wings and raucous honkings. The orchard is bare of leaves, but a few late red apples still cling to gnarled bare branches.

"We'll start early in the morning, about eight o'clock, for the apple butter takes a long time to cook down," she explains. "Some we'll cook down in the washhouse in the deep wash kettle there; a bunch of it will be cooked outside in lard-rendering kettles, and the rest we'll bake in shallow pans in the ovens in the house," says Lydia.

Most of the women meet the day before to prepare the apples, coring and slicing them, but leaving the skins on. Stored in five-gallon lard cans with sugar and a bit of cider, the apples are transferred to their cooking pots the following morning, and slowly and carefully simmered until they become a coarse dark mass. The women use long wooden paddles to stir the apple butter to keep it from scorching. "You really have to watch it at the end of the cooking; it burns real easy," warns Lydia.

After cooling slightly, the apple butter is dipped out with deep saucepans and forced through hand food mills or coarse sieves to make a smooth butter. Cinnamon is added to taste. At the end of the day, the apple butter is divided evenly among the group and taken home in the lard cans, then canned the next day for the winter to come.

Other frolics include quilting, cider making, butchering, and during the summer, making large amounts of jams and jellies. Elderberry and grape season is always a time for jelly frolics organized by the women, since the elderberries are so pesky small and grape jelly is so time-consuming to prepare. Many hands and much conversation make tedious preparation more enjoyable.

Husking bee frolics are centered on the husking and shelling of harvested dried popcorn; this is a young people's frolic and is held in a barn. The evening ends with singing and, of course, popped corn and lemonade.

At threshing time, the men come together to harvest the wheat, oats, or spelt. A threshing machine, run off a generator, is an expensive piece of equipment and is owned by a group of farmers, so they all help each other during the threshing season. The wives come together to prepare and serve abundant meals. Before school starts in the fall, there is a frolic to clean the schoolhouse, inside and out, to cut the grass, and to spruce up the play equipment, softball field, and outdoor privvies.

Of course, a central feature of any frolic is food. Each participant will have brought along a sturdy, portable recipe to share, augmented by food contributed by the host family. If the frolic is an all-day event, the group will stop at noon for a hearty meal of soup and cornbread, casseroles brought in by the women, plus different kinds of pies. If men are helping in the work, the food is more substantial and will include chicken, meat loaf, or pork chops along with vegetables and salads—all foods that can be prepared and toted along to reheat on site or served at room temperature. Any of these foods would be ideal for a potluck or bring-a-dish supper.

> The Nathan Chupps had a Jake Detweiler Reunion last Saturday. There were 145 there and 28 missing. Most of us slept there and had dinner and supper before going home. Others stayed over Sunday too, and went to church. We picked up a load of cheese enroute home for our store. Grandma Bethie stayed with the Dennis Headings family while we were gone.
>
> **—KINGSTON, WI**

> The three of us here had a most pleasant surprise last evening when 3 buggies arrived with "meals on wheels." My sister and husband, Alma and Enos Bender, also sat in on the chicken and ice cream supper, beings they happened to arrive at a most auspicious time.
>
> **—PANAMA, NY**

Spicy Oven-Fried Chicken

Serves 6

FRIED CHICKEN is prepared for many of the large carry-in dinners. The woman who gave me this recipe had used it for the wedding of her friend's daughter, and with some help from the neighbors baked 963 pieces of chicken. She counted every one of them. "You people should go into the catering business," I suggest. "Oh no, the English would want us to work on Sundays and we won't do that," she answered.

> $\frac{1}{3}$ cup vegetable oil
> $\frac{1}{3}$ cup ($\frac{2}{3}$ stick) butter
> $\frac{1}{2}$ cup all-purpose flour
> $\frac{1}{2}$ cup cracker meal
> $\frac{1}{2}$ cup yellow cornmeal
> $1\frac{1}{2}$ teaspoons Easy Garlic Salt (page 266)
> $1\frac{1}{2}$ teaspoons paprika
> $1\frac{1}{2}$ teaspoons ground sage
> 1 teaspoon salt
> 1 teaspoon black pepper
> $\frac{1}{4}$ teaspoon dried red pepper flakes
> 4 pounds chicken pieces (legs, thighs, breast
>   halves), approximately 14 pieces

▨ Combine the oil and butter in a shallow cooking pan (a jelly-roll pan is perfect) and place in an oven set to 375°F. to melt. Set aside.

▨ In a large paper sack, combine the flour, cracker meal, cornmeal, and seasonings. Roll the chicken pieces, 3 at a time, in the melted oil–butter mixture, then drop them in the sack and shake to coat. Place on a dish or wax paper.

▨ Place the coated chicken in the pan, skin side down. Bake for 45 minutes, then use a spatula to turn the pieces and bake 5 to 10 minutes longer, or until the top crust begins to bubble. Serve hot or cold, but the crust texture is better if the chicken is not refrigerated before eating. If you can afford the calories, the pan drippings make a divine gravy for potatoes or biscuits.

Succulent fried chicken is ready to be served to a busload of hungry tourists at an Amish farm close to Shipshewana, Indiana.

Mexican Baked Chicken

AMISH AND MENNONITE cooks have embraced both Mexican and Italian cookery with enthusiasm; they like the way seasonings of these two cuisines can dress up some of their otherwise plain dishes. Oregano, cumin, and chili powder are available in all the small groceries, of course, as well as in the bulk food stores that the Amish prefer to frequent. Buying a pound of cumin at a time is not unusual if one is going to can thirty quarts of chili.

This chicken recipe is one of those easy dishes that we all depend on; not only is it well seasoned but the chicken doesn't have to be browned first, saving time, mess, and calories. It can be made with skinless chicken pieces as well, though I do prefer it with the skin myself. Since it's good the second day, it finds its way into lunch boxes as well.

> 2 14$\frac{1}{2}$-ounce cans stewed tomatoes
> 2 tablespoons chili powder
> 1$\frac{1}{4}$ teaspoons ground cumin
> 1$\frac{1}{2}$ teaspoons fresh oregano, or $\frac{1}{2}$ teaspoon dried crushed
> $\frac{1}{2}$ teaspoon salt
> 4 pounds chicken pieces, such as breast halves, legs, thighs

▧ Preheat the oven to 400°F. Grease a 9 × 13-inch flat glass baking dish.

▧ Pour the tomatoes into the dish. Add 1$\frac{1}{2}$ tablespoons of the chili powder, 1 teaspoon of the cumin, and all the oregano; mix well. Mix the remaining chili powder and cumin with the salt and rub on the chicken parts. Arrange the chicken skin side up on top of the tomato mixture. Bake uncovered for 30 minutes, then remove from the oven and baste with the tomato sauce. Return to the oven and bake for 15 minutes longer or until the chicken is tender. Serve hot with rice or refried beans, or both.

Amish Filling with Chicken

WE PROBABLY WOULD CALL this a dressing or stuffing, but with lavish amounts of chicken pieces added, it makes a good one-dish meal. It is always brought to large Amish and Mennonite gatherings. Most of the regional restaurants have it on their menus, and serve it with deep yellow chicken gravy.

The bread must be cubed and dried in advance; three days is the right amount of time. The whole mixture can be frozen before baking; thaw it partially and then bake, allowing approximately 15 to 20 minutes extra baking time.

> 1 to 1$\frac{1}{2}$ loaves good white bread, crusts removed
> 2 pounds chicken thighs or mixed pieces
> 1 bay leaf
>   Salt and pepper
> $\frac{1}{4}$ cup finely diced carrot
> 1 cup diced potato
> $\frac{1}{2}$ cup (1 stick) butter
> 3 eggs
> 2 cups milk
> 1 tablespoon powdered sage
> 2 teaspoons celery seeds
> $\frac{1}{2}$ cup finely chopped celery
> $\frac{1}{4}$ cup minced fresh parsley
> 2 tablespoons melted butter

▧ Three days before preparing the filling, remove the crust from the bread. (You can feed it to the birds.) Cut the bread into small cubes and spread on a baking sheet. Allow to dry, covered lightly, for 3 days. Measure out 2 quarts of the cubes and reserve, freezing any extra cubes for another time.

▧ In a large stockpot, over medium-high heat, cover the chicken with water and add the bay leaf and a pinch of salt and pepper. Cook for approximately 20 minutes or until the chicken is tender. Meanwhile, combine the carrot and potato in a small saucepan, cover with water, and cook over medium-high heat for 8 to 10 minutes, until just tender; drain and set aside to cool.

▨ Remove the chicken from the broth, cool slightly, then discard the skin and bones. Chop the chicken coarsely and set aside.

▨ Preheat the oven to 350°F. In a large sauté pan, melt the butter. Add the bread cubes and brown them about 3 minutes, stirring constantly. Set aside. In a large bowl, beat the eggs, then stir in the milk, sage, celery seeds, and ½ teaspoon each salt and pepper. Add the bread cubes and toss lightly. Fold in the chopped chicken, carrot, potato, celery, and parsley. Pour the melted butter into a 9 × 13-inch pan, and then add the dressing. Bake for 1 hour or until the top of the dressing is nicely browned and puffy. Serve hot, with chicken gravy, if desired.

Savory Pork Pie

Serves 6

A MOST SATISFYING SAVORY DISH, pork pie is also an ideal buffet dish that is good for carry-in suppers (it travels well in the buggy or the car). It can also be topped with pie crust (page 270) instead of the biscuits. The meat mixture can be made several days in advance, but do not freeze it because of the potatoes; thawed, they have an unpleasant, mushy texture. When doubling the recipe, use a 15 × 12-inch oval casserole.

> 1 tablespoon vegetable oil
> 1 pound lean fresh pork loin, cut into
>   bite-size pieces
> 1 cup water
> 1 bay leaf
> 2 large potatoes, peeled and cut into
>   bite-size pieces
> 1 medium onion, coarsely chopped
> 1 celery rib, chopped
> 2 cups Chicken Stock (page 267) or
>   1 16-ounce can chicken broth
> ⅛ teaspoon coarsely ground black pepper
> ⅛ teaspoon grated nutmeg
> ¼ teaspoon salt

> 1 tablespoon fresh minced thyme, or
>   ½ teaspoon dried
> ½ tablespoon Worcestershire sauce
> ½ cup minced fresh parsley
> ¼ cup milk
> 2½ tablespoons flour

BISCUITS
> 1 cup all-purpose flour
> ½ teaspoon salt
> ½ teaspoon sugar
> 1¼ teaspoons baking powder
> ⅛ teaspoon celery seeds
> ⅛ teaspoon coarsely ground black pepper
> 3 tablespoons cold butter
> ½ cup milk

▨ Heat the oil in an 11-inch sauté pan (not a nonstick pan—the meat doesn't brown as well) and add the pork. Sauté until the pork is browned, about 10 minutes. Add the water and bay leaf, cover, and bring to a boil, then reduce the heat and simmer for 30 to 40 minutes, or until the pork is tender.

▨ Add the potatoes, onion, celery, and stock. Continue simmering for 20 minutes, then add the seasonings. In a small jar, combine the milk and flour and shake to form a smooth paste. Add this to the meat mixture and cook 5 minutes longer, stirring all the while until the mixture thickens. Be sure the mixture is bubbling up in the center of the pan. Transfer the mixture to a 2-quart (12 × 7-inch) baking pan. (This portion of the recipe can be done 2 days in advance.)

▨ MEANWHILE, MAKE THE BISCUITS, either by hand or in the food processor: Combine the flour, salt, sugar, baking powder, celery seeds, and pepper. Drop in the butter and work with a pastry blender or process until coarse crumbs form. Add the milk all at once and blend until just mixed. Using a cookie scoop or tablespoon, drop the biscuits (8 or 9) on top of the warm meat mixture. Bake for 10 minutes, or until the biscuits are golden brown. Serve immediately.

BARN

RAISING

DINNER

When there's a need for a barn in an Amish or Mennonite community, church members from near and far rally round to donate their time, tools, and materials for the job. Plans are drawn up carefully, so the crew of several hundred can raise a large barn in a day. The women volunteer food and time to prepare the meals. This spectacular outpouring of effort illustrates the Bible reference to "bear one another's burdens," taken literally by the Amish, who come together in mutual aid.

The raising can be either for a new barn or to rebuild an old one that has burned down, which is not uncommon. The Amish do not believe in lightning rods, so many fires begin because of electrical storms. Their belief is that if a fire comes, it is God's will.

The foundation of cement blocks is laid in advance. One man is in charge of the actual raising of the barn, and he delegates tasks to the carpenters; nothing is prefabricated.

Here is a list of food to be prepared for one barn raising in Pennsylvania:

- 24 loaves of bread
- 5 pounds butter
- 21 crocks potatoes
- 4 large roasters of beef with gravy
- 8 crocks carrots, boiled and buttered
- 3 crocks cucumber pickle
- 45 large jars applesauce
- 12 crocks sweet apple schnitz and prunes
- 350 doughnuts
- 5 gallons maple syrup
- 45 lemon drop pies

There is usually enough food left over for all women and children who are there to help—anywhere from 50 to 90 additional folk.

Ham Loaf

... to 12

... carry-in entrees for
... ite cooks, and many
... loaf is spicy with
... sugar in the bot-
... e loaf as it cooks.
... for it also has
... dients; ground
... supermarkets
... es not, make

...ed fresh parsley
... ground mustard
$^1\!/_2$ teaspoon salt
$^1\!/_2$ teaspoon coarsely ground pepper
$^1\!/_2$ cup dark brown sugar, packed
Scant $^1\!/_2$ teaspoon ground cloves
$^1\!/_4$ teaspoon grated nutmeg

▨ Preheat the oven to 350°F. In a small mixing bowl, soak the bread crumbs in the milk. Add the eggs and mix well. In a large mixing bowl, combine the ground ham, beef, parsley, mustard, salt, and pepper and the milk mixture; combine thoroughly.

▨ In a small bowl, combine the brown sugar, cloves, and nutmeg. Sprinkle evenly in the bottom of a 9 × 5-inch loaf pan. Transfer the meat to the pan and pat it in firmly, leaving no air holes. Bake for 1$^1\!/_2$ hours; remove the loaf from the oven and allow to stand for 5 minutes before cutting into slices. The cold leftovers make very good sandwiches.

PRECEDING PAGES: In Amish and Mennonite communities, barns such as this are built by hundreds of neighbors in one day.

Creamy Noodle and Ground Beef Casserole

Serves 6 to 8

WHEN I GO INTO AMISH HOMES and inquire about their recipes for publication, the cooks say, "Now wouldn't you like my recipe for chop suey? Or pizza?" I always have to decline, for it is the old country recipes I'm after, so they will be recorded and kept—as oddities, if nothing else. Here is one of their really good versions of what is sometimes called Johnny Marzetti. I don't have a clue who he is, but he certainly is not Amish.

This dish is rather like a lasagne, only made with thinner noodles. It tastes and looks great and assembles easily. Most important, it can be made in advance, and it travels well—by buggy or car.

2 cups (a 16-ounce container) sour cream
2 cups (a 16-ounce container) small-curd cottage cheese
$^1\!/_4$ cup finely chopped onion
2 tablespoons minced fresh parsley
1 7- to 8-ounce package medium egg noodles
1 tablespoon vegetable oil
2 pounds lean ground round or well-trimmed chuck
2 6-ounce cans tomato paste
1 tablespoon minced fresh basil, or 1 teaspoon dried
1 tablespoon minced fresh oregano, or 1 teaspoon dried
1 teaspoon salt
$^1\!/_2$ teaspoon coarsely ground black pepper

▨ In a small mixing bowl, combine the sour cream, cottage cheese, onion, and parsley; set aside. In a large saucepan, cook the noodles according to the package directions. Drain and set aside.

▨ Heat the oil in a large sauté pan, over medium heat, and add the ground beef, stirring now and then until the meat is no longer pink. Drain off all liquid and discard. Stir in the tomato paste, basil, oregano, salt, and pepper and simmer for 5 minutes.

■ Preheat the oven to 325°F. Grease a 9 × 13-inch pan and begin layering as follows: one-third of the meat sauce, one-half of the noodles, and one-half of the sour cream mixture. Repeat these layers, ending with the meat sauce. Bake uncovered for 1 hour or until the casserole is golden brown and bubbly. Allow to stand for 15 minutes, then serve.

Creamy Escalloped Potatoes and Ham

Serves 4 to 6

THIS WELL-SEASONED VERSION of escalloped potatoes with a generous amount of ham is a favorite at all the local potlucks in Amish or Mennonite country.

I make the sauce in the microwave; it is much faster than on the stove top.

> 4 cups (about 5 medium) potatoes, peeled and sliced 1/2 inch thick
> 3 tablespoons butter
> 1/3 cup chopped onion
> 3 tablespoons all-purpose flour
> 1 teaspoon salt
> 1/4 teaspoon ground mustard
> 1/4 teaspoon coarsely ground black pepper
> 1/8 teaspoon ground red pepper
>   Dash of hot red pepper sauce
>   Dash of grated nutmeg
> 2 1/2 cups whole milk
> 1/2 pound cooked ham, julienned
>   Paprika

■ Preheat the oven to 350°F. Place the potatoes in a medium saucepan and cover with water. Bring to a boil over medium-high heat and cook for 3 minutes; drain and set aside.

■ Place the butter and onion in a 2-quart microwave/ovenproof dish or 4-cup measuring cup. Cover and microwave on high for 3 to 5 minutes or until the onion is transparent. Stir in the flour, salt, mustard, peppers, hot pepper sauce, and nutmeg until smooth. Whisk in the milk. Microwave another 12 minutes, whisking

every 3 minutes, until smooth and slightly thickened. (Or melt the butter in a saucepan, add the onion, and sauté until it is softened; add the flour, salt, mustard, peppers, pepper sauce, and nutmeg. Cook over medium heat until the mixture bubbles up in the center. Add the milk all at once and whisk and stir until thickened.)

■ Grease a 2-quart dish; layer half of the potatoes, all of the ham, then the remaining potatoes. Pour the sauce over all, making sure it gets down into all the layers. Sprinkle with paprika and bake immediately (or refrigerate until needed) for 35 minutes or until the mixture bubbles up in the center. Serve hot.

Creamy Kidney Bean Salad

Serves 6

WHEN THE RAMER FAMILY moved from Wakarusa to the Argos, Indiana, area, their barn was built before the house was. The father, Ben Ramer, moved a house trailer to the barn site and stayed there, leaving his five sons at the other farm. Sixty-five men came from their church to put in the cement blocks for the foundation. Then for the final raising, eighty-five men arrived by a rented bus. Mrs. Ramer served substantial meals both times, twice a day. Salads such as this often are served at such barn raisings, along with fried chicken, filling, noodles, and lots of desserts.

> 2 1-pound cans red kidney beans, drained
> 4 hard-cooked eggs, peeled and coarsely chopped
> 1 medium onion, chopped
> 2 celery ribs, chopped
> 1/2 cup chopped fresh parsley
> 1/4 cup sweet pickle relish
> 1/3 cup mayonnaise, or more to taste
> 2 tablespoons sugar
> 1 teaspoon cider vinegar
> 1/4 teaspoon celery seeds

■ In a large bowl, combine the beans, eggs, onion, celery, parsley, relish, mayonnaise, sugar, vinegar, and celery seeds; mix well. Cover and chill for several hours before serving.

Green Beans
with Mustard Sauce

Serves 4 to 6

SUNDAY NIGHT SINGINGS are a favorite diversion for the Amish, and the young people have Sunday night singings of their own at a different house from where their parents are singing. The songs are sung in English or a Pennsylvania Dutch dialect. The dialects vary; when Amish from a German-based community visit a Swiss-Amish community, they speak English, for they are unable to understand each other's dialects. Also, at the Swiss gatherings, yodeling is very popular.

This dish might be prepared for supper after the yodeling is over. The sauce elevates the simple vegetable to gourmet status. It is also a good use for frozen beans, which most Amish families have in their rented freezer locker in a nearby town.

> 2 pounds young green beans, tailed and rinsed, or 1 20-ounce bag frozen cut green beans
> $\frac{1}{4}$ cup ($\frac{1}{2}$ stick) butter
> 2 tablespoons prepared mustard
> 2 tablespoons light brown sugar, packed
> $\frac{1}{2}$ teaspoon salt
> 2 tablespoons fresh lemon juice
> 3 tablespoons cider vinegar
> $\frac{1}{4}$ cup chopped fresh parsley
> 1 teaspoon fresh thyme, or $\frac{1}{4}$ teaspoon dried
> 1 teaspoon fresh savory, or $\frac{1}{4}$ teaspoon dried
> $\frac{1}{4}$ teaspoon coarse black pepper

■ In a large saucepan, steam the green beans over hot water until tender, about 8 minutes. Drain and place in a serving dish. (If using frozen beans, cook according to package directions and drain.)

■ In a small saucepan, combine the butter, mustard, brown sugar, salt, lemon juice, vinegar, parsley, thyme, savory, and pepper. Heat slowly over medium heat until the butter has melted and all the ingredients are blended. Pour over the hot green beans and serve.

Sweet Baked Sauerkraut
with Tomatoes

Serves 6

BUGGY DESIGNS VARY from area to area. In Indiana, some of the communities permit only open buggies; others have closed buggies. Both are black in color. Some have back windows, some don't. In Pennsylvania, the buggy tops are gray. When a teenage girl is fifteen or sixteen years old, she may be permitted to drive the horse and buggy into town, but never alone. "And it does depend a lot on the horse," admitted one conscientious father.

This recipe, given to me by Don Bright, one of the chefs in the prep kitchen who worked with me on the Heirloom Recipes series, is similar to the sauerkraut casseroles made by the Amish. His version has meat in it and is a quick one-dish meal; it is also good for reheating and sending along in a thermos for lunch or to take to potlucks.

> 1 pound ground beef, turkey, or herbed sausage
> 1 medium onion, chopped
> 1 pound sauerkraut, very well drained
> $\frac{1}{2}$–$\frac{3}{4}$ cup light or dark brown sugar, packed, or to taste
> 1 cup (10-ounce can) tomato puree
> 1 small bay leaf, halved
> $\frac{1}{4}$ teaspoon salt
> $\frac{1}{4}$ teaspoon ground black pepper

■ Preheat the oven to 350°F. In a deep saucepan, over medium heat, sauté the meat and onion together until the meat begins to brown, 5 to 10 minutes. Drain off any excess fat.

■ Stir in the sauerkraut, brown sugar, tomato puree, bay leaf, salt, and pepper. Transfer to a greased shallow 2-quart casserole and bake for 35 to 45 minutes or until bubbling in the middle. Remove the bay leaf and serve immediately.

Bright annual flowers border the vegetable garden at this Amish farmhouse. The buggy in the background is large, obviously designed to transport a big family.

Escalloped Cheese and Rice

Serves 6 to 8

YOU WILL LIKE THIS creamy rice dish; it is very much like a savory rice pudding (without the raisins, of course), and it is perfect with fried chicken or barbecued ribs and a lot of other things, too. It reheats well.

> ¼ cup (½ stick) butter or bacon fat
> 2 tablespoons finely chopped onion
> 2 tablespoons finely chopped green bell pepper
> 3 tablespoons all-purpose flour
> ½ cup evaporated milk
> ½ cup water
> ½ teaspoon salt
> 1 teaspoon black pepper
> 1½ cups grated extra-sharp Cheddar cheese
> ½ cup chopped fresh parsley
> 3 cups cooked long-grain white rice
> 4 slices dense whole-grain bread,
>   processed into crumbs
>   Additional butter, for topping
>   Paprika

▪ Preheat the oven to 375°F. Coat a 2-quart flat baking dish with nonstick cooking spray.

▪ In a small saucepan, melt the butter over low heat. Add the onion and green pepper and sauté until the onion begins to color, about 5 minutes. Add the flour and cook, stirring, until the mixture bubbles up in the center of the pan, about 5 minutes. Slowly pour in the evaporated milk and water, whisking until smooth. Add the salt, pepper, cheese, and parsley, continuing to whisk until the cheese is melted. Stir 1 cup of the cooked rice into the cheese sauce. Pour the remaining plain rice into the baking dish and top with the sauce-rice mixture. Sprinkle with the bread crumbs and dot with butter. Dust with paprika.

▪ Bake for 25 minutes or until the top is slightly brown and bubbly. Serve immediately.

Country Peach Cobbler

Serves 10 to 12

AS IT BAKES, the sugar- and nutmeg-garnished cobbler rises to the top of this dish, leaving the peaches below, a very satisfactory arrangement.

Alas, a conventional 9 × 13-inch baking dish is just not big enough for this cobbler. If you don't have a larger pan, use the 9 × 13-inch, *plus* a small casserole or pie pan to hold about one-fifth of the mixture. Bake the smaller dish for a shorter period of time, about 30 minutes.

> 1 cup (2 sticks) butter
> 2 cups granulated sugar
> 2 cups all-purpose flour
> 1 tablespoon baking powder
> ¾ teaspoon salt
> ½ teaspoon grated nutmeg
> 1½ cups milk, at room temperature
> 5 cups peeled and thinly sliced fresh peaches,
>   or 2 20-ounce bags frozen, thawed
>   partially on paper towels; they should still
>   be crispy with ice crystals

TOPPING
> 1 cup dark brown sugar, packed
> ½ cup granulated sugar
>   Grated nutmeg

▪ Preheat the oven to 350°F. Place the butter in a 10 × 14-inch pan and place the pan in the preheating oven and melt the butter.

▪ Meanwhile, in a large bowl, whisk together the sugar, flour, baking powder, salt, and nutmeg. Add the milk and whisk until the mixture is combined; don't overbeat. (The batter is quite thin.) Pour the batter over the melted butter, but do not mix it in. Part of the butter comes to the top; not to worry. Layer the peaches (no pattern is necessary) on top of the batter.

▪ MAKE THE TOPPING: In a small bowl, combine the brown and granulated sugars. Sprinkle over the top of the peaches, and then sprinkle nutmeg liberally over all. Bake for 50 to 60 minutes, or until the top of the cobbler is a deep golden brown and bubbling up in the center. Serve warm with thick cream or ice cream.

Bushel Oatmeal
Church Cookies

Makes 5 dozen

ACTUALLY, THESE PROPORTIONS yield an eighth of a bushel of cookies, which is enough for most of us. However, the Amish do need *bushels* of cookies to serve after church, for the average congregation numbers about 100 people. The recipe is very moist because of the applesauce, and they keep well packed in airtight containers.

> 1½ cups dark brown sugar, packed
> 1 cup solid vegetable shortening
> 2 eggs
> 2 tablespoons molasses or sorghum
> 2 teaspoons vanilla extract
> 3 cups all-purpose flour
> 1½ cups plus 2 tablespoons quick-cooking
>   oats (not instant)
> 1½ teaspoons ground cloves
> ¾ teaspoon baking powder
> ¾ teaspoon baking soda
> 1½ teaspoons salt
> ¾ cup unsweetened applesauce
> 1 cup chopped English walnuts
> ¾ cup raisins, plumped (page 270)

■ In a large mixer bowl, cream the brown sugar and shortening together until light and fluffy, about 4 minutes. Add the eggs one at a time, then mix in the molasses and vanilla.

■ Preheat the oven to 375° F. In another mixing bowl, whisk together the flour, oats, cloves, baking powder, baking soda, and salt. Add the dry ingredients to the sugar mixture alternating with the applesauce, beginning and ending with the dry ingredients; mix well. The dough appears quite moist, but not to worry. Fold in the nuts and raisins.

■ Using a 1½-inch cookie scoop or a heaping tablespoon, drop the batter onto parchment-lined baking sheets. Bake for 12 to 13 minutes or until the cookies are firm in the middle when touched with your finger. Cool the cookies on the baking sheet for 3 to 5 minutes and then transfer to a wire rack and cool completely.

Gingersnap
Rhubarb Crisp

Serves 6

THE YOUNG AMISH GIRL who gave me this recipe said she takes it to "work days," a monthly gathering of young married Amish women in her neighborhood. They meet at each other's houses on the last Tuesday of every month to work together at whatever needs to be done—canning, painting walls, special heavy cleaning, sewing of clothes—everything but quilting. That is always done with the older women.

Of course, they bring their small children, and it provides an opportunity for a day of productive fellowship, to talk and laugh, and share a noon meal together.

> 1 cup gingersnap crumbs (about 20 cookies),
>   homemade or bought
> ½ cup quick-cooking oats (not instant)
> ¼ teaspoon grated nutmeg
> 2 pounds fresh rhubarb, cut into ½-inch pieces
>   (about 6 cups)
> 1 cup granulated sugar
> ½ cup light brown sugar, packed
>   Red food coloring (optional)
> 2–3 tablespoons butter

■ Preheat the oven to 350° F. In a small bowl, combine the gingersnap crumbs, oats, and nutmeg. In a large bowl, combine the rhubarb and sugars. Add a few drops of red food coloring to tint the mixture light pink, if desired.

■ Grease a 2-quart flat casserole and sprinkle ¼ cup of the crumb mixture on the bottom. Add half of the rhubarb and top with ½ cup of the crumb mixture. Add the rest of the rhubarb and top with the remaining crumbs. Dot the top of the mixture with butter and bake for 35 to 40 minutes, or until the top of the crisp is browned and bubbling up in the center. Serve warm with cream or a scoop of ice cream.

Mincemeat Tea Bread

Makes 1 loaf; serves 10

QUICK BREADS, those made without yeast, can be lifesavers for busy cooks. With the addition of a homemade bread, a plain meal becomes distinctive, even memorable.

This quick bread is far better than average; the mincemeat gives it real character and keeps it moist. I use the Delicate Pear Mincemeat on page 162, but any kind will work. This loaf freezes very well, too.

> 2 cups all-purpose flour
> $^1\!/_2$ cup sugar
> 1 $^1\!/_2$ teaspoons baking powder
> $^1\!/_2$ teaspoon baking soda
> $^1\!/_2$ teaspoon salt
> 1 egg
> $^1\!/_4$ cup vegetable oil
> 1 tablespoon grated orange zest
> 2 tablespoons orange juice
> 2 cups mincemeat

▓ Preheat the oven to 350° F. Grease a 9 × 5 × 3-inch loaf pan and set aside.

▓ In a large mixing bowl, whisk the dry ingredients together; set aside. In a mixer bowl, beat the egg. Add the oil, orange zest and juice, and mincemeat and blend thoroughly. Gradually add the dry ingredients and mix until all ingredients are just moistened; do not overmix. Pour into the prepared pan and bake for 60 to 65 minutes or until a toothpick or metal skewer inserted into the center comes out clean and the top of the loaf is golden brown.

▓ Tip out of the pan onto a baking rack, cover with foil and a terry cloth towel, and allow to cool completely. Cut into thin slices and serve with butter or cream cheese.

CLOCKWISE FROM TOP LEFT: Mennonite builders assist the Methodists. A view through a buggy wheel gives a partitioned view of the world. Amish couples never hire baby-sitters; they take their children with them everywhere. Kohlrabi is popular raw as a crudite or cooked and pureed.

Date Pudding Trifle

Serves 24

TO CREATE THIS HEAVENLY dessert, chewy date cake squares are alternated with layers of a rich homemade butterscotch pudding and dates. The trifle is lavishly topped with whipped cream garnished with toasted walnuts. Sprinkling a bit of crème de cacao over the date cake is a worldly touch the Amish would disdain, but I quite like it that way.

Make this dessert twenty-four hours in advance of serving. Ordinarily, I prefer to make trifles in cut-glass bowls to show off the pretty layers, but since this is just a brown and white mixture, it can be assembled in any deep attractive bowl or even a soup tureen.

CAKE

1 teaspoon baking soda
1 tablespoon softened butter
1 cup coarsely chopped dates
1 cup boiling water
1½ cups all-purpose flour
1 cup granulated sugar
½ teaspoon ground mace
¼ teaspoon ground cardamom (see Note)
⅛ teaspoon salt
1 egg, slightly beaten
½ cup coarsely chopped English walnuts

PUDDING

4 cups milk
⅔ cup all-purpose flour
2 cups dark brown sugar, packed
⅛ teaspoon salt
4 egg yolks, beaten
¼ cup (½ stick) butter
2 teaspoons vanilla extract

TO ASSEMBLE

9–12 tablespoons crème de cacao (optional)
18 pitted dates, halved
Double recipe Whipped Topping (page 271)
¾ cup toasted English walnuts (page 270)

Preheat the oven to 350° F. Grease a 9 × 9-inch cake pan. In a medium bowl, combine the baking soda, butter, dates, and boiling water. Set aside to cool.

PREPARE THE CAKE: In a large bowl, whisk together the flour, granulated sugar, mace, cardamom, and salt. Add the egg to the cooled date mixture, then pour the date mixture over the dry ingredients, add the nuts, and gently combine. Transfer the batter to the prepared pan and bake the cake for 30 to 35 minutes, or until the middle of the cake springs back when touched lightly with your fingertip. Remove from the oven and allow to cool completely.

PREPARE THE PUDDING: Heat 3 cups of the milk over hot water in a double boiler; do not allow the milk to boil. In a gravy shaker or glass jar with a lid, combine the remaining 1 cup of milk and the flour and shake vigorously until a smooth paste forms. Pour the flour mixture into a medium bowl and whisk in the brown sugar and salt. Whisk in 1 cup of the hot milk, then add all the sugar-milk mixture to the milk in the double boiler. Cook the mixture, whisking all the while, until thick, about 8 minutes.

Whisk in the egg yolks, butter, and vanilla. Cook 5 minutes longer. Remove from the heat and transfer to another container. Place a piece of plastic wrap directly on top of the hot pudding and cool completely. Refrigerate until needed.

ASSEMBLE THE TRIFLE: Cut the cooled cake into 3 pieces. Cut one piece in half lengthwise, then cut each half into 3 strips; there will be 6 strips. Cut each strip into 10 cubes and set aside on a platter in a separate pile. Repeat with the remaining 2 pieces. Or if you are going to use the crème de cacao, spread the cake pieces out in even layers on a large cookie sheet; sprinkle each third with 3 or 4 tablespoons crème de cacao and allow the cake to stand for 15 minutes.

Place one-third of the cake cubes in a 3-quart bowl. Arrange 12 date halves over the cake, then spread one-half of the cooled pudding on top of the cake. Repeat with cake, date halves, pudding, cake, date halves. Spread the whipped topping over the last layer, then sprinkle toasted walnuts on top of the whipped cream. Cover the bowl with plastic wrap and refrigerate for 24 hours. This is quite firm, so it can be served on small dessert plates.

NOTE: Cardamom is a favorite German spice but if you don't have it, substitute $\frac{1}{4}$ teaspoon ground ginger.

Date Treasures

Makes 3 dozen cookies or 36 mini-cupcakes

THIS IS MIDWAY BETWEEN a cookie and a mini-cupcake, a delightful confection. The recipe is very old, and very good. The combination of the stuffed dates with the deep brown cakelike cookie, all topped with frosting, is a taste and texture delight and they can be presented as cookies or cupcakes; no one will quibble.

> 36 pitted dates
> 36 small walnut halves
> 2 tablespoons ($\frac{1}{4}$ stick) butter
> $\frac{1}{2}$ teaspoon vanilla extract
> $\frac{1}{4}$ cup dark brown sugar, packed
> 1 egg
> $\frac{1}{3}$ cup all-purpose flour
> $\frac{1}{4}$ teaspoon baking powder
> $\frac{1}{2}$ teaspoon baking soda
> $\frac{1}{8}$ teaspoon salt
> $\frac{1}{4}$ cup sour cream

BROWN BUTTER FROSTING
> 2 tablespoons ($\frac{1}{4}$ stick) butter
> $\frac{1}{2}$ cup plus 1 tablespoon confectioners' sugar
> 1 teaspoon vanilla extract
> Dash of salt

Preheat the oven to 350°F. Stuff each date with a 2-lobed walnut half; set aside. (If the walnut halves are too large, cut them down a bit with a small sharp knife to make them fit the dates.)

In a large mixer bowl, cream the butter, vanilla, and brown sugar together. Add the egg and mix thoroughly. In a small mixing bowl, whisk together the flour, baking powder, baking soda, and salt and then combine with the creamed mixture; blend well. Add the sour cream and blend again. Stir the filled dates into the batter.

Using a tablespoon, drop a date with some batter on it onto a parchment-lined or greased baking sheet or into a greased mini–muffin pan cup, making sure there is a date in each cookie. Bake for 10 to 12 minutes or until lightly browned. Remove from the pan with a spatula to a rack to cool. If making mini-cupcakes, leave in the pans for 10 minutes, then loosen the edges of the cake from the tin with a knife, and tip out on a rack to cool. Cool completely before frosting.

PREPARE THE FROSTING: In a small saucepan, melt the butter over medium-high heat. Continue to cook until the butter turns a rich, nutty brown; do not burn. Add the confectioners' sugar, vanilla, salt, and enough hot water to make a spreading consistency. Cool slightly and then frost each cookie or cake. More hot water can be added to the frosting as needed if the frosting becomes too firm as it cools.

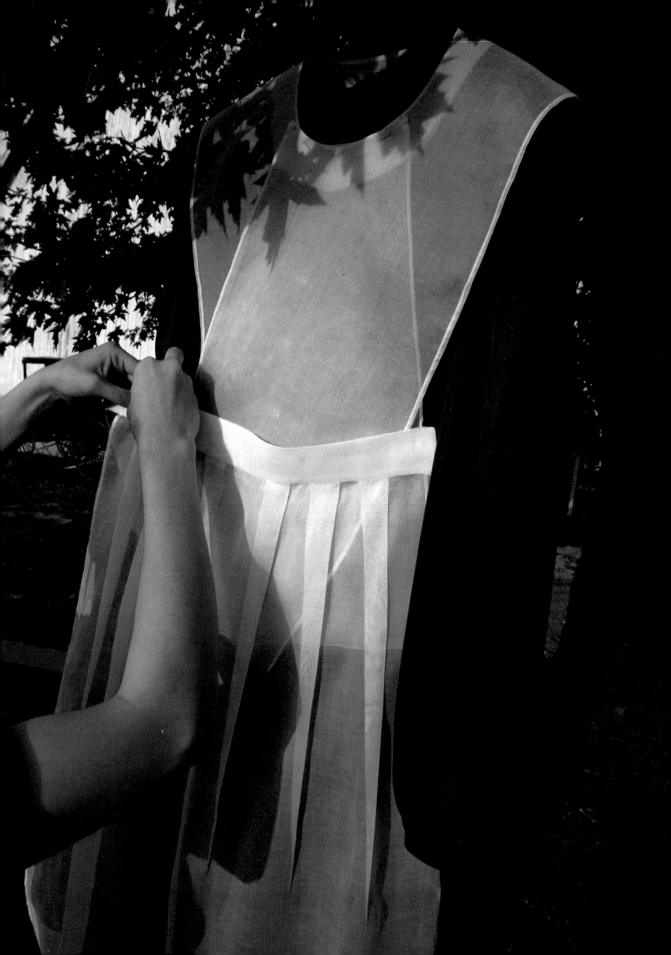

10
FAMILY
MILESTONES

Meat Loaf Stuffed with Cheese ❖ Oyster Noodle Casserole ❖ Boiled Fresh Beef Brisket with Mustard Sauce ❖ Chicken Pot Pie ❖ Meat Loaf with Sweet and Sour Sauce ❖ Potato Dressing Balls ❖ Roesti (Swiss Mennonite Brown Potatoes) ❖ Mashed Sweet and White Potatoes ❖ Orange-Glazed Baked Ham with Rosemary ❖ Versatile Rice and Pecan Stuffing ❖ Butternut Squash with Buttery Pumpernickel Crumb Topping ❖ Gingered Carrots with Raisins and Honey ❖ Honey Mustard Dressing ❖ Ruby Cranberry Sauce ❖ German Chocolate Oatmeal Cake with Caramel Topping ❖ Fresh Fruit Cup ❖ Amish Matrimony Cake ❖ Carmel Tapioca Pudding

It is the observation of the rites of passage within the home that helps bind the Old Order Amish so tightly. The more worldly Mennonites might meet in churches as a group, but the intent is the same: to keep the family intact. Births are greeted with pleasure, as are birthdays and "Sister Days," a custom in some areas where sisters visit each other regularly and share a meal. Even if most of the social affairs, such as picnics and frolics, are attended by family members, certainly there is no dearth of things to do in an Amish and Mennonite community. This would include funerals and weddings as well. Both of these events have their own separate traditions, social mores, and food traditions.

Funerals are heavily attended. The appearance of relatives and friends from other states is expected and appreciated. Death is accepted as part of God's plan for the world; the bereaved are surrounded by family and friends, who take over the family's work during this period.

The body is returned to the home after embalming by the local undertaker, dressed in a white shroud made by the women, and placed in an open, handcrafted casket for viewing for one or two days. The funeral is conducted at the house and is similar to the regular three-hour church service, with the men sitting on one side of the room, the women on the other. The long, medieval German hymns are spoken, however, instead of being sung.

Food is prepared usually for two meals, and it is all brought in by friends. If an unusually large number of people are expected and the weather permits, Amish barns are cleaned and tables are set up there to handle the crowds. The Mennonites meet in their churches that have large community rooms. There is little loud lamenting, for these people live by the words of the biblical poet, "To everything there is a season."

Weddings are much happier affairs, important social occasions especially for the Amish, since the whole community has a stake in the marriage. This couple and their future children will carry on the tradition of emphasizing the home, farm, and church as the center of their lives. Wedding customs vary from community to community; however, in all instances, the

FROM 'THE BUDGET'

LATE FALL ISSUE

Last week was a busy week for the E. A. Rabers as they made final preparations for the Thursday wedding of their daughter Susie to Lester Mast. Lester's parents, Levi and Mary, came on Tuesday, and spent a good part of the day on Wednesday helping Evelyn bake five different kinds of pies. One of them was that Pennsylvania favorite, shoo-fly pie. —**ALMYER, ONTARIO, CANADA**

young couple is required to join the church before they marry. Once married, this is a union forever. Divorce is not an option.

Most weddings are performed in November and December, after all the crops are harvested. To allow the bride's family to concentrate on the planning and cooking, the weddings are generally held at a friend's house. However, the work is done by the bride's family and the host family is kept well informed of everything going on, as they assist and turn their house and barns over to the bridal party.

We stopped at the Alton Hershberger house, where we'd heard there was to be a wedding. The large maple tree in front was completely teepeed. Anne Hershberger, the hostess for the wedding, stood in the doorway, ruefully shaking her head. "These kids really get carried away sometimes. We'll have to get the paper all taken off before Thursday and the wedding." Actually, she didn't seem too displeased.

As at funerals, the guests are fed two meals. The community Sunday bench wagon is brought in, plus those from other communities. The furniture is removed from the living area, and the straight backless benches are set up. The triple-wide door openings enable everyone to see the service.

A couple of days before the wedding, long tables are set up for the wedding couple and their party—there may be forty couples in all. The table coverings are white paper, and in some cases, so is the tableware. The bride does not have a china pattern, nor is she registered for gifts. After the wedding service, a lavish midday meal is immediately served, often featuring special dishes as well as traditional family fare. The menus of the two occasions—weddings and funerals—are similar; however, there is an emphasis on cakes instead of pies at wedding meals. There are pans of fried chicken and filling, whole glazed hams, possibly a turkey, potato salad, bean salad, casseroles of all kinds, and, of course, noodles. The bread is homemade and served along with homemade jams and pickles. There are many desserts, plus a tall wedding cake, with additional sheet cakes in the same flavor. It's a meal that would do most English families proud for any holiday meal or reunion gathering.

The group eats in two shifts, men and women sitting separately, and the older people served first. However, in the evening, the parents leave and the young people are permitted to eat together. They then go to the barn, weather permitting, for an evening of singing. In some communities, a harmonica, guitar, or accordion provides the accompaniment. After much merriment, the married couple retires, the buggies are hitched up, and the friends go home.

> There were over 600 guests in the Mennonite church house for the Overholt wedding and I think all the seats were filled. The same was true for the reception held in the gymnasium. There was such an abundance of food that a goodly part of the carry-in meal the next day consisted of the largess from the wedding feast.
> **—FILMORE, NY**

> Relatives received the death message of Bishop Wesley Zimmerman of Montezuma, GA. Several van loads from here will be going to the funeral on Thursday. Close to a thousand people are expected to attend and Bishop Dan I. Bontrager will officiate.
> **—SUGARCREEK, OH**

Meat Loaf Stuffed with Cheese

Serves 6 to 8

MEAT LOAVES SUCH AS THIS one would be served at a wedding meal, and made in tripled or quadrupled recipes. When guests arrive, often with food, each buggy and horse is marked in chalk with matching numbers so they can be paired up again after the day is over.

> ¼ cup quick-cooking tapioca
> ½ cup chili sauce
> 2 pounds lean ground beef or turkey
> 1½ cups fine soft bread crumbs
> ¼ cup finely chopped onion
> ½ cup minced fresh parsley
> 1 garlic clove, minced
> 1 tablespoon minced fresh thyme, or
>   1 teaspoon ground (optional)
> ½ teaspoon salt
> ¼ teaspoon freshly ground black pepper
> ¼ pound extra-sharp Cheddar cheese, shredded

■ Preheat the oven to 350° F. In a large mixing bowl, mix the tapioca and chili sauce. Allow to stand for 5 minutes. Crumble in the beef, then add the bread crumbs, onion, parsley, garlic, thyme, salt, and pepper. Mix lightly, using your hands if necessary. Divide the mixture into 2 equal portions.

■ On a piece of wax paper, mold one portion into a 5 × 7-inch rectangle and flip into the center of a greased 9 × 13-inch baking dish. Top with the shredded cheese. Shape the remaining meat and place the same way on top of the cheese, pinching the edges of the meat layers together to enclose the cheese. Bake the loaf for 55 minutes or until firm and browned.

■ Remove from the oven, cover lightly with foil, and allow to stand for 10 minutes, then cut into slices and serve hot.

The cheese industry is an important one for Amish farmers, who sell their milk to local cheese makers. Very good buys are available at nearby groceries.

SPECIAL
Ko-jack
Cheese

Disco (Ko-Jack)

HEINI'S
LOWER MILK
FAT CHEESE

HEINI'S
LOWER MILK
FAT CHEESE

Amish Cheese Country Gold (Lon

HONEYVILLE GENERAL STORE

CLOCK

KING

Oyster Noodle Casserole

Serves 6

OYSTERS ARE ONE LUXURY the Amish and Mennonites permit themselves, despite their high price. Their affection for this mollusk goes back to the 1800s, when oysters were plentiful and sold as snack food on the streets of Philadelphia. The local Pennsylvania Dutch, Mennonites, and Amish shoppers adored them, and they have never gone out of fashion, though buying them on the street is a treat long gone.

Oyster dressing is a holiday tradition in many families, as is oyster stew. However, the combination of oysters and noodles is an inspired marriage, and a nice change from the conventional bread dressing. The tarragon is my addition.

> 3 tablespoons butter
> 3 tablespoons minced onion
> 1 tablespoon finely minced green bell pepper
> 3 tablespoons all-purpose flour
> 1¼ cups milk
> 1 teaspoon minced fresh tarragon, or ¼
>   teaspoon dried (optional)
> ¼ teaspoon grated nutmeg
> ¼ teaspoon celery salt
> ⅛ teaspoon ground black pepper
> ⅛ teaspoon hot red pepper sauce
> 2 tablespoons chopped fresh parsley
> 1 8-ounce package thin egg noodles, cooked and
>   drained
> 1 pint oysters, drained

> TOPPING
> 2 tablespoons melted butter
>   Approximately 25 round rye crackers,
>   roughly crushed to equal 1 cup
>   Paprika

■ In a sauté pan, melt the butter over medium heat, add the onion and green pepper, and sauté until the onion is golden, about 8 minutes. Whisk in the flour, and allow the mixture to bubble up in the center of the pan. Add the milk all at once and whisk the mixture smooth, cooking until it thickens. Stir in the tarragon, nutmeg, celery salt, black pepper, hot pepper sauce, and parsley and remove from the heat.

■ Preheat the oven to 350°F. Grease a 2-quart soufflé dish and transfer half the noodles to it. Top with the drained oysters, then the remaining noodles. Pour the sauce over all, and with a fork, make tunnels down into the noodles and oysters so the sauce reaches them.

■ PREPARE THE TOPPING: In a small bowl, combine the butter and crackers and sprinkle on top of the casserole. Dust with paprika and bake for 45 to 55 minutes, or until the top of the casserole is browned and bubbly. Remove from the oven, cover with a towel or foil, and allow to stand for 10 minutes. Serve hot.

Boiled Fresh Beef Brisket with Mustard Sauce

Serves 4, with some leftovers for sandwiches

THIS IS A FRESH BRISKET, not corned, and you may have to order it in advance from your butcher. It is a popular cut with Amish cooks, for they are accustomed to and, indeed, prefer slow-cooked meals. The meat is so tender and flavorful that it's worth the extra baking time; however, it certainly doesn't take much time to assemble it.

> 4 pounds boneless beef brisket
> 5 cups Beef Stock (page 267) or canned beef
>   broth
> 3 cups water
> 1 medium onion, cut into quarters
> 2 medium carrots, cut in half
> 2 celery ribs with leaves, halved
> 1 small dried red pepper, or ½ teaspoon dried
>   red pepper flakes
> ½ teaspoon salt
> 1 bay leaf

> MUSTARD SAUCE
> 1 cup mayonnaise
> ½ cup grainy horseradish mustard
> ⅓ cup chopped fresh parsley

■ Preheat the broiler. Line a 12 × 17-inch baking pan with foil and place the meat on it. Broil the meat 6 inches from the heat for approximately 5 to 7 minutes on each side, or until it is richly browned. Turn the oven down to 325° F.

■ Transfer the meat to a deep, heavy pan or stockpot, and add the stock and water. The meat should be covered by the liquid, so add more if necessary. Add the onion, carrots, celery, red pepper, salt, and bay leaf. Bake for 1 ½ hours, turn the meat over, and continue baking for another 1 ½ hours, or until tender. (The meat should still hold together.) Transfer the meat and place on a cutting board, cover with foil, and allow to stand for 10 minutes. Reserve the cooking liquid and 1 carrot.

■ While the meat rests, prepare the sauce: In a medium bowl, whisk together the mayonnaise and mustard. Add enough of the reserved cooking liquid to make a thin sauce. Chop the reserved carrot finely and stir into the sauce along with the parsley.

■ Slice the meat in thin slices against the grain and serve immediately with the mustard sauce.

Chicken Pot Pie

Makes one 9 × 13-inch pie; serves 6 to 8

THIS DISH IS SO POPULAR in some communities that Mennonite churches hold chicken pot pie suppers as fund-raisers. People drive in from miles around, and serving 300 hungry folk would be considered just a modest success.

It makes a hearty meal and is a good family dish, too. My nephew Eric, who, with his brother and sister polished off the entire dish, evaluated it by saying mournfully, "the only thing wrong with it is that it's gone."

5 pounds chicken breasts, legs, and thighs
2 medium carrots, halved
3 celery ribs, halved
1 medium onion, quartered
6 whole cloves
1 bay leaf

SAUCE
⅓ cup butter
½ cup all-purpose flour
1 tablespoon minced fresh thyme, or 1 teaspoon dried
¾ teaspoon salt
¼ teaspoon ground mustard
½ teaspoon ground white pepper
½ cup fresh or frozen peas, thawed
½ cup chopped fresh parsley

Pastry for 1-crust pie (page 270)

■ In a large stockpot, combine the chicken pieces, carrots, celery, onion, cloves, and bay leaf. Cover completely with water 2 inches above the chicken. Cover, bring to a boil, lower the heat, and simmer for 20 to 30 minutes or until the chicken is done and the vegetables are tender. Remove the chicken from the pot, cool slightly, then remove the meat, discarding the skin and bones; set aside. Remove the carrots from the pot, chop finely, and set aside. Strain the stock through a sieve into a bowl and discard the celery, onion, bay leaf, and cloves. Allow the stock to cool completely in the refrigerator and then skim the congealed fat off the top and discard. Measure out 5 cups of stock for the sauce; refrigerate or freeze the rest for another use.

■ MAKE THE SAUCE: In a large sauté pan, melt the butter over medium heat. Add the flour and stir the mixture constantly until it bubbles up in the pan. Add the reserved 5 cups of chicken stock all at once; whisk and stir until the mixture bubbles up; you may need to add a bit more stock if the mixture is too thick. (Freeze the remaining stock for another time.) Stir in the thyme, salt, mustard, and white pepper. Add the reserved chicken and carrots, peas, and parsley; mix well.

■ Preheat the oven to 350° F. Transfer the chicken mixture to a greased 13 × 9-inch glass dish. Roll out a thick pastry crust to fit the top of the dish and place it over the chicken filling. Crimp the edges and slash the top to allow steam to escape. Bake for 1 hour or until the juices in the middle begin to bubble. Transfer to a wire rack; cool for 10 minutes before serving.

SUCCESSFUL
CREAM
SAUCES

One of the biggest problems in adding cream to sauces is curdling. If cream is added to a sauce base that is too hot, especially one that is very vinegary or has quite of bit of fruit juice or alcohol in it, the proteins in the cream coagulate too fast, which causes it to curdle. Dishes with less dairy fat curdle most readily, meaning skim milk is risky and half-and-half is not as safe as heavy cream.

To prevent curdling by heat, first remove the saucepan with its hot mixture from the stove. Stir several tablespoons of the hot mixture into the cream one spoonful at a time to temper it. Transfer the warmed cream back into the hot mixture in a slow, thin stream, whisking constantly. Return the pan to low heat and continue cooking until the mixture is heated through.

If curdling does occur, in spite of all your good intentions, you can save the sauce if you apply first aid the moment you see the sauce begin to separate. Remove the pan from the stove and immediately whisk in several drops of ice water or very finely chopped ice. The drop in temperature may prevent the curdling.

If you become desperate, cool the mixture and zap it in the food processor. It won't be perfect, but may very well be usable.

Meat Loaf with Sweet and Sour Sauce

Serves 6

MEAT LOAVES ARE POPULAR main dishes since they can be put in the oven and be mostly ignored until serving time. They are perfect for carry-in meals, and the leftovers make good sandwiches for the lunch bucket.

The Amish travel long distances to family affairs, such as weddings and funerals, and for just plain visiting. Traveling by train and bus is acceptable, but generally the Amish hire what is called an "Amish taxi driver"—an English neighbor who has a passenger van, or even a fleet of them, and will drive them to their destination for a fee.

SAUCE
1/2 cup ketchup
1/4 cup brown sugar, packed
2 teaspoons prepared mustard
2 tablespoons cider vinegar
1/2 teaspoon grated nutmeg

MEAT LOAF
2 eggs
2 small onions, chopped
1/2 cup minced fresh parsley
1 teaspoon salt
1/2 teaspoon black pepper
1 cup cracker crumbs
2 pounds lean ground beef

▧ Preheat the oven to 350°F.

▧ MAKE THE SAUCE: In a small bowl, combine all of the sauce ingredients and mix thoroughly; set aside.

▧ MAKE THE LOAF: Beat the eggs slightly in a large bowl. Add half the sauce, the onions, parsley, salt, pepper, and cracker crumbs. Crumble in the meat and mix lightly with your hands. Pat the mixture into a loaf shape and place in the center of a greased 9 × 13-inch baking dish. Bake for 40 minutes, then pour the remaining sauce over the top of the loaf and bake the loaf 10 minutes longer. Remove the loaf from the oven and allow to stand for 5 to 10 minutes before slicing.

Potato Dressing Balls

Makes about 20 balls; serves 8

MY NIECE, MARY ELLEN, did the first test on this recipe and brought it to the house. She declared excitedly as she entered the kitchen, "These are out of this world!" Well, if you've been raised in the bread belt as we have, you do get lyrical about dressings and stuffings. This is a most appealing carbohydrate combination, terrific with either poultry or pork dishes.

A mélange of mashed potatoes, bread cubes, and perfectly balanced seasonings, these baked balls are a different and satisfying way to present dressing. The balls can be served with gravy, but that is optional; they are good by themselves.

3–4 medium white potatoes, peeled and cut
    into 1-inch cubes
2 tablespoons butter
1 cup chopped celery
1/2 cup chopped onion
1/4 cup minced fresh parsley
2 eggs
18 slices soft bread, torn into small pieces,
    including the crusts
1 cup melted butter
1 cup milk
1/4 teaspoon hot red pepper sauce
1/4 teaspoon dried thyme, or 1 teaspoon minced
    fresh
1 teaspoon rubbed sage
1/2 teaspoon salt
1/4 teaspoon coarsely ground black pepper

▧ In a medium saucepan, cover the potatoes with cold water and bring to a boil over medium-high heat. Cook, covered, for 20 to 25 minutes or until tender; drain. Transfer to a mixer bowl and beat until the potatoes are smooth; set aside.

▧ In a medium skillet, melt the butter over medium heat. Add the celery and onion, and sauté for 10 minutes or until transparent. Add the parsley and set aside.

▧ Preheat the oven to 375°F. In a large mixing bowl, beat the eggs well and stir in the bread, melted butter, milk, hot pepper sauce, thyme, sage, salt, and pepper. Add the sautéed vegetables, combine, then stir in the mashed potatoes. Using an ice cream scoop (or a ¹/₃-cup measure), form the dressing into approximately 20 balls and place on a buttered baking sheet (or into buttered muffin tins). Bake for 25 minutes or until they are golden brown. Serve hot.

NOTE: The uncooked dressing balls can be frozen; to serve, bake the unthawed balls at 375°F. for 45 minutes.

Roesti

SWISS MENNONITE BROWNED POTATOES

Serves 6 to 8

THIS APPETIZING POTATO DISH is a specialty of any community of Mennonites with strong ties to Switzerland. It's terrific accompanied with grilled meats. Originally, roesti was made with either fresh or previously boiled potatoes that were then shredded. A very quick and improved way, which saves heaps of time, is to use frozen shredded potatoes. Prepared in a heavy black iron skillet or an electric skillet, the potatoes have a deep golden brown crust. The green pepper and marjoram are my additions. To loosen the frozen mass of potatoes, bang the unopened bag on the kitchen counter.

> ¹/₄ cup bacon fat or vegetable oil
> ²/₃ cup chopped onion
> 1 tablespoon finely minced green bell pepper (optional)
> 1 26-ounce bag frozen shredded potatoes, unthawed but in a loose mass
> ¹/₄ teaspoon salt
> ¹/₂ teaspoon freshly ground black pepper
> 1 teaspoon fresh minced marjoram, or ¹/₃ teaspoon dried (optional)
> ¹/₄ cup minced fresh parsley
> 1 cup shredded Swiss cheese

Heat the fat or oil to 275°F. in an electric skillet, or in a sauté pan over medium heat, then toss in the onion and green pepper and sauté about 4

minutes, until the onion begins to color. Add the frozen potatoes, seasonings, and parsley and combine. With a metal spatula, pat the potato mixture firmly into the skillet, forming a dense patty.

Increase the electric skillet heat to 300°F., or medium high if using a sauté pan, cover, and cook the potatoes for 6 minutes, or until they turn deep golden brown on the bottom. With the spatula, turn the potatoes over by sections, pat down again firmly, cover, and continue sautéing until the bottom is again a deep golden brown, 3 to 4 minutes longer. Sprinkle the cheese on top, and continue cooking until the cheese melts. Cut into wedges and serve immediately.

Mashed Sweet and White Potatoes

Makes 3¹/₂ cups

THIS VEGETABLE DISH has a subtle flavor and is a nice change from plain mashed white or sweet potatoes, good as both of those are. It's an attractive golden color, too. The buttermilk lends an interesting tang; you can add a chunk of butter if you like. Make the potatoes in advance and keep warm in a double boiler or slow cooker.

> 2 large sweet potatoes (about 1 pound), peeled and cut into 1-inch cubes
> 2 large white potatoes (about 1 pound), peeled and cut into 1-inch cubes
> 1¹/₂ cups water
> 8 garlic cloves, peeled (optional)
> ¹/₂ teaspoon salt
> ¹/₂ cup buttermilk

In a 3-quart saucepan, combine the potatoes, water, garlic if using, and salt. Bring to a boil, reduce the heat, and cook about 25 minutes or until tender. Drain the potatoes and place in a mixer bowl. Add the buttermilk and beat until smooth and fluffy. Serve hot.

Orange-Glazed Baked Ham with Rosemary

Serves 12, with leftovers

HAMS ARE CONSIDERED a special treat among the Amish and are reserved for important occasions. A whole or half a ham would be served to the immediate family for a birthday dinner or Easter meal; for a large group, a creative Amish cook might make a ham loaf (page 186) or ham balls (page 78), which extends the costly ham a lot further. I find the Mennonites serve ham more frequently than the Amish.

The hams available in our supermarkets today are generally cooked during their processing, have the rind and bones removed, and need only to be heated to 140°F. to set the glaze. If the ham has a rind, leave that on throughout most of the cooking time to baste the meat. Cut off the rind for the last ½ to 1 hour of baking, then stud the ham with cloves and add the glaze. If the meat has no rind, you can stud it with cloves at the beginning of the baking.

> 1 boneless ham half (approximately 4 pounds)
> 30 whole cloves
> ¼ cup orange marmalade or apricot jam
> ½ cup dark brown sugar, packed
> 2 tablespoons prepared horseradish mustard
> 2 teaspoons fresh rosemary leaves, or 1
>   teaspoon dried, crumbled

■ Preheat the oven to 325°F. Line a 9 × 13-inch dish with foil, add a baking rack, and place the ham on the rack. Insert the whole cloves into the ham and bake for 1½ hours, or until the meat thermometer registers 130°F.

■ Meanwhile, in a 2-cup measure, combine the marmalade, brown sugar, mustard, and rosemary. Microwave on high for 3 minutes. Drizzle the sauce over the ham and bake ½ hour longer or until the ham registers 140°F. and the outside of the ham is crusty and sugary brown. Baste occasionally. Remove from the oven and allow the ham to stand for 10 minutes before carving.

■ Slice thinly (an electric knife is ideal for this) and serve hot or cold.

THE PERFECT HAM

Place the ham, straight from the refrigerator, in a shallow roasting pan and cover the pan tightly with foil. Insert a meat thermometer through the foil into the meat, making certain it does not touch bone or fat. Roast in a 325°F. oven; it is not necessary to preheat the oven unless ham weighs 2 pounds or less. Remove the ham from the oven when the thermometer registers 135°F.; the temperature will continue to rise to 140°F. Allow the ham to stand for 10 minutes for easier carving.

Type of Ham	Weight (pounds)	Cooking Time (minutes per pound)
FULLY COOKED SMOKED BONELESS HAM*		
Portion	1½–2	30–33
Half	3–4	20–23
Whole	6–8	17–20
Whole	9–11	13–16
FULLY COOKED SMOKED BONE-IN HAM		
Half	6–8	14–17
Whole	14–16	12–14
Cooked ham**	1½–2	23–25
	3	21–23
	5	17–20
	8	15–18

*Add ½ cup water to roasting pan.
**Add juices from can to roasting pan; do not cover.

Versatile Rice and
Pecan Stuffing

Serves 6

THOUGH MOST TURKEYS AND roasting hens are stuffed with a bread dressing, occasionally a more creative cook substitutes something different. I certainly like this herby rice stuffing because of its flavor and texture. This mixture will stuff either a three-pound roasting chicken or six game hens. If making for an average size turkey, say twelve pounds, use four times as much stuffing.

> 2 tablespoons butter
> 2 tablespoons chopped onion
> 2 tablespoons chopped celery
> 1 tablespoon minced fresh parsley
> 2 cups cooked long-grain white rice
> $1^1/2$ teaspoons minced fresh thyme,
> $^1/2$ teaspoon dried (optional)
> $^1/2$ teaspoon salt
> 1 teaspoon finely minced fresh sage, or $^1/4$
>   teaspoon dried
> $^1/4$ teaspoon coarsely ground black pepper
> $^1/4$ teaspoon celery seeds
> $^1/8$ teaspoon grated nutmeg
>   Pinch of ground cloves
> $^1/2$ cup chopped pecans or English walnuts

▦ Preheat the oven to 325°F. If baking the dressing separately, grease a 1-quart flat baking dish and set aside.

▦ In a medium sauté pan, over medium-low heat, melt the butter. Add the onion, celery, and parsley and sauté the onion until it begins to color, about 4 minutes, stirring now and then. Add the cooked rice, thyme, salt, sage, pepper, celery seeds, nutmeg, cloves, and nuts; toss together until well mixed. Stuff the bird, or transfer the mixture to the prepared dish and bake for 30 minutes. Serve immediately.

Butternut Squash with
Buttery Pumpernickel
Crumb Topping

Serves 6

THIS IS SUCH a good way to present that autumn favorite, butternut squash. The texture, flavor, and color of the pumpernickel crumbs are a perfect complement to the pureed orange squash. The Amish sometimes substitute molasses or sorghum for the maple syrup, and that's good, too.

You can prepare the whole dish, ready for baking, several days in advance, if you so choose. It keeps very well covered and refrigerated.

> 1 3-pound butternut squash
> $^1/2$ cup ground pecans
> 4 large slices pumpernickel bread, processed
>   into crumbs (2 cups)
> 2 tablespoons melted butter
> 1 tablespoon maple syrup
> $^5/8$ teaspoon salt
> 2 tablespoons unsalted butter, cut into small
>   pieces
> $^1/4$ teaspoon black pepper

▦ Preheat the oven to 425°F. Line a flat 3-quart baking dish with foil and grease the foil. Cut the squash in half lengthwise and scoop out the seeds. Place the squash cut side down in the baking dish and bake for 1 hour or until the squash is tender. You may have to cut off the large seedy end, for it will be done first, and let the stem end bake longer by itself.

▦ Toast the pecans for a few seconds in the microwave and set aside. Toast the pumpernickel crumbs, 1 cup at time, in the microwave for 1 minute, tossing with a fork now and then to even the drying. (The time will vary from microwave to microwave.) Set aside. In a medium mixing bowl, combine the melted butter, maple syrup, and $^1/8$ teaspoon salt; mix well. Add the nuts and bread crumbs, and toss to coat; set aside.

■ Scoop the cooked squash from its shell and place in a medium mixing bowl. Add the butter, $1/2$ teaspoon salt, and the pepper, and mash thoroughly until it is smooth. Transfer to a greased flat 2-quart casserole and sprinkle with the topping. (The casserole can be refrigerated until needed at this point.)

■ Preheat the oven to 350°F. and bake the squash for 45 minutes or until the topping is quite browned and the center of the dish is hot when touched with your finger.

Gingered Carrots with Raisins and Honey

Serves 4 to 6

THESE BAKED CARROTS with raisins and a touch of honey, lemon, and ginger add real zip and color to a winter meal, or even an Amish wedding.

> 1 pound carrots, peeled and thinly sliced
> $1/4$ cup dark raisins
> $1/4$ cup ($1/2$ stick) butter
> 3 tablespoons honey
> 1 tablespoon fresh lemon juice
> $1/4$ cup minced fresh parsley
> $1/4$ teaspoon ground ginger
> $1/4$ teaspoon salt
> $1/4$ teaspoon coarsely ground black pepper

■ In a medium saucepan, over medium-high heat, cook the carrots in about 3 cups of water for 5 to 7 minutes; drain. Stir in the raisins, butter, honey, lemon juice, parsley, ginger, salt, and pepper.

■ Preheat the oven to 375°F. Transfer the carrot mixture to a 1-quart baking dish and bake, uncovered, for 35 minutes or until the carrots are very tender and nicely glazed. Serve while hot.

Honey Mustard Dressing

Makes 1 $3/4$ cups

YES, HONEY MUSTARD DRESSING has found its way to Quilt Country. This one gets distinction from the addition of allspice and red pepper flakes. I prefer the rice vinegar (available in the Asian foods section of most supermarkets) and using part olive oil for a more delicate balance of flavors.

Prepare the greens and pass the dressing in a bowl with a ladle so the diner can be as generous or chary as he likes.

> 2 tablespoons honey
> 2 tablespoons water
> $1/8$ teaspoon ground allspice
> 1 tablespoon plus 1 teaspoon dry mustard
> $1/4$ cup Dijon mustard
> $1/4$ cup cider or unseasoned rice vinegar
> 1 cup vegetable oil, or $1/2$ cup vegetable and $1/2$ cup olive oil
> $1/4$ teaspoon dried red pepper flakes

■ In a blender, mix the honey and water. Add the allspice, mustards, vinegar, oil, and red pepper flakes, blending after each addition. Let stand for at least 30 minutes before serving to allow the flavors to blend.

NOTE: Add 1 teaspoon curry powder to make a curried honey mustard dressing.

Ruby Cranberry Sauce

Makes 4 cups

PREPARE THIS UNADORNED country cranberry dish several days in advance. Generally, I make quite a bit and freeze some to have on hand during the summer to serve with meat pies and other turkey dishes. The amount of pectin in the berries varies from year to year, so sometimes this will be quite runny, other years quite thick. Add more orange juice after baking, if needed.

I present this startling magenta condiment in an antique footed compote dish with a matching lid. In the Midwest, these are called engagement bowls, and Amish women display them in china cupboards that are similar to a hutch.

> 3 1/4 cups sugar
> 2 cups hot water
> 1 teaspoon ground cinnamon
> 2 12-ounce bags cranberries, washed, drained, and looked over
> 3 tablespoons grated orange zest

■ Preheat the oven to 350°F. Combine the sugar, water, and cinnamon in a 9 × 13-inch glass baking dish and place in the oven for 15 minutes or until the sugar dissolves, stirring occasionally. Add the cranberries and bake, uncovered, for 45 minutes without stirring.

■ Remove from the oven and stir in the orange zest. Let the mixture stand until cooled, without stirring. If you think the sauce is a bit too thick, and this will vary, add a bit of orange juice. Ladle into jars and refrigerate until needed. Serve in ramekins or sauce dishes.

German Chocolate Oatmeal Cake with Caramel Topping

Makes one 9 × 13-inch cake; 12 to 16 pieces

MOST AMISH WEDDINGS TAKE place in the fall, after the summer work is completed; November is a popular month. With all of the guests who come, it takes a lot of preparation and planning for this event. There is always a wedding cake, of course, but other cakes will be served too, such as this soft, moist, yet great-textured cake. Hint: the chewy topping goes down into the corners of the pan so the end pieces are best.

> 1 cup quick-cooking oats (not instant)
> 1/2 cup (1 stick) butter, at room temperature
> 4 ounces (4 squares) German sweet chocolate, broken into small pieces
> 1 1/4 cups milk, scalded (see Note)
> 1 1/2 cups all-purpose flour
> 1 cup granulated sugar
> 3/4 teaspoon salt
> 1 teaspoon baking soda
> 1 cup light brown sugar, packed
> 3 eggs, lightly beaten
> 1 teaspoon vanilla extract

> TOPPING
> 6 tablespoons (3/4 stick) butter
> 3/4 cup light brown sugar, packed
> 1/4 cup heavy cream or evaporated milk
> 1/2 cup chopped pecans

■ Preheat the oven to 350°F. Grease a 9 × 13-inch pan. (If using a glass dish, lower the heat to 325°F.)

■ In a medium mixing bowl, combine the oats, butter, chocolate, and hot milk; cover with a plate and let stand for 20 minutes.

■ Meanwhile, in a large mixing bowl, whisk the flour, granulated sugar, salt, and baking soda together. Add the brown sugar, eggs, vanilla, and chocolate mixture; mix well. Pour into the prepared pan and bake for 35 minutes or until the top springs back when touched lightly with your finger. Spread immediately with the topping.

■ PREPARE THE TOPPING: In a small saucepan, over medium-high heat, mix the butter, brown sugar, and cream; bring to a boil. Stir constantly for 2 minutes or until slightly thickened. Pour over the hot cake and sprinkle the top of the cake with the pecans. Cool completely before serving.

NOTE: Scalded milk is milk heated just to the boiling point; tiny bubbles will form around the edges of the pan. Remove the pan from the heat but don't let it cool.

HOW TO BAKE
A PERFECT CAKE

Always preheat the oven 10 minutes before baking. Shiny metal pans produce the lightest, most tender cakes; darker metal pans can cause excess browning. Coat the pans' sides and bottoms with shortening —don't use butter or vegetable oil. Then dust the pans with flour. Or use Baker's Joy, a combination of  shortening and flour in an aerosol can; it is an ideal product and widely available.

Stagger the pans on the center rack, so they don't touch each other or the sides of the oven. If all the pans won't fit on one rack, bake a layer by itself; don't bake one layer below the other.

Don't open the oven door until the minimum baking time has elapsed. Then press the middle of the cake with your fingertip; the cake should spring back.

The cake will also appear just to be shrinking from the sides of the pan. If the cake is not quite done, bake 2 to 3 minutes longer and test again. Repeat as necessary. Don't overbake. For a moister cake, immediately cover the hot cake with foil and a terry cloth towel, and allow it to cool completely.

To frost a layer cake, transfer the cake to its serving plate. Slide four strips of wax paper underneath the edges of the cake to catch the drips of frosting. Frost the sides, then the top of the cake. Store cakes with cream cheese or whipped cream frosting in the refrigerator, and if they are butter-based cakes, bring them to room temperature before serving; the flavor of the cake will be more apparent and the texture more tender.

Fresh Fruit Cup

Serves 16

THIS MAKES A LARGE AMOUNT, since it is served at large gatherings such as weddings or engagement parties. However, any leftovers can be frozen, then used at a later time.

The simple addition of vanilla and brown sugar enhances this refreshing dish and a touch of Fruit-Fresh, a brand name for ascorbic acid, or vitamin C, will keep fresh fruits from darkening. Ordinarily, it is found in the canning section of your grocery.

Sweet woodruff is a German herb, used most frequently in America as a groundcover, and is a most attractive, hay-scented garnish. It is a traditional component of May bowls (*mailbowle*), a punch of German May wine; I like to garnish sangria with a few leaves as well. The Amish and Mennonites use sweet woodruff in sausages and candies.

> 2 tablespoons fresh lemon juice
> 1/4 cup granulated sugar
> 1/4 cup light brown sugar, packed
> 1 teaspoon vanilla extract
> 1 teaspoon Fruit-Fresh
> 1 fresh pineapple, peeled, cored, and cut into
>   chunks
> 1 pink grapefruit, peeled and sectioned
> 2 small cantaloupe, cut into balls
> 1 honeydew melon, cut into balls
> 2 bananas, sliced into rounds
> 2 large peaches, peeled and sliced
>   Large bunch of red seedless grapes, halved
>   Fresh mint or sweet woodruff leaves
>   (optional)

◼ In a large mixing bowl, mix the lemon juice, sugars, vanilla, and Fruit-Fresh until the sugar is dissolved. Add all the fruit and toss gently. Cover tightly and chill for 2 hours, until serving time, stirring lightly now and then. Garnish with mint or sweet woodruff leaves, if desired, and serve cold.

Amish Matrimony Cake

Makes 48 one-inch square pieces

THIS RECIPE FROM LANCASTER, Pennsylvania, is oddly named, at least to me, since it is more like a date bar cookie than a cake. But the flavor is as nice as the name and it is easy to prepare. This is served at the second meal at some weddings, when just the young people are there, hence its name. I like serving it as a cookie, but this recipe could also be cut into 12 squares and topped with whipped cream or ice cream and served as dessert.

> 3 cups quick-cooking oats (not instant)
> 2 cups all-purpose flour
> 1 1/4 cups light brown sugar, packed
> 1/2 teaspoon baking soda
> 2 teaspoons grated nutmeg
> 2 teaspoons ground cinnamon
> 1 teaspoon salt
> 1 cup (2 sticks) cold butter

FILLING
> 1 pound chopped dates
> 1 cup granulated sugar
> 1 1/2 cups water
> 2 teaspoons vanilla extract
> 2 teaspoons grated orange zest
> 1/4 teaspoon salt

◼ Preheat the oven to 375°F. Grease and flour a 9 × 13-inch baking pan; set aside.

◼ In a mixing bowl, whisk together the oats, flour, brown sugar, baking soda, nutmeg, cinnamon, and salt. With a pastry blender or pastry fork (or food processor), cut in the butter. The mixture should be crumbly, like apple crisp topping. Transfer three-quarters of the mixture to the prepared pan and press down firmly and evenly; set aside.

■ PREPARE THE FILLING: In a medium saucepan, over medium heat, mix the dates, granulated sugar, water, vanilla, orange zest, and salt. Bring to a boil and cook until the mixture bubbles up in the center of the pan and begins to thicken. Spread the mixture over the crust and sprinkle with the remaining crumbs. Bake for 30 minutes or until lightly browned on top. Remove from the oven, cool completely, then cut into bars.

Caramel Tapioca Pudding

Makes 1½ quarts; serves 12

THIS IS ONE VERSION of a classic Amish and Mennonite dessert that appears on every regional restaurant menu and at most family gatherings, including weddings.

The wedding ceremony takes most of the morning, with everyone seated. Finally, the couple rises for the final blessings from the bishop. They are dressed in the usual dark unadorned clothes, and she carries no flowers, nor do they exchange rings. The honeymoon will be traveling about visiting relatives. And everywhere, they will surely be served tapioca pudding.

2 egg yolks
3½ cups plus 3 tablespoons water
¾ cup quick-cooking tapioca
½ teaspoon salt
¼ cup (½ stick) butter
1½ cups dark brown sugar, packed
½ teaspoon mace
⅛ teaspoon baking soda
¾ teaspoon butterscotch extract
1 cup heavy cream, whipped

■ In a medium bowl, beat the egg yolks until light and creamy; set aside. In a large saucepan, combine the 3½ cups of water, tapioca, and salt. Let the mixture stand for 5 minutes to soften the tapioca, then cook over medium heat, constantly, for 3 to 4 minutes. Remove from the heat and add 1 cup of the hot tapioca to the beaten yolks, ¼ cup at a time. Gradually stir the egg mixture back into the tapioca. Still on medium heat, bring the tapioca mixture to a full boil, about 4 minutes, and keep stirring. The surface should be bubbly. Set aside.

■ In another large saucepan, over medium heat, melt the butter. Stir in the brown sugar, mace, baking soda, and remaining 3 tablespoons of water. Cook until the sugar is dissolved; the mixture will be foamy. Remove from the heat. Add ¼ cup of this mixture to the tapioca; whisk to combine. Stir the tapioca back into the brown sugar sauce and return to the stove. Bring once again to a full boil, over medium heat, about 4 minutes. Remove from the heat and stir in the butterscotch extract. Cool to room temperature. Using a rubber spatula, fold in the whipped cream. Transfer to a cut-glass bowl or container, cover, and chill.

11
GROWING
UP
AMISH

Knepp ("Buttons") Soup ❖ Macaroni and Cheese ❖ Billy Goat Cookies ❖ Amish Boiled Cookies ❖ Apple Dumpling Pudding ❖ Amish Church Peanut Butter Spread ❖ Peanut Butter Whoopi Bars ❖ Caramel Corn with Chocolate Drizzles ❖ Popcorn Birthday Cake ❖ Never-Fail Fudge ❖ Super Toffee ❖ Apple Butter Roly-Poly Biscuits ❖ Chocolate Gravy and Biscuits

TO THE AMISH community, children are considered a gift from God. Speaking very generally, the average Amish family has eight children, though there is a traceable pattern of even larger families in communities that are more remote from modern society. The Old Order Amish

especially are trying to increase their communities, which in turn enables them to further preserve their special lifestyle and culture.

Children are also an economic asset for rural life where farming depends on human and animal power alone. At the beginning of their marriage, a young couple starts out living on a farm of approximately 90 acres. If they have many male children, they will be able to expand that farm, eventually and with good farming practices, to 160 acres. This is considered a large farm and one that can satisfactorily support a large family.

Amish children are expected to work about the farm at an early age (though this is not different from rural English children), as soon as they can toddle. There is strong identification with the parents, who are constantly busy, without other examples of alternative patterns of behavior to observe.

During the day, the little girls sweep the porch and kitchen with a broom, and dust-mop the living room and bedrooms. They assist in the

FROM 'THE BUDGET'
WINTER ISSUE
Our youth group, along with the sponsors, went to Mammoth Springs on the 23rd. They spent some time fishing, had a picnic lunch and played softball and volley ball.
—SUMMERSVILLE, MO

kitchen, learning to peel potatoes, cut out cookies, and form bread loaves. By the time they are ten years old, the girls are doing some straight seam sewing on their own dresses and aprons. Outside, in the fruit garden, strawberries and blueberries are to be picked, and as they grow older, the children are allowed to clamber up ladders to pick cherries and other fruits.

And the Amish children are always surrounded by other children; the babies especially are attended by the girls when the mothers are otherwise engaged. By the time a female is sixteen years old, she knows exactly how to run a house, plant and harvest a garden, and raise a family. When she marries, generally at about eighteen years of age, marriage and its responsibilities hold no surprises for her.

The boys, who look like miniature men in their drop-fall trousers and black straw hats, consider it their right—indeed, their childish duty—to follow their fathers or older brothers around. Although they get in the way, nonetheless the fathers are patient and start teaching the boys from the beginning how to be responsible adults and farmers.

Yet the outside world encroaches. Expensive running shoes might suddenly appear on the feet of a teenager, and the whole community will be in an uproar; this is precisely the type of status clothing that the adults will not tolerate. Leather belts are forbidden, as are neckties. The young men are clean shaven until they marry, when they are permitted to grow a full beard.

For young women, such things as lipstick, expensive shampoos, and moisturizer will never be of concern. From a fashion point of view, women are more conservative than men, and their mode of dress has not changed much since the early 1700s.

Amish parents recognize that their teenagers need to explore the English world before they make a lifetime commitment to the faith. The boys (but not all of them) especially might flirt with the outside for a while. It is not unknown for a group of Amish boys to buy an old pickup truck and keep it in town, along with a set of English clothes, so that on Saturday nights they can experiment with the twentieth century. On hot summer nights, they might hold surreptitious parties in a cornfield, with boom boxes and beer. The farmer, who can hear the unaccustomed music blaring from the green jungle of six-foot-tall cornstalks, gnashes his teeth, but can never find the source.

These happenings, though gossiped about and not encouraged, are accepted philosophically as a rite of passage. No one considers family counseling or has confrontational meetings. Wisely, the community knows that young people must not be forced or manipulated into baptism, marriage, and the Amish faith. The ultimate decision to reject the outside world is one they must make willingly, for they are entering a life of denial and separation.

More isolated than other children, the Amish children have a strong idea of who they are and where they are going. They know the rules. Yet their lives are not without the pleasures and joys of childhood. Amish yards are dotted with trampolines and sandboxes, and there is always a pond for swimming and fishing. Volleyball is a popular sport enjoyed by both sexes. In the winter, there are ice skating and sleighing parties, as well as singing, candy, and popcorn parties—all thoroughly enjoyed by the participants and carefully supervised by the parents. Amish parents plan school-related activities, such as spelling bees, picnics, and outings to local zoos. At night, there are singings, Bible study meetings, and frolics.

Despite cultural differences, Amish children's food preferences are much like English kids'. They prefer smooth mixtures, such as mashed potatoes, macaroni and cheese, peanut butter, puddings, chocolate-based desserts, Mexican food, and candy. Carbonated soft drinks are purchased only as a special treat; lemonade and homemade fruit juices are the alternatives.

> The young group that went to Romania to help with the church building came home last Friday. They had supper and a singing at the Gideon Millers on Sunday night. —HARTLEY, DE

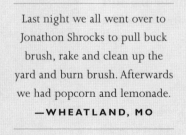

> Last night we all went over to Jonathon Shrocks to pull buck brush, rake and clean up the yard and burn brush. Afterwards we had popcorn and lemonade. —WHEATLAND, MO

Knepp ("Buttons") Soup

Serves 6

MY HUSBAND SAYS these chewy, quick dumplings resemble soft matzo balls. They are quite unlike the soft, cakelike dumplings I usually prepare, and I suspect this is the kind of dumpling his mother made. In Pennsylvania, round dumplings are called "gnepp," from the German word *knöpfen*, meaning "buttons." In Iowa Amish communities, where I discovered this recipe, the word is spelled with a K.

I use homemade stock for the broth. It is a substantial soup; these dumplings are not for sissies.

> 2 cups all-purpose flour
> 2 teaspoons baking powder
> $1/2$ teaspoon celery salt
> $1/2$ cup milk
> 1 egg
> 2 tablespoons melted butter
> 6 cups Beef or Chicken Stock (page 267)
>   Minced fresh herbs

■ In a large bowl, whisk together the flour, baking powder, and celery salt. Pour the milk into a 2-cup measure, add the egg and butter, and beat to combine. Make a well in the flour and pour the milk-egg mixture into it. Stir until a stiff dough forms; if the batter looks too dry, add a bit more milk, 1 tablespoon at a time. It will look raggedy even when it's ready to drop, and that's all right. Cut the dough in half, cover, and allow to stand for 10 minutes.

■ With scissors, cut the dough into 1-inch pieces or buttons. These will double in size as they cook. Meanwhile, bring the stock to a boil in a large, shallow pan and gradually add the buttons to the hot broth. Cover, turn heat to low, and simmer the mixture for 12 minutes; *do not lift the lid* during the cooking period.

■ Ladle the hot soup into bowls and strew the top of the soup with fresh herbs of any kind. Serve immediately.

Every available pair of hands goes to the field to get in the crops when rain in on the horizon.

Macaroni and Cheese

Serves 6 to 8

MACARONI AND CHEESE tops the list of favorites with most children, Amish or not. This version, so well seasoned with onion, Worcestershire, and dry mustard, is a real treat. You might want to make a double recipe and freeze the extra casserole.

> 8 ounces uncooked elbow macaroni
> 6 tablespoons (¾ stick) butter
> 3 tablespoons all-purpose flour
> 2 cups milk
> 3 tablespoons finely minced onion
> 2 teaspoons Worcestershire sauce
> ¾ teaspoon celery salt
> ¼ teaspoon ground white pepper
> ¼ teaspoon ground dry mustard
> 2 cups grated extra-sharp Cheddar cheese
> ¼ cup finely minced fresh parsley
> ½ cup bread crumbs

▓ Preheat the oven to 350°F. Coat a 2-quart flat baking dish with nonstick cooking spray.

▓ In a large saucepan, over high heat, bring water to a boil and then add the macaroni and cook until tender, about 6 minutes, or according to package directions. Drain and pour the macaroni into the prepared dish; set aside.

▓ In a medium saucepan, melt 4 tablespoons of the butter; add the flour and whisk and cook over low heat until the mixture bubbles. Add the milk all at once, plus the onion, Worcestershire, celery salt, pepper, and mustard. Increase the heat to medium, and continue whisking until the mixture bubbles up again in the center. Add the cheese gradually and return to a boil, whisking smooth.

▓ Pour the sauce over the macaroni and mix well. Combine the parsley and bread crumbs, and sprinkle over the top of the macaroni; dot with the remaining 2 tablespoons butter. Bake until golden brown and bubbly, 30 to 35 minutes. Serve hot.

Billy Goat Cookies

Makes 6 dozen

I AM AMUSED BY SOME of the recipe names I find in Amish and Mennonite cookbooks and while away many minutes trying to find rational explanations for them. For instance, could this name have come about when a pet goat jumped up on an unattended picnic table and gobbled up all the cookies? (This would be typical goat behavior. They are mischievous and fond of cookies, I daresay.)

However they got their name, these are extremely good date cookies—soft, scented with orange and cardamom (indicating a Scandinavian or German goat, maybe?), and topped with a meltingly good orange frosting that is also used on Soft Orange Frosted Cookies (page 151). These are more intensely flavored the second day after baking, if you can ignore them for that long.

> 4 cups all-purpose flour
> 2 teaspoons salt
> 1 teaspoon ground cardamom
> ½ teaspoon baking soda
> 1 cup (2 sticks) butter, at room temperature
> 2 cups sugar
> 3 eggs
> ½ cup sour cream
> 1 teaspoon vanilla extract
> 2 tablespoons grated orange zest
> 2 cups chopped dates
>   Orange Frosting (page 151)

▓ Preheat the oven to 350°F. In a large bowl, whisk together the flour, salt, cardamom, and baking soda; set aside.

▓ In a mixer bowl, beat the butter for a few seconds, then gradually beat in the sugar, creaming for 2 minutes. Add the eggs one at a time, blending well after each. Add the sour cream, vanilla, and orange zest and combine. Gradually add the dry ingredients, mixing well, then stir in the dates.

▓ Using a 1½-inch cookie scoop or by heaping tablespoons, drop the cookie dough onto ungreased or parchment-lined cookie sheets about 2 inches apart. Bake the cookies for 13 minutes, or until lightly golden brown. Remove to a rack to cool completely, then frost. Place wax paper between the layers of cookies in airtight storage containers and store or freeze until needed.

Amish Boiled Cookies

Makes about 45 cookies

THESE APPEAR IN MANY Amish cookbooks and are also sometimes called funeral cookies, since they can be made in a hurry and taken to the grieving family. There's no baking at all involved; the cooking process takes place on top of the stove.

I must tell you, I didn't expect to like them. Well, was I surprised! They have a wonderful chocolate peanut butter flavor and slightly chewy texture. And they're so easy to make. Let your children help with these; you will be creating confirmed cooks!

> 1/2 cup (1 stick) butter
> 1/2 cup milk
> 2 cups sugar
> 3 tablespoons unsweetened cocoa
> 1/2 cup regular (not low-fat) peanut butter
> 1 teaspoon vanilla extract
> 1/4 teaspoon salt
> 3 cups quick-cooking oats (not instant)
> 1/2 cup coarsely chopped pecans

In a small saucepan, over medium heat, mix the butter, milk, sugar, and cocoa; bring to a boil and cook for 1 minute. Remove from the heat and stir in the peanut butter, vanilla, and salt. Mix in the oats and pecans. Using a small cookie scoop or a teaspoon, drop onto wax paper and allow the cookies to stand, unrefrigerated, for 1 hour. Store in an airtight container, with wax paper between the layers.

Apple Dumpling Pudding

Makes 26 to 28 small dumplings; serves 6

WHAT A QUICK AND tempting dessert this is. The base is canned applesauce, all spiced up and then topped with soft nutmeg-scented dumplings. It might be old-fashioned Amish, but it is twentieth-century good.

> 1 46-ounce jar (6 cups) sweetened applesauce
> 3/4 cup light brown sugar, packed
> 1 teaspoon grated nutmeg
> 1/2 teaspoon ground cinnamon
> 2 cups all-purpose flour
> 4 teaspoons baking powder
> 1/2 teaspoon salt
> 1 egg
> 3 tablespoons melted butter
> 2/3 cup milk, at room temperature
>   Heavy cream, for serving

In a large saucepan or sauté pan, combine the applesauce, brown sugar, 3/4 teaspoon of nutmeg, and the cinnamon; heat over medium-low heat until the sugar is dissolved and the sauce is bubbling.

Meanwhile, in a medium mixing bowl, whisk together the flour, baking powder, salt, and remaining 1/4 teaspoon nutmeg. In a small bowl, beat the egg and stir in the butter and milk. Make a well in the dry ingredients and pour in the egg mixture. Stir together until just moistened and stiff. Drop by heaping tablespoonfuls (or use a 1 1/2-tablespoon cookie scoop) onto the bubbling applesauce; cover and cook for 20 minutes. Do not lift the cover during cooking time or the dumplings will fall. Transfer to sauce dishes (the Amish call them "nappies") and serve with cream.

OVERLEAF: Jumping toward the sky on the trampoline is a very pleasant way to while away a summer afternoon.

Amish Church Peanut Butter Spread

Makes 5 cups

AFTER SUNDAY CHURCH SERVICES, the entire congregation gathers together for a meal, which is provided by the family hosting the services. Over the years, these meals have become more simple, especially if the congregation is a large one.

The menu varies from community to community; however, there is always coffee and cookies, either Bushel Oatmeal Church Cookies (page 191) or the big soft White Dropped Amish Church Sugar Cookies (page 62) plus bread and butter or peanut butter spread. In many states, this interesting spread is made up by the dishpanfuls and slathered on homemade bread. It is a creamy beige, soft, frosting-like mixture and sounds dreadful, but is disgustingly good. It is so popular that many Amish and Mennonite stores sell it to visiting English shoppers. Kids love it, and I've not seen an adult scorn it, though they hate themselves when they eat it. But not the Amish.

    1 18-ounce jar peanut butter
    2 cups light corn syrup
    1 13-ounce jar marshmallow creme

■ In a large mixer bowl, combine all of the ingredients and beat vigorously until well blended. Serve on fresh bread.

Peanut Butter Whoopie Pies

Makes 43 pies or filled cookies

I AM FOND OF the chocolate whoopie pies prepared by the Amish and have a delectable recipe for them in the first Quilt Country cookbook. So when I found this peanut butter version at the farmer's market in Bird-in-Hand, Pennsylvania, I was overjoyed.

COOKIES
    ⅔ cup regular (not low-fat) peanut butter
    ⅔ cup butter, at room temperature
    4 cups light brown sugar, packed
    4 eggs, at room temperature
    5 cups all-purpose flour
    2 teaspoons baking powder
    1 teaspoon salt
    4 teaspoons baking soda, dissolved in 6 tablespoons boiling water
    1 teaspoon vanilla extract

FILLING
    ⅓ cup peanut butter
    ⅓ cup milk
    ½ teaspoon salt
    3 cups confectioners' sugar
    1 tablespoon hot water

■ Preheat the oven to 350°F. Line 2 baking sheets with parchment paper or foil.

■ Make the cookies: In a mixer bowl, cream together the peanut butter and butter until blended. Add the brown sugar and cream well, about 1 minute. Add the eggs one at a time, blending well after each addition.

■ In a mixing bowl, whisk together the flour, baking powder, and salt. Gradually add to the sugar mixture and mix well. Add the baking soda and water and the vanilla and combine again.

■ Using a 1½-inch cookie scoop or by heaping tablespoons, drop the dough onto the baking sheets. Bake for 10 to 12 minutes or until the centers of the cookies spring back when touched with your finger. (The middle of this cookie remains a bit chewy.) Transfer the cookies to a wire rack and cool before filling.

■ Prepare the filling: In a mixer bowl, beat the peanut butter, milk, and salt together. Then beat in the confectioners' sugar and hot water. Spread the flat side of one cookie with approximately 2 teaspoons of filling and top with a second cookie, flat side down, to make a sandwich or pie. Repeat with remaining cookies and filling. Transfer to airtight tins or containers and store or freeze.

Caramel Corn with Chocolate Drizzles

Makes 16 cups

POPCORN AND COCOA is a favorite treat for the visiting grandchildren everywhere, and in Amish homes, the children might be allowed to make caramel corn for entertainment. However, making caramel corn in large amounts is also a cottage industry for some Amish women, who sell it at roadside stands or local Amish groceries.

The Amish do not use microwaves, but since this is the easiest way to make the caramel, I have adapted their recipe to the twentieth century. If you prefer, you can skip the chocolate, which is a bit messy to eat; however, it is a fine addition to this old favorite.

> 16 cups popped popcorn
> 1 cup cashews, almonds, or peanuts (optional)
> 1 cup light brown sugar, packed
> $\frac{1}{2}$ cup (1 stick) butter
> $\frac{1}{4}$ cup light corn syrup
> 1 teaspoon vanilla extract
> 1 teaspoon salt
> $\frac{1}{2}$ teaspoon baking soda

> CHOCOLATE DRIZZLE
> 1 cup milk chocolate morsels
> 1 teaspoon solid vegetable shortening

▓ Line 2 baking sheets with foil; set aside. Combine the popped popcorn and nuts in a brown paper bag (12 × 17 inches); set aside. In a microwave-safe bowl, combine the brown sugar, butter, corn syrup, vanilla, and salt. Microwave on high for $4\frac{1}{2}$ minutes. Remove and immediately add the baking soda, whisking until the mixture is thoroughly combined. Pour over the popcorn and cashews and shake. Fold down the top of the bag and place in the microwave on high for 90 seconds, remove, and shake; repeat for 60 seconds, 40 seconds, and 30 seconds. Pour onto the prepared baking sheets and spread out to cool.

▓ PREPARE THE CHOCOLATE DRIZZLE: Combine the chocolate morsels and shortening in a microwave-safe bowl. Microwave for 1 minute on high; stir. Microwave again at 20-second intervals until the mixture is melted. Immediately drizzle the chocolate over the caramel corn. Let cool completely until firm and then break into clusters and store in a tightly covered container.

Popcorn Birthday Cake

Serves 10 to 20

THIS WHIMSICAL CONFECTION is made in addition to a regular birthday cake for an Amish and Mennonite child and is served topped with birthday candles. Though it is great for small-fry, the adults gather round this too, if they think no one is looking.

> 12 cups popped popcorn
> 1 12-ounce package blanched peanuts (no skins)
> 6 tablespoons ($\frac{3}{4}$ stick) butter
> 1 10.5-ounce bag marshmallows
> 1 teaspoon vanilla extract
> $\frac{1}{2}$ teaspoon salt
> 1 12-ounce package mini M&M baking pieces

▓ Generously butter a 10-inch tube pan and set aside. Place the popcorn and peanuts in a large mixing bowl. In a medium saucepan, over low heat, melt the butter and marshmallows together, stirring constantly. Add the vanilla and salt and stir.

▓ Immediately pour the mixture over the popcorn mixture and partially mix with your buttered hands. Add the baking pieces and mix again, still using your hands. Press into the prepared pan and let stand 1 hour or overnight.

▓ Unmold the cake onto a serving plate. Top with birthday candles or serve as is. It can be cut, but it is more fun to pull it apart and eat it without ceremony.

CANDY MAKING HINTS

❖ Use a candy thermometer to give yourself peace of mind.

❖ Don't make substitutions for the ingredients listed in the recipes.

❖ Don't halve or double the candy recipes. Make one recipe at a time.

❖ Don't make candy on rainy or damp days because high humidity will prevent the candy from setting up.

❖ Cook the candy mixture at a moderate, steady rate over the entire surface of the mixture. Cooking the mixture too slowly causes the candy to become too hard; if cooked too slow, the candy tends to become soft.

❖ Don't store different kinds of candies together because hard candies will get soft, and also candies do "trade" flavors.

❖ Fudge, pralines, toffee, and caramels freeze well and can be stored for up to a year.

❖ After removing candy from the freezer, let it stand at room temperature before opening the container. This prevents moisture from collecting on the surface.

Never-Fail Fudge

Makes 150 one-inch pieces

CANDY MAKING IS a time-honored family recreation for the Amish, as it is among the Mormons. Fudge is the most popular candy and is made mostly in the winter months.

There are two kinds of fudge: the sugary kind with a bit of grit, and the smooth kind, which is much easier to make. I happen to like both, but this version is quite foolproof. It makes a lot, too, so it is nice to give away or freeze. It is not necessary to use a candy thermometer, but if it gives you added confidence, do use it. Actually, the timing alone is adequate.

> $4^{1}/_{2}$ cups sugar
> 1 12-ounce can evaporated milk
> 2 7-ounce milk chocolate bars, broken into pieces
> 1 12-ounce package semisweet chocolate morsels
> 1 7-ounce jar marshmallow creme
> 1 teaspoon salt
> 1 teaspoon vanilla extract
> $1^{1}/_{2}$ cups coarsely chopped English walnuts

▦ Butter a 10 × 15-inch pan; set aside. In a large saucepan over medium-high heat, combine the sugar and evaporated milk. When it begins to boil, insert a candy thermometer, lower the heat to medium low, and cook until the temperature reaches 236° F. (softball), approximately 10 minutes, stirring constantly.

▦ Remove from the heat, add the chocolate bars and morsels, and stir until melted. Add the marshmallow creme, salt, vanilla, and nuts; beat with a wooden spoon until the mixture is glossy, 2 to 3 minutes. Pour into the pan and chill in the refrigerator. Cut into pieces and store; it freezes well.

This Amish boy is hoping his father will bid on this dog when it comes up for auction.

Super Toffee

Makes 4½ quarts, plus 1 quart of crumbs

MENNONITE CHURCH WOMEN in Summersville, Missouri, come together at Christmas time to make this celestial toffee, using the local pecans. The profits are used for their Sunday school. The recipe does make an enormous amount, which is perfect, since it is so nice for holiday gifts. When you break up the toffee you'll create lots of small crumbs, which are ideal to sprinkle on top of ice cream sundaes or Caramel Tapioca Pudding (page 215).

> 1½ pounds pecans
> 2 tablespoons (¼ stick) melted butter
> ¼ teaspoon salt
> 26 plain milk chocolate bars (1.55 ounces each)
> 1 pound (4 sticks) butter (no substitutes)
> 4 cups sugar

■ Preheat the oven to 375° F. In a food processor, finely chop the nuts (you'll need to work in batches) and transfer to a 12 × 16-inch pan. Drizzle the melted butter over the top, sprinkle very lightly with salt, and toss. Bake for 8 to 10 minutes, stirring twice. Set aside to cool.

■ Meanwhile, unwrap all the candy bars and set aside. When the nuts have cooled, transfer half to a bowl and set aside. Spread the remaining nuts evenly on the baking sheet and top with 13 of the chocolate bars, breaking them up if you want to.

■ In a deep, heavy 3-quart pan, melt the butter over low heat. Gradually whisk in the sugar. If the butter doesn't integrate into the sugar, use an electric hand mixer; it should be a thick creamy mass. Turn up the heat to medium low. Stir constantly with a wooden spoon at this point. Insert the candy thermometer. The mixture begins to darken immediately, marbling even. Don't leave it! Wipe down the sides of the pan 2 times with a dampened paper towel wrapped around a knife, or a pastry brush dipped in water—this keeps the sugar crystals on the sides of the pan from turning the candy back again to sugar.

■ When the candy thermometer reaches 250° F., stop stirring; the candy is nearly ready to pour. When the mixture reaches 300° (this took about 13 minutes on my stove), pour immediately over the prepared nuts and chocolate. Top the hot toffee with the remaining chocolate bars, using a small rubber spatula to smooth the chocolate once melted. Top with the reserved nuts, and with the back of a metal spatula, pat the nuts into the melted chocolate. Set aside to cool.

■ The chocolate needs to be firm before breaking into pieces, so place the tray in the refrigerator for 30 minutes to 1 hour. When the chocolate is firm, loosen the toffee patty with the tip of a knife and break into large chunks, then into smaller pieces with a cleaver. I made rough pieces, about 1 to 1½ inches in size. (I should warn you the nuts scatter a bit around the kitchen.) Store the crumbs in the refrigerator, and the candy too, or freeze both until needed. Bring almost to room temperature before serving.

Apple Butter Roly-Poly Biscuits

Makes 2 rolls; each serves 8

BASED ON A ROLLED-OUT biscuit dough that's made richer by the addition of cottage cheese, this quick hot bread filled with apple butter is wonderfully good. Some Amish families eat it in a bowl with milk poured over it. However, it is equally fine simply spread with butter, and is the way we do it. It would make a terrific after-school treat. This dough can also be rolled out and cut into biscuits, omitting the apple butter.

1 egg
¼ cup milk, at room temperature
1 cup small-curd cottage cheese (not low-fat),
    at room temperature
2 tablespoons melted butter
2 cups all-purpose flour
1 tablespoon sugar
4 teaspoons baking powder
1 teaspoon salt
½ cup apple butter
    Ground cinnamon

▨ Preheat the oven to 425°F. In a large bowl, whisk the egg slightly. Add the milk, cottage cheese, and butter and mix well. In a medium bowl, whisk together the flour, sugar, baking powder, and salt. Add the dry ingredients all at once to the egg mixture and blend by hand just until the mixture is combined. Add a bit more milk, a teaspoon at a time, if necessary, to make the dough come together.

▨ Turn the dough out onto a lightly floured surface; cut in half. Pat or lightly roll out one portion of dough into a rectangle about 6 × 10 inches. Spread the dough with ¼ cup of the apple butter, leaving one long edge free of the apple butter, about 1 inch in. Sift cinnamon liberally over the top. Beginning with the long side opposite the apple butter–free edge, firmly roll up the dough jelly-roll fashion and, with a large spatula, transfer the roll to a greased baking sheet, seam side down. Repeat with the remaining dough and apple butter. Bake the rolls for 15 to 17 minutes, or until nicely browned and an instant-read thermometer registers 190°F. If the rolls begin to overbrown before they are done, cover loosely with foil.

▨ Allow the rolls to stand for a few minutes, then cut into slices and serve hot with butter.

NOTE: To use this dough for biscuits, do not divide the dough in half, but pat or roll out the dough to ½ inch, and cut with a biscuit cutter. Bake at 425°F. for 12 minutes. Makes nine 2½-inch biscuits.

Chocolate Gravy and Biscuits

Makes 3 cups sauce; serves 4 to 6

BELIEVE IT OR NOT, this really is a breakfast dish. The recipe first came to me from Arkansas, and later appeared in a Missouri Mennonite cookbook. I tried it out of curiosity—an odd sort of dish, and not exactly what I prefer in the morning, but I can well imagine children loving it. In all truthfulness, it is very similar to Cottage Puffs (page 86). Anyway, it ought to be recorded, so here 'tis.

½ cup sugar
¼ cup all-purpose flour
1 heaping tablespoon unsweetened cocoa
2 cups milk
⅛ teaspoon salt
1 tablespoon butter
1 teaspoon vanilla extract
6–8 Best Ever Biscuits (page 46)

▨ In a deep saucepan, whisk together the sugar, flour, and cocoa. Blend in the milk. Bring the mixture to a boil over medium heat, stirring constantly with the whisk. Continue to cook and whisk for 3 more minutes, or until the mixture is thick. Remove from the heat and stir in the salt, butter, and vanilla.

▨ Split and reheat the biscuits in the microwave. Place 2 or 3 halves on each plate and top with the hot chocolate gravy and serve immediately with tall glasses of milk.

NOTE: The recipe can be doubled. Poured into individual dishes and chilled, it makes very good chocolate pudding.

12

CHANGING TIMES,

FAMILIAR

FAVORITES

Meaty Ham Bone Vegetable Soup ❖ Creamy Reuben Soup ❖ Tender Chili

Pork Chops ❖ Beef Pot Roast with Cider ❖ Incredibly Tender Beef Stew

❖ Shake-It-in-the-Bag Catfish ❖ Amish Roast Chicken and Potatoes with

Garlic ❖ Barbecued Meatballs with Tomato Cumin Sauce ❖ Chicken Baked

in Cream ❖ Lamb and Creamy White Beans ❖ Tomato Sour Cream Gravy

❖ Real Old-Fashioned Mashed Potatoes ❖ Tomato Bread Pudding ❖ Tomato

Aspic with a Touch of Horseradish ❖ Fluffy Cornbread in a Skillet ❖ Apple

Ice Cream with Maple Apple Topping ❖ Four-Day Coconut Cake ❖ Golden

Mace Cake with Lemon Sauce ❖ Chocolate Angel Delight ❖ Blueberries

with Nutmeg Dumplings ❖ Pineapple Gingerbread Upside Down Cake

❖ Baked Coconut Butter Cream Pie ❖ Brown Sugar Dumplings

GRAPPLING with the twentieth century is as difficult for the Amish as it is for us, and as this book and year near completion, it is easy to see the Amish are changing. Divorcing themselves from politics, rejecting membership in public organizations, and refusing to be exposed to mass media have kept the collective Amish Community intact.

Still, the outside world has become an important part of the Amish community's own economy. With soaring land prices, the Amish father can no longer provide a farm for each of his children. To support the large families, many Amish males have entered the English workforce, with collective permission from their bishops and congregations. A large percentage of what the Amish produce is sold to the outside world, and cottage industries are an important part of their economy.

Though standing apart, some of the Amish view the novelty of their involvement with the English as enriching and fascinating. My friend Rebecca Haarer, who is an Amish culture and quilt consultant in Shipshewana, Indiana, recently taught Amish quilting techniques (with a translator) to a group of Japanese girls who were participating in an exchange program from nearby St. Mary's College in South Bend, Indiana. After the lecture, the class was served

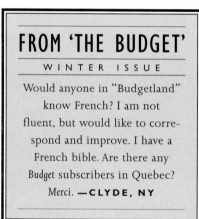

their noon meal at an Amish farmhouse, sampling fried chicken, mashed potatoes, green beans, corn, Jell-O salads, tapioca pudding, iced tea, and all sorts of pies. It was hard to tell who had the most fun, the Japanese or the Amish.

Increasingly, it is possible for English visitors to partake of a meal such as this for a fee, say $10 per person, in Amish communities. It is a good way for the women to supplement the family's income. The meals Levi and Mildred Schmucker serve in their house became so popular they found it necessary to build a special structure next to the house just for their "almost restaurant business." Still, Mildred tries to keep this side of her life in perspective: "I'm not going to serve any meals during March," she declares. "I'm taking a month off just to clean house. For me, the serving of the meals is really just a hobby, not a real business." Yet it is obvious that she does it well and enjoys it immensely. Still, she adds, "I wouldn't do it if my husband didn't approve."

The Schmuckers give about fifty dinners a year, most of them in the summer and arranged with two weeks' advance notice. A busload of forty folks is the usual number. Rising at 2:30 A.M. on these days (they all go to bed at 9:00 P.M. the night before), Mildred and two neighbor women make bread and pies first so they can cool.

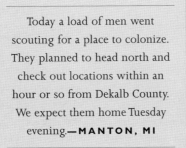

David Coblentz and Wilmer Eby are planning on going to Romania next week along with a work crew to help out with the building project near the new children's home.
—SUMMERTOWN, TN

Levi cleans the dining room, washes the windows, sets the tables, and does any necessary garden work in the already impeccably groomed yard. Mildred says she could do the baking the day before, but feels better about the meal if she does the baking the day it is to be eaten.

Mildred also goes once every other year to meet with her pen pals—other Amish women from all over the country with whom she has corresponded for six years. Seven women are in this group; one writes a letter, then sends it on. The second person reads the letter, adds her news, and sends it on to the third person. It is quite a lengthy epistle by the time it arrives back to Mildred, who starts a new one. The women are from Texas, Kansas, Oklahoma, Illinois, Michigan, Ohio, and Indiana. For their reunions, they generally meet in Indiana or Ohio, which are centrally located, and spend three delightful days together, exchanging gossip, news, and recipes face to face.

Mildred and her husband, though devout, con-

Today a load of men went scouting for a place to colonize. They planned to head north and check out locations within an hour or so from Dekalb County. We expect them home Tuesday evening.**—MANTON, MI**

servative house (Old Order) Amish scorning electricity and cars, are still more involved with the English community than most, not only through their successful business but also because their daughter, an only child, has a hearing disability and is enrolled in the nearby public school. Mildred's father, a bishop, encouraged them to enter the child in the public school system since it had an excellent program for the deaf, something the local Amish schools did not offer. Like English parents everywhere, they wanted what was best for their child. Mildred personifies the attitudes of some of the more contemporary Amish: "We think it's important to share our life with others and make new friends."

The supper table also reflects the changes in Amish cultures everywhere, and Amish cooks are more interested in integrating new recipes into their menus than they were when I first started working with them in 1988. Though sun-dried tomatoes and extra-virgin olive oil are hardly staples in their kitchens, such ethnic fare as Tex-Mex cuisine— which uses many of the staple ingredients they always have on hand, such as corn, tomatoes, cheese, and peppers—is turning up more frequently. Yet even when they incorporate "newfangled" ingredients or reflect a culture far removed from their rural existence, the dishes served up in these country kitchens are indisputably homey, simple, and good. At least in that way, things will remain unchanged in Quilt Country.

Meaty Ham Bone Vegetable Soup

Makes 18 cups, or 12 generous servings

IN THE FALL, the tall, dried wheat stalks ripple and sigh in the wind, and the kildeer call from the fading goldenrod along the roadsides. It is hearty soup weather and this one, based on a meaty ham bone, is a perfect cool-weather dish. This recipe makes a huge amount, so it is perfect for entertaining, but leftovers don't freeze well.

2 tablespoons vegetable or peanut oil
3 medium onions, chopped
1 red or green bell pepper, chopped
1 meaty ham bone
12 whole peppercorns
1 bay leaf
3 quarts water or Chicken Stock (page 267)
4 medium potatoes, peeled and cut into
    bite-size ($^3/_4$-inch) chunks
1 small head cabbage, cored and coarsely
    shredded
1 28-ounce can chopped tomatoes, juice
    included
1 tablespoon minced fresh marjoram, or
    1 teaspoon dried
1 tablespoon minced fresh thyme, or 1 teaspoon
    dried
$^1/_8$ teaspoon hot red pepper sauce
    Black pepper and a bit of sugar to taste
1 cup coarsely chopped fresh parsley

In a large stockpot, heat the oil over medium heat and add the onions and bell pepper. Sauté until the vegetables are softened and beginning to color, about 10 minutes. Add the ham bone, peppercorns, bay leaf, and water or stock. Cover and bring the mixture to a boil, then simmer 1 hour. Skim off the foam and discard.

Add the potatoes, cabbage, and tomatoes, cover partially, and continue cooking for 1 hour; the potatoes should be tender. Add the rest of the ingredients except the parsley, and simmer 10 minutes longer. Stir in the parsley and serve immediately in large soup bowls, with hot bread.

Creamy Reuben Soup

Serves 8

THE REUBEN SANDWICH is now a popular dish in Amish communities, probably because of the sauerkraut, so a Reuben soup was an inevitable innovation. Adding the skim milk to the soup first will keep the soup from curdling.

3 tablespoons butter
$^1/_2$ cup finely chopped onion
$^1/_4$ cup finely chopped celery
3 cups Chicken Stock (page 267), or
    1$^1/_2$ 16-ounce cans chicken broth
$^1/_4$ cup quick-cooking tapioca
1 cup sauerkraut, well drained
$^1/_2$ pound deli-sliced corned beef, shredded
1$^1/_2$ cups skim milk
1$^1/_2$ cups whole milk
12 ounces Swiss cheese (not low-fat), shredded
    Salt and pepper
6–8 slices rye bread, toasted and quartered

In a stockpot, melt the butter over medium heat. Add the onion and celery and sauté until the onion begins to color, about 5 minutes. Stir in the stock and tapioca, and remove from the heat; let the mixture stand for 5 minutes.

Put the soup back on the stove and bring to a boil over medium heat, stirring frequently. Reduce the heat, uncover, and simmer 5 minutes longer. Stir in the sauerkraut and corned beef, then add the skim milk first, then the whole milk and 1 cup of the shredded cheese. Cook and stir frequently for 30 minutes until slightly thickened. Season with salt and pepper to taste.

Preheat the broiler. To serve, ladle soup into 8 ovenproof bowls, top each with several pieces of the toasted bread, and sprinkle with the remaining cheese. Place under the broiler until the cheese is melted. Serve immediately.

Dried corn is stored in outdoor wire cribs, providing livestock with provender all winter long.

Tender Chili Pork Chops

Serves 6

FRESH, DOUBLE-THICK pork chops are one of the benefits of butchering time. This is when you use up some of that homemade chili sauce (page 163), though you can also use store-bought. The long, slow cooking, combined with the chili sauce and vinegar, really tenderizes the thick pork chops.

> $1/4$ cup all-purpose flour
> $1/2$ teaspoon salt
> $1/2$ teaspoon freshly ground pepper
> $3/4$ teaspoon ground ginger
> 6 pork chops, 1 inch thick, all fat removed
> 2 tablespoons vegetable oil
> $1/2$ cup finely chopped onion
> 2 garlic cloves, finely minced
> $1/2$ cup Beef Stock (page 267) or canned broth
> $1/2$ cup chili sauce
> 3 tablespoons cider vinegar
> 2 tablespoons light or dark brown sugar, packed
> 1 tablespoon minced fresh thyme, or
> $\qquad$ $1/2$ teaspoon dried
> $\qquad$ Fresh thyme sprigs, for garnish

▩ In a shallow dish, combine the flour, salt, pepper, and ginger. Dredge the chops in the flour, shaking off any excess. In a large sauté pan, over medium to medium-high heat, heat the oil. Brown the chops well, about 10 minutes on each side; remove to a platter.

▩ Add the onion and garlic to the pan and sauté until the onion is soft, about 5 minutes. Stir in the stock, chili sauce, vinegar, brown sugar, and minced thyme. Return the chops to the pan and spoon the sauce up over them. Cover, and simmer the chops on top of the stove over very low heat for 1 hour, or until tender. Add more broth if necessary. Or the chops can be baked at 300°F., basting occasionally, for 2 hours. Serve hot, garnished with thyme.

Beef Pot Roast with Cider

Serves 6 to 8

SLOW-COOKING POT ROASTS are still popular in Amish and Mennonite communities, since most of the women are at home all day. And they have access to very good beef. Most families now have the beef butchering done by a local butcher and frozen locker shop, for handling a ponderous 1,000-pound steer is much more difficult than butchering a 300-pound pig. Coping with a pig is considered a frolic.

Most local beef cattle graze on pasture, fodder crops, and silage, all free of additives such as hormones and antibiotics. Many English town folk are willing to drive quite a few miles to patronize Mennonite butcher shops.

I use red wine in this dish, but that is very non-Amish.

> $1/4$ cup vegetable oil
> 1 4-pound beef chuck roast, all fat removed
> 2 medium onions, chopped
> $1/4$ cup all-purpose flour
> 2 tablespoons minced fresh sage, or
> $\qquad$ $1 1/2$ teaspoons dried
> 1 cup cider (or dry red wine)
> 4 cups Beef Stock (page 267) or canned beef broth
> 1 tablespoon Worcestershire sauce
> 1 tablespoon cornstarch (optional)
> $1/2$ cup water or stock (optional)
> $\qquad$ Salt and freshly ground pepper
> $\qquad$ Fresh sage leaves, for garnish

▩ Heat the oil in a large roasting pan (I use an 11-inch sauté pan) over high heat. Brown the meat in the hot oil, turning with tongs, until all sides are well browned, 10 to 12 minutes. Remove the meat from the pan and set aside. Lower the heat to medium, add the onions, and cook until browned, 5 to 7 minutes.

Preheat the oven to 325°F. Stir the flour into the sautéed onions and cook for 2 to 3 minutes, stirring often; the mixture should bubble up in the bottom of the pan. Add the sage, cider, and stock, and whisk and stir until smooth. Return the meat to the pan and bring to a boil over medium heat. Cover the pan and place in the oven. Bake until the meat is very tender, 2½ to 3 hours. Turn the meat with tongs and spatula twice during the cooking process.

Remove the cooked meat to a platter and cover with foil to keep warm. Skim the fat off the liquid in the pan (or use a paper towel to blot it up), and stir in the Worcestershire. Reduce the sauce by approximately one-third over medium heat, 8 to 10 minutes. If the gravy is too thin, blend the cornstarch and water in a shaker jar and slowly stir into gravy until it bubbles and becomes thickened. Season to taste with salt and pepper. Slice the beef ¼ inch thick against the grain and serve with the pan gravy. Garnish with sage leaves.

Incredibly Tender Beef Stew

Serves 6

AN AMISH COOK WOULD never throw out anything that could be added to another dish, and that would certainly include leftover coffee. And the coffee is the secret of this superb stew.

The coffee is a great meat tenderizer, and beef prepared this way melts in your mouth. Some people like to drop dumplings (see page 266) on top of this dish twenty-five minutes before the stew is done; I'm one of them.

 1 cup all-purpose flour
 1½ teaspoons salt
 ½ teaspoon black pepper
 3 tablespoons minced fresh thyme, or
  1 teaspoon dried
 3 pounds lean chuck roast, trimmed of fat, cut
  into 1-inch cubes
 3 tablespoons vegetable oil

 5 cups Beef Stock (page 267) or canned beef
  broth
 1 cup strong brewed coffee
 1 tablespoon Worcestershire sauce
 1 teaspoon paprika
 1 teaspoon sugar
 3 tablespoons ketchup
 6 medium potatoes, peeled and quartered
 2 medium onions, quartered
 6 medium carrots, peeled and quartered
 ½ cup peas, fresh or frozen
  Minced fresh thyme

Place the flour, ½ teaspoon of the salt, ¼ teaspoon of the pepper, and the thyme in a paper bag and shake to blend. Add the beef, a few pieces at a time, and shake to coat. In a large stockpot, heat the oil over medium-high heat. Add the beef to the stockpot and brown each piece on all sides; don't overcrowd the pan or the meat won't brown properly. Work in batches if necessary.

When the meat is browned, add the stock, coffee, Worcestershire, paprika, sugar, ketchup, and remaining salt and pepper; stir to combine. Add the potatoes, onions, and carrots. Reduce the heat to low, cover, and simmer for 2 hours. Add the peas and continue cooking for 15 to 30 minutes or longer until the meat is very tender. (If a thicker stew is desired, thicken the mixture with 1 tablespoon cornstarch dissolved in 3 tablespoons of water.) Ladle into shallow bowls and serve hot, garnished with fresh thyme.

NOTE: If you are adding dumplings, drop them in after the peas have cooked for 5 minutes and let the dumplings cook for 25 minutes. The flour from the dumplings will thicken the stew mixture enough so you will not need to add any cornstarch.

THE HOME OF ELIAS RUFF

RST. PORK with
FRESH SAUERKRAUT
MASHED POTATOES
and SWEET-SOUR RED CABBAGE

GERMAN MEATLOAF with
DUTCH POTATOES
and FRESH GREEN BEANS w/BACON

FRESH APPLE DUMPLINGS
or
RED RASPBERRY COBBLER

GRABILL, INDIANA

Shake-It-in-the-Bag Catfish

Serves 6

LAKE FISHING IS A PERMITTED pastime for Amish men, and this simple method of preparation is used for many kinds of freshwater fish. If the fisherman has a good day, the whole family gets together for a fish fry. The fish is fried in deep Dutch ovens, but for the rest of us, a deep-fryer or electric fry pan is an ideal way to prepare this fish since you can so easily control the temperature.

My deep-fryer is large and requires a lot of oil; possibly yours won't take three bottles of peanut oil. I make this dish after I've finished frying doughnuts, since the fryer is out, then I discard the fat, for it does take on fishy overtones. Serve the golden brown fish with a dilled tartar sauce (page 268).

> Peanut oil, for deep-frying
> 10 6-ounce fresh or thawed frozen catfish
>   fillets
> 1 1/2 cups yellow cornmeal
> 1 tablespoon plus 1 teaspoon salt
> 1 tablespoon plus 1 teaspoon black pepper

■ Heat the oil in a deep-fryer to 375° F. Wash the fillets, drain, and pat dry. In a large paper or plastic bag, combine the cornmeal, salt, and pepper. Add the catfish to the bag 2 pieces at a time. Shake until well coated and set aside on paper towels to dry a bit, about 5 minutes. Dip all of the fish before you begin frying

■ Deep-fry the fillets, 3 at a time, for 7 minutes or until golden brown, turning as needed. Remove with tongs and drain on paper towels. Serve immediately.

Amish Roast Chicken and Potatoes with Garlic

Serves 4

THE AMISH HAVE ALWAYS raised their chickens in the free-range manner, and now their deliciously succulent birds are popping up on fashionable menus in cities across the country, where they are prized for their superior flavor. Late one afternoon, I was interviewing Esther Bontrager in her kitchen about bushel cookies, and she said, "Say, I've got to start supper. I'll talk while I fix the chicken." Then she prepared a version of this dish (without the thyme), and as it cooked and I scribbled, I thought I had never smelled anything more delicious in my whole life. "There's no recipe," she said. "Just throw the potatoes and stuff around the chicken and pour over some butter and broth and fresh lemon." All dinners should be so simple. And this one really is.

> 1 fresh free-range roasting chicken,
>   approximately 4 pounds
> 2 handfuls fresh thyme (optional)
> 1 large onion, cut into chunks
> 4 red-skinned potatoes, 2 inches in diameter,
>   sliced 3/4 inch thick
> 6 garlic cloves, skin on
> 1/2 cup (1 stick) butter
> 1 cup Chicken Stock (page 267)
>   or canned broth
> 1/2 lemon, seeded
>   Salt and freshly ground pepper

■ Preheat the oven to 425° F. Rinse and clean the chicken well and pat dry with a paper towel. Place the chicken breast side up in a shallow 15 × 12-inch greased pan. Separate the skin from the breast meat with your fingers and insert a liberal amount of thyme between the two. Place another handful of thyme inside the cavity.

■ Scatter the onion chunks, potato slices, and garlic cloves around the chicken. In a measuring cup, heat the butter and chicken stock together in the microwave; pour over the chicken and vegetables. Squeeze the lemon half over the chicken and place the lemon in the cavity of the chicken along with the thyme. Add salt and pepper to the chicken and vegetables to taste.

■ Bake the chicken for 30 minutes, then turn it over, back side up, and baste with the pan juices. Lower the heat to 350° F. and bake the chicken 20 to 30 minutes longer, basting occasionally, or until a meat thermometer inserted into the thigh registers 180° F. and the potatoes are tender.

■ Remove the chicken from the oven and, keeping it covered, allow it to rest for 10 minutes. Carve and serve with the vegetables and pan juices.

Barbecued Meatballs with Tomato Cumin Sauce

Serves 10 to 12

WE MIGHT THINK of meatballs as a humble dish, and ordinarily they are. But not this Mennonite recipe—it yields outstanding meat balls! They are well seasoned with a great sweet-and-sour sauce, and their texture, owing to the oats, is exceptional.

> 3 pounds lean ground beef
> 1³⁄4 cups milk
> 2 cups quick-cooking oats
> 2 eggs, slightly beaten
> 1 cup minced onion
> 1 tablespoon chili powder
> 1 tablespoon ground cumin
> ¹⁄2 teaspoon minced garlic
> 2 teaspoons salt
> ¹⁄2 teaspoon coarsely ground black pepper
>
> SAUCE
> 2 cups tangy ketchup
> 1¹⁄2 cups light brown sugar, packed
> ¹⁄2 teaspoon minced garlic
> ¹⁄2 cup minced onion

■ Preheat the oven to 350° F. In a large mixing bowl, mix the beef, milk, oats, eggs, onion, chili powder, cumin, garlic, salt, and pepper. Using your hands or a scoop, form into 2-inch balls. Place in an ungreased 9 × 13-inch pan and bake for 15 minutes. Remove from the oven and drain off the fat.

■ MEANWHILE, PREPARE THE SAUCE: In a medium saucepan, over medium heat, stir together the ketchup, brown sugar, garlic, and onion. Cook over medium heat until the sugar is dissolved. Pour the sauce over the meatballs, cover, and continue baking for 45 minutes longer. Serve with mashed potatoes (page 247) or Macaroni and Cheese (page 222).

Chicken Baked in Cream

Serves 4 to 6

THIS OLD COUNTRY-STYLE recipe is hard to beat. An Amish or Mennonite farm wife would serve it with mashed potatoes and green peas. The beauty of this dish is that it can slowly bake most of the morning as the women work; the finished chicken is very tender and makes its own pan gravy.

> ¹⁄2 cup all-purpose flour
> ³⁄4 teaspoon salt
> ¹⁄2 teaspoon coarsely ground black pepper
> ¹⁄2 teaspoon paprika
> 1¹⁄2 teaspoons poultry seasoning
> 2 tablespoons butter
> 2 tablespoons vegetable oil
> 8–9 chicken pieces, legs, thighs, breasts (about 4 pounds), skin on or removed
> 2 cups heavy cream
> Paprika
> Minced parsley or sage leaves, for garnish

■ Preheat the oven to 300° F. In a large paper bag, combine the flour, salt, pepper, paprika, and poultry seasoning. In a large sauté pan, melt the butter with the oil over medium-high heat. Shake the chicken pieces, 2 or 3 at a time, in the flour mixture. Place the floured chicken in the pan and sauté on both sides until golden brown, 8 to 10 minutes.

■ Transfer the browned chicken to a 9 × 13-inch baking dish and pour the cream over the chicken pieces. Sprinkle additional paprika over the chicken, cover, and bake for 2 hours or until the chicken is tender. Garnish with parsley or sage and serve immediately.

SHUNNING
PRACTICES

The custom of shunning is responsible, in part, for the stability of the Amish community. Those who teach a false doctrine, those who cause division and dissension among the group, and those who live in open sin are all candidates for shunning. Interpreted by the Bible, this means avoidance, and the believer is to avoid those who are not following the tenets of their faith. The shunned do not share meals with the family, nor are they spoken to by anyone in or out of the family. Spouses sleep apart.

The Amish insist that shunning is not considered punishment, but rather is a way to bring the sinner back into good grace, in the eyes of the congregation and of God. It is a powerful tool for giving coherence and controlling their society. Shunning is not entered into lightly and is used only when a church member falls short of the group's expectations.

Shunning is an admittedly strong way to govern unconventional behavior, and it works. Some offenders leave the church, but not many—only one in four shunned people takes this step. And if the person leaves the faith, the shunning continues anywhere from several months to several years, depending on the strictness of the community. It is not unusual for those individuals who do choose to leave to become Mennonites and to stay in the same area, eventually becoming reconciled with their more conservative families.

Lamb and Creamy White Beans

Serves 8 to 10

LAMB IS NOT WIDELY consumed among the Amish and many have never even tasted it. However, some farmers are discovering that wool is an easy cash crop, providing dollars in an early spring season when the farm is not otherwise productive. In these communities, lamb and mutton are becoming popular meats. In Indiana, lamb is more commonly found than in many other states, owing to the influence of British immigrants, who helped settle this part of the country.

This thrifty recipe stretches the tender lamb meat to serve ten. Served with corn muffins and a pitcher of maple syrup to pour over the muffins, it makes hearty eating.

> 2 cups dried navy beans, soaked overnight in
> water to cover
> 3 pounds lamb shoulder chops, with bone in
> 1 medium carrot, chopped
> 1 medium turnip or parsnip, chopped
> 1 large onion, chopped
> 1/3 cup chopped fresh parsley
> 1 garlic clove, chopped
> 1 tablespoon minced summer savory, or
> 1 teaspoon dried (optional)
> 1 bay leaf
> 1/2 teaspoon celery salt
> 3/4 teaspoon salt
> 1/2 teaspoon pepper
> 2 cups Chicken Stock (page 267), or
> 1 16-ounce can chicken broth
> 2 tablespoons butter
> 1/2 cup half-and-half

■ Drain the soaking liquid from the beans and discard. In a slow cooker or crockpot bowl, combine the beans, lamb chops, carrot, turnip or parsnip, onion, parsley, garlic, savory, bay leaf, celery salt, salt, pepper, and stock. Cook over high heat for 15 minutes, then lower the temperature to low and continue cooking for about 8 hours or until the meat is done.

■ When the chops are cooked and tender, remove from the cooker, and cut into cubes, discarding all bones. Return the meat to the cooker, then add the butter and half-and-half. Stir and allow to heat through, 5 to 10 minutes. Serve with corn muffins.

NOTE: During the cooking period, check occasionally to see if the beans have soaked up the stock. Add additional stock or water if needed.

Tomato Sour Cream Gravy

Serves 6 to 8

A FIRST COUSIN to tomato gravy, this creamy sauce is always served over mashed potatoes or fried mush. It is one of those recipes that came into being because the ingredients were available and it was another way to use canned tomatoes. I know it sounds weird, but it is quite good. This is considered a winter dish in most Amish communities.

> 1 28-ounce can stewed tomatoes
> 1/2 cup sour cream
> 3 tablespoons all-purpose flour
> 1 teaspoon sugar, or more to taste
> 1/4 teaspoon salt
> 1/4 teaspoon pepper

■ In a medium saucepan, cook the tomatoes over medium-high heat, uncovered, for about 10 minutes or until the liquid is somewhat reduced.

■ In a 2-cup glass measure, whisk together the sour cream, flour, sugar, salt, and pepper. Add enough of the hot tomatoes to make 1 cup and mix well. Pour this mixture back into the saucepan with the remaining hot tomatoes and stir and cook until the mixture thickens. Serve hot over mashed potatoes or fried mush.

Real Old-Fashioned Mashed Potatoes

Makes 4 cups

SINCE I GREW UP with farm-cooking experience, I never realized there could be a recipe for mashed potatoes; you just knew how to make them. However, this method, which infuses the dish with the subtle essence of bay leaf and nutmeg, should move out of the oral tradition and into a written version. The Amish, who are always interested in trying new fruit and vegetable varieties, raise a lot of Yukon Gold potatoes, and they are excellent for this dish.

Sometimes I add the pulp of a roasted garlic head or a few minced chives to this recipe, and then it is really party fare. If you are making this for a large group and want to get it done several hours ahead of time, transfer the mashed potatoes to a slower cooker (crockpot) and keep on low until ready to serve. (Keep that hint in mind for Thanksgiving!)

> $2\frac{1}{2}$ quarts cold water
> 1 teaspoon salt
> 1 bay leaf
> 2 pounds medium Idaho or Yukon Gold
>   potatoes, peeled and quartered
> $\frac{1}{4}$ cup ($\frac{1}{2}$ stick) unsalted butter, chilled and
>   cut into 4 equal slices
> $\frac{1}{2}$ cup hot milk, or more as needed
>   Rounded $\frac{1}{4}$ teaspoon grated nutmeg
>   Salt and freshly ground black pepper

▓ In a large saucepan, combine the water, salt, bay leaf, and potatoes. If the potatoes are not covered by at least 2 inches, add more water. Bring to a boil, then reduce the heat to medium and cook, partially covered, for 25 to 30 minutes or until quite tender when pierced with a fork.

▓ Drain the potatoes thoroughly, remove the bay leaf, and mash slightly with an electric mixer. Gradually add the butter, milk, and nutmeg, and continue beating the potatoes until smooth and creamy, adding a bit more milk if necessary. Season to taste with salt and pepper and serve hot.

Tomato Bread Pudding

Serves 6

TOMATOES PREPARED in an escalloped fashion have always been a quick country vegetable dish, since the pantry always is stocked with plenty of tomatoes and bread. This version is such a sturdy recipe you can skip the potatoes or rice without a qualm.

> 2 15-ounce cans stewed tomatoes with onion
>   and green pepper
> 1 bay leaf
> $\frac{1}{4}$ cup light or dark brown sugar, packed
> $\frac{1}{4}$ teaspoon coarsely ground black pepper
> $\frac{1}{8}$ teaspoon salt
> $\frac{1}{4}$ cup ($\frac{1}{2}$ stick) butter
> 8 slices firm bread, crusts removed, cut into
>   1-inch cubes
> 2 tablespoons minced fresh parsley or chervil

▓ In a deep saucepan, combine the tomatoes, bay leaf, brown sugar, pepper, and salt. Simmer over medium heat for 5 minutes. Remove the bay leaf and discard.

▓ Preheat the oven to 400° F. Meanwhile, place the butter in a 2-quart flat glass baking dish and melt in the oven or microwave. Add the bread and parsley, and toss well to combine. Pour the tomato mixture evenly over the bread, but do not combine. Bake the tomatoes for 30 minutes, or until the top is puffy and golden brown. Serve hot.

Tomato Aspic with a Touch of Horseradish

Serves 8

I CAN'T EXPLAIN MY WEAKNESS for aspic, especially since I don't care for molded salads. From our travels about the country, I observe that such salads are most popular in the South and in the Midwest. You certainly won't find them in New York or Los Angeles. However, the sharpness of this dish often counterpoints another milder seasoned dish quite perfectly.

If you hanker to be fancy, this can be jelled in individual molds or a 1-quart mold. Present it on Boston lettuce and serve with a mayonnaise seasoned with a bit of onion and bell pepper or with Creamy Tomato Dressing (page 142).

> 1 ½ cups water
> 2 3-ounce packages lemon gelatin
> 2 cups vegetable cocktail, such as V-8
> ½ cup chili sauce
> ¼ cup minced fresh parsley
> 2 tablespoons minced onion
> 1 teaspoon prepared horseradish

▧ In a medium saucepan, bring the water to a boil and whisk in the gelatin until it is dissolved. Add the vegetable cocktail, chili sauce, parsley, onion, and horseradish; mix well. Pour into a lightly oiled 8-inch square pan. Chill for 3 hours or until firm. Cut into squares to serve.

Buggies are a major investment for the Amish and last many years. Unlike automobiles, the styles do not change every year.

Fluffy Cornbread in a Skillet

Serves 8

THIS IS CORNBREAD LIKE my mother prepared —soft, light, cakelike in texture. The Amish often serve this with soups, and in the spring, when maple syrup is being made, the cornbread is served in sauce dishes with lots of maple syrup poured over the top.

I bake mine in a black iron "spider," but you could use any heavy skillet or a 10-inch round cake pan.

> 1 cup milk
> 1 cup water
> 2¼ cups yellow cornmeal
> 2 cups buttermilk
> 1 teaspoon baking soda
> 3 eggs
> 1 teaspoon salt
> 2 tablespoons melted butter

■ Preheat the oven to 375° F. if using a glass container, 400° F. if using metal. In a saucepan, combine the milk and water. Bring to a boil over medium-high heat, then gradually add 2 cups of the cornmeal, stirring constantly. (It will be quite crumbly, not like mush, as you might expect.) Transfer to a mixer bowl and set aside.

■ Measure the buttermilk into a 4-cup measure or medium bowl and whisk in the baking soda. Set aside for 5 minutes; it will puff a bit. In a mixer bowl, beat the eggs until very light and add the salt. Add the cornmeal mixture gradually, beating until very smooth. Add the buttermilk mixture and blend, then add the melted butter and combine.

■ Pour the batter into a greased 2-quart flat glass baking dish or skillet. Sprinkle the top with the remaining cornmeal. Bake for 20 minutes or until firm and golden brown. Serve hot.

Apple Ice Cream with Maple Apple Topping

Serves 10 to 12

THIS RECIPE CAME ABOUT in an interesting way, as do so many of the Amish-Mennonite recipes. Lucy Chupp had a dab of leftover baked apples and decided to add them to her husband's ice cream mixture—and lo, a new ice cream flavor was born. It turned out so well, the family requested she always make ice cream that way. For a special treat, she serves this on top of freshly baked warm doughnuts. Now that's a knockout dessert!

Lucy's husband makes their ice cream in an old-fashioned five-gallon ice cream freezer, but this recipe is designed for a smaller ice cream maker. For ease and best results, break the recipe down into two days' prep.

For freezing the ice cream, I use a Donvier ice cream maker with great success. This low-priced gadget can be purchased at some kitchen supply stores (page 286) or in large department stores. The metal churn should be placed in the coldest part of the freezer a day in advance of preparing the ice cream. Prepare the apple filling and the ice cream base the day before, too. Chilling the cream base overnight gives the finished dessert more volume.

FILLING AND TOPPING
> 8 medium cooking apples, such as Jonathan or Yellow Delicious, peeled, cored, and coarsely sliced
> 1½ cups maple syrup
> 1 cup honey
> 1 teaspoon grated nutmeg

ICE CREAM
> 2 cups half-and-half
> 1 cup whole or skim milk
> ½ cup granulated sugar
> ½ cup light brown sugar, packed
> ¼ cup nonfat dry milk
> ¼ teaspoon salt
> 5 egg yolks, whisked to break them up
> 1 tablespoon vanilla extract

■ Preheat the oven to 350°F.

■ MAKE THE FILLING AND TOPPING: In a greased 9 × 13-inch flat baking dish, combine the apples, syrup, honey, and nutmeg. Bake the apples for 1 hour and 15 minutes, or until they are very tender. Remove from the oven, cool, cover lightly with plastic, and chill until very cold, preferably overnight.

■ With a slotted spoon, dip out 1 cup of the apples and transfer to a food processor or blender. Add ¼ cup of the syrup. Process until the apples are rather finely chopped but not pureed —you want some apple texture in this mixture. Set aside in the refrigerator until needed. Reserve the remaining apples and sauce for topping.

■ MAKE THE ICE CREAM: Fill the bottom of a double boiler about two-thirds full of water and bring to a simmer. Meanwhile, in the top of the double boiler, combine the half-and-half, milk, sugars, dry milk, and salt. In a small bowl, whisk the egg yolks and vanilla together and add to the cream mixture in the double boiler. Mix thoroughly and insert a candy thermometer. Cook over simmering water, stirring often with a wooden spoon or spatula, until it reaches between 165° and 180°F. (Don't let the temperature go over 180°F., or the mixture will curdle. If this *does* happen, whiz the cooked mixture in the food processor until smooth, then proceed with the recipe.) Keep the temperature in that range for 10 to 15 minutes, still stirring. The mixture will thicken.

■ Empty the hot water from the bottom of the double boiler and refill with cold water and lots of ice cubes. Replace the top of the double boiler. Stir the mixture now and then, replenishing the ice cubes if needed. When the custard base is cool, place plastic wrap directly on the surface and refrigerate overnight.

■ Read the manufacturer's instructions on how to prepare the ice cream. After about 10 minutes of processing (the ice cream will be soft, like cake batter), add the reserved chopped apples and continue freezing until stiff peaks form, about 5 more minutes. Transfer the mixture to the freezer and allow the ice cream to ripen for several hours, or serve immediately, with the reserved apples and sauce poured over each individual serving.

Four-Day Coconut Cake

Serves 12

THOUGH THEY ARE likely to apologize for it, the Amish do use boxed cakes, and I well understand that, for they work harder than we English do and with fewer conveniences. And for the uninitiated home baker, box cakes can save the day, especially if they are dressed up a bit.

This cake from a regional Amish cookbook is, well, fabulous—and I hardly ever use that word. Since it must be made well in advance of serving, it is ideal for entertaining.

> 1½ cups sugar
> 2 cups sour cream
> 6½ cups flaked coconut
> 1 18-ounce box French Vanilla cake mix

■ In a mixer bowl, combine the sugar, sour cream, and coconut. Transfer to a tightly covered container and refrigerate for 24 hours.

■ Prepare and bake the cake in two 9-inch layer pans according to the package instructions. Cool the cake and remove from the pans, then chill the cake layers completely in the refrigerator.

■ Spilt each layer in half. Divide the filling into fifths (I do this by lightly scoring the top of the mixture with a knife). Place one-fifth of the coconut mixture between each layer. Then, using the remaining two-fifths of the filling, frost first the sides and then the top of the cake. Store tightly covered in the refrigerator for 2 or 3 days before serving. Cut into wedges and serve.

HOME REMEDIES

When you begin talking to the Amish, you realize how much we have lost of what was once common knowledge and practice in our society. In the early years of our country, many natural plants and substances were used for healing, and some of these methods are still practiced today by the Amish. These include drinking a tablespoon of cider vinegar and honey in a half-glass of water for arthritis as well as weight loss. An application of plain cider vinegar soothes itchy skin. Cranberry juice is used for urinary and bladder infections, and crushed cranberries are a good poultice for animal bites. Sorghum syrup helps dry scalp and dandruff, and molasses and butter soothe dry coughs.

Dandelion wine is used when one's heart seems to be beating too slowly and dandelion greens are good for the kidneys. Herbal teas are used as general tonics, as are red clover blossom,

corn silk, chamomile, and elderberry flowers. Thistle root is for rheumatism, sage tea for an upset stomach, and blackstrap molasses for arthritis. All the teas are made the same way: ¼ cup dried leaves or roots, 2 cups of boiling water, and a little honey.

Honey is a familiar remedy. For irritability and exhaustion, the recommended dosage is 4 teaspoons a day for several months. For slight scalds or burns, apply honey immediately; it will heal the burn rapidly. Twitching of the eyelids or at the corner of the mouth can be cured by taking 2 teaspoons honey at each meal. Muscle cramps can also be cured by taking 2 teaspoons honey at each meal. For minor burns, cut an aloe vera leaf and apply the sap.

Golden Mace Cake with Lemon Sauce

Serves 9

A CAKE WITH A HOT SAUCE poured over it is sometimes called a "cottage pudding" and was devised as a way to use leftover or stale cake, as the hot sauce softens the dried cake. The combination was so successful that some cooks started making simple yellow butter cakes and serving them fresh with the hot sauce. This dish is still well loved in country kitchens and served in rural restaurants.

> 1 $\frac{1}{4}$ cups all-purpose flour
> 1 cup sugar
> 1 $\frac{1}{2}$ teaspoons baking powder
> $\frac{1}{2}$ teaspoon salt
> $\frac{1}{4}$ rounded teaspoon mace
> $\frac{1}{3}$ cup butter, at room temperature
> $\frac{3}{4}$ cup milk, at room temperature
> 1 egg, at room temperature
> 2 teaspoons vanilla extract

> SAUCE
> 2 eggs, well beaten
> 2 cups sugar
> 1 cup (2 sticks) butter
> $\frac{1}{2}$ cup water
> $\frac{1}{3}$ cup fresh lemon juice
> $\frac{1}{2}$ teaspoon almond extract

▓ Preheat the oven to 350°F. Grease and flour a 9-inch square pan.

▓ Combine the flour, sugar, baking powder, salt, and mace in a mixer bowl. Add the butter, milk, egg, and vanilla and blend for 30 seconds on low speed, scraping the bowl constantly. Turn the mixer to high and beat 3 minutes longer, scraping the bowl occasionally.

▓ Pour the batter into the prepared pan and bake for 35 to 40 minutes, or until the cake is golden brown and begins to shrink from the sides of the pan. Remove from the oven, cover with foil and a terry cloth towel, and cool.

▓ MAKE THE SAUCE: In a medium saucepan, combine all of the ingredients. Bring to a boil over medium heat and cook, whisking now and then, until it thickens, about 8 minutes. Cut the cooled cake into squares and transfer to individual serving bowls or deep plates. Ladle the hot sauce over the cake and serve immediately.

Chocolate Angel Delight

Serves 16

THIS RECIPE CAME to me from Lucy Stuckey, an Amish lady in Maryland who always makes it for her family's Easter dinner, and once in a while for her friends when they come to quilt. Since she makes her own egg noodles, which use just the egg yolks, she always has plenty of egg whites left over, so she makes the angel food cake that forms the base of this dessert from scratch. However, store-bought angel food cake works just as well. This smooth, elegant dessert reminds me of a chocolate trifle and makes oodles—perfect for a large gathering.

> $\frac{1}{2}$ cup finely chopped English walnuts
> $\frac{1}{2}$ cup finely chopped black walnuts (see Note)
> 1 teaspoon vegetable oil
> 1 10-inch 16-ounce Angel Food Cake (page 90)
> 1 12-ounce package semisweet chocolate chips
> 2 tablespoons sugar
> 2 tablespoons water
> 4 jumbo or 5 large eggs, separated
> 2 cups heavy cream
> 2 teaspoons vanilla extract
> $\frac{1}{8}$ teaspoon salt

▓ Place the walnuts on a large paper plate and drizzle the oil over them; toss to mix. Microwave for 4 to 5 minutes, stirring once. Set aside to cool.

▓ Tear the cake into bite-size pieces and set aside. (This step, and the nut toasting, can be done a day in advance.)

Place the chocolate chips, sugar, and water in the top of a double boiler and heat over barely moving water for about 10 minutes. (The water should be "smiling," as the Amish say.) Stir occasionally until smooth. The mixture might start to firm up; if so, remove the top pan from the bottom one and proceed with the recipe. Meanwhile, beat the egg yolks thoroughly until they begin to lighten. Gradually add to the melted chocolate mixture and blend until smooth. Set the mixture aside to cool.

Beat the egg whites until they are stiff and hold a peak. Add one-quarter of the egg whites to the chocolate mixture first to lighten it, then fold in the remaining whites.

Whip the cream, vanilla, and salt together until the cream is stiff and holds a peak. Add about one-fifth of the whipped cream to the chocolate mixture to lighten it, then fold in the remaining cream, then the nuts and cake pieces. Do not overblend—the mixture should be light and puffy.

Transfer to a large 2-quart glass serving dish, cover, and refrigerate until needed.

NOTE: If black walnuts are not available, you can use all English walnuts or even pecans.

Blueberries with Nutmeg Dumplings

Serves 6

A DOWN-HOME DESSERT of blueberries simmered in apple juice with just a touch of almond topped with fluffy nutmeg dumplings—what a fine way to end a light summer supper. To further enhance this dessert, pass a pitcher of cream or a bowl of lightly sweetened yogurt.

3 cups apple juice
$\frac{1}{4}$ cup quick-cooking tapioca
1 quart fresh blueberries, or 32 ounces frozen
$\frac{1}{3}$ cup sugar, or more to taste
$\frac{1}{2}$ teaspoon almond extract

DUMPLINGS
1 cup all-purpose flour
$1\frac{1}{2}$ teaspoons baking powder
$\frac{1}{2}$ teaspoon salt
$\frac{1}{4}$ teaspoon grated nutmeg
1 tablespoon sugar
1 egg
1 tablespoon vegetable oil
6 tablespoons milk

In a large saucepan, combine the apple juice and tapioca; allow to stand for 5 minutes. Add the blueberries, sugar, and almond extract. Cover and bring to a boil, then lower the heat and simmer for 2 to 3 minutes, or until the tapioca is transparent.

MEANWHILE, PREPARE THE DUMPLINGS: In a medium bowl, whisk together the flour, baking powder, salt, nutmeg, and sugar. In a small bowl, beat the egg slightly, and whisk in the vegetable oil and milk. Pour over the dry ingredients and stir to just blend; do not overmix. The batter will be quite stiff.

Drop the batter by $\frac{1}{4}$ cups onto the simmering blueberries, cover tightly, and continue cooking over low heat for exactly 25 minutes. Do not lift the lid during this time, or the dumplings will fall. Transfer the warm dumplings and sauce to individual dishes and pass the cream or yogurt.

Pineapple Gingerbread Upside Down Cake

Serves 12

DELICIOUS. UNUSUAL. Delightfully rich and pretty. And the topping is a bit crunchy. The cake is tastier if made the day before; individual pieces can be reheated in the microwave. I serve this with a bit of English Pouring Sauce (page 275) or Whipped Cream Topping (page 271).

You can also substitute maraschino cherries, which I personally abhor (though Amish and Mennonite bakers do use them); the candied ones are better. I can rarely find candied fruit in my local grocery stores, except in November and December, so I always buy extra to freeze and have on hand all year long.

> ¾ cup (1½ sticks) butter, at room temperature
> 1 20-ounce can pineapple slices in heavy syrup
> 1½ cups dark brown sugar, packed
> 10 candied cherries
> 1½ cups all-purpose flour
> 1 teaspoon baking soda
> 1 teaspoon ground ginger
> ½ teaspoon ground cinnamon
> ½ teaspoon salt
> 1 egg
> ½ cup light or dark molasses

■ Preheat the oven to 350°F. Coat a 10-inch round cake pan with nonstick cooking spray. Place 1 stick of butter in the pan and put into the preheating oven to melt.

■ Meanwhile, drain the pineapple, reserving ½ cup of the syrup. When the butter is melted, add 1 cup of the brown sugar to the pan, mix it into the butter, then evenly pat it out with your fingers. Arrange as many pineapple rings on top as will fit, then cut the remaining rings into wedges and place them in any openings still available. Place cherries in the pineapple ring centers.

■ In a medium bowl, whisk together the flour, baking soda, ginger, cinnamon, and salt; set aside. In a mixer bowl, cream the remaining ¼ cup butter and ½ cup brown sugar together for 3 minutes. Add the egg and molasses and blend.

■ Heat the reserved pineapple juice in the microwave. Add the dry ingredients to the creamed mixture alternately with the hot syrup, beginning and ending with the flour. Pour the batter evenly over the pineapple-lined pan and smooth it out with a rubber spatula.

■ Bake the cake for 35 to 40 minutes, or until the cake begins to shrink away from the sides of the pan and the top springs back when touched with your finger.

■ Remove the cake from the oven to a rack and allow to cool for 5 minutes. Invert it onto a 12- or 15-inch round platter. If all the topping does not fall out onto the top of the cake, quickly use a metal spatula to release the sugar mixture and pat it onto the cake. The sugar will firm up rapidly, so work fast. Cool, cut into wedges, and serve.

Baked Coconut Butter Cream Pie

Makes one 9-inch pie; serves 6

BUTTERY YELLOW, delicate in flavor, the filling for the pie can be made two or three days in advance and refrigerated. Just before pouring it into the lightly baked shell, whisk the mixture to recombine all the ingredients.

Since I belong to the school of baking the pies the day they are to be eaten, this recipe earns high marks in my book!

> Pastry for 1-crust 9-inch pie shell, lightly baked (page 270)
> 2 eggs
> ¼ cup sugar
> 1 tablespoon all-purpose flour
> ⅛ teaspoon salt
> 1 tablespoon melted butter
> 1½ teaspoons vanilla extract
> 1 cup light corn syrup
> 1 cup milk
> 1⅓ cups flaked coconut
> Ground cinnamon

Preheat the oven to 350°F. Roll out the pastry and line a 9-inch pie pan. Prick the pastry all over with a fork and bake for 6 to 8 minutes, checking frequently to prick air bubbles and to pat the sides up with a fork if the pastry begins to slip down. Remove from the oven and cool completely.

In a large mixer bowl, beat the eggs until they are broken up. In a small bowl, combine the sugar, flour, and salt and gradually add to the eggs. Add the butter, vanilla, and corn syrup and combine; do not overmix. With a mixing spoon, stir in the milk and the coconut. The mixture should not be too bubbly.

Pour the coconut mixture into the prebaked shell and sift cinnamon over the top. Bake for 45 to 50 minutes, or until the pie is still a bit shaky, puffy in the middle, but not completely firm. Remove from the oven and transfer to a rack to cool completely before serving.

Brown Sugar Dumplings

Serves 8 to 10

HUMBLE INGREDIENTS, but nonetheless this is a most appealing and quick-to-prepare dessert —just the sort of dessert that Amish and Mennonite cooks depend on to round out a meal. The tender, soft, and puffy dumplings enhanced by dates and nuts bake on top of a brown sugar sauce flavored with orange. Serve with a pitcher of milk or cream. Any leftovers can be reheated in the microwave.

SYRUP
    2 cups dark brown sugar, packed
    2 cups water
    1 tablespoon butter
    1 1/2 teaspoons grated orange zest
    1 teaspoon vanilla extract
    3/4 teaspoon grated nutmeg
    1/8 teaspoon salt

DUMPLINGS
    2 cups all-purpose flour
    1 cup light brown sugar, packed
    2 teaspoons baking powder
    1/2 teaspoon salt
    3/4 cup milk
    1 tablespoon melted butter
    1 teaspoon vanilla extract
    1/2 cup chopped nuts
    1/2 cup chopped dates

Preheat the oven to 350°F.

MAKE THE SYRUP: In a saucepan over medium heat, combine the syrup ingredients. Cook for approximately 5 minutes or until the sugar is dissolved and the butter melted. Pour into a greased 9 × 13-inch baking dish; set aside.

MAKE THE DUMPLINGS: In a mixing bowl, whisk together the flour, brown sugar, baking powder, and salt. Add the milk, melted butter, vanilla, nuts, and dates and mix well. Using a 1 1/2-inch cookie scoop or by heaping tablespoon, drop into the syrup; this will make 28 dollops of batter. Bake the dumplings for 40 minutes or until golden brown and the syrup is bubbly. Serve warm in sauce dishes with a pitcher of milk.

NOTE: The syrup can be made a day in advance.

GOOD
NIGHT

[GUD NACHT]

❖

COME DECEMBER, the smaller lakes and ponds are icy and glitter in the sunlight. The landscape is still filled with color; wild sumac heads, oval and musty red, cover the bushes. Scarlet-stemmed dogwoods fill the marshes, and brown cattail heads fray out to a silky beige. By this time, the cornfields are golden stubbles and the trees are groves of deep velvety gray. The landscape is an ever-changing delight, and its observance is one of the great pleasures of Amish life. The evening sky first turns purple, then hot pink with streaks of gold. The martens dive and swoop in the dying light. Thin fingers of mist rise in the valleys. The first quaver of the little gray screech owl signals the end of the day, and in the orchard, the silent moon watches through the trees.

13
THE
BASICS

Easy Garlic Salt ❖ Butter Dumplings ❖ Chicken Stock ❖ Beef Stock ❖ Greens for Salad ❖ Really Good Tartar Sauce ❖ Toasted Nuts ❖ Plumped Dried Fruits ❖ Perfect Pie Pastry ❖ Meringue Topping ❖ Whipped Cream Topping ❖ Hot Lemon Sauce ❖ Chocolate Fudge Frosting ❖ Chocolate Glaze Frosting ❖ Basic Butter Frosting ❖ Most Delicious Coconut-Pecan Filling and Frosting ❖ Quick Streusel Topping ❖ Foamy Sauce ❖ English Pouring Sauce

EVERYTHING YOU find in this chapter is mentioned elsewhere or is referred to in other recipes in this cookbook. This chapter is the only place I duplicate recipes from earlier books. For instance, you will find the same no-fail Perfect Pie Pastry here as in my other books. You shouldn't have to use two cookbooks when you are doing one of my recipes, unless you want to, of course!

Easy Garlic Salt

Makes ½ cup

THIS HAS A MUCH better flavor than the store-bought stuff, and really comes in handy.

> 3 garlic cloves
> ½ cup kosher salt

In a measuring cup, quarter the garlic cloves. Add the salt and cover loosely. Allow the mixture to stand 3 days, stirring occasionally. Leave the garlic in the salt until it is completely dried —the time varies; don't worry about it. Remove the garlic, transfer the mixture to salt shakers, and cover tightly. Use as a seasoning on grilled meats, in soups and sauces, and with cheese and garlic toast.

Butter Dumplings

Serves 4 to 6

WHAT A WONDERFUL recipe this is! These puffy light dumplings can be simmered on top of any liquid, such as a stew or soup.

> 1 cup all-purpose flour
> 1½ teaspoons baking powder
> ½ teaspoon salt
> 1 tablespoon cold butter
> 1 egg, beaten
> 6 tablespoons milk
> 1 heaping tablespoon finely minced fresh
>   parsley

In a medium bowl, whisk together the flour, baking powder, and salt. Cut in the cold butter with a pastry blender or fork until the mixture resembles coarse oatmeal. Add the egg, milk, and parsley. Blend lightly; don't overmix. Drop by tablespoonfuls (approximately 6) on top of the simmering liquid. Cover tightly, and cook over medium-low heat for 20 minutes; do not lift the cover during the cooking period. Serve in bowls, topped with butter.

Chicken Stock

THERE ARE SOME VERY good canned chicken broths on the market that I use, such as Campbell's Healthy Request. If you do use canned broth, choose one of the reduced-sodium products, which tend to have better flavor and won't unbalance the seasonings in your dish. But, time permitting, this homemade stock is really very nice to have on hand. It freezes well.

> 1 roasting chicken (4 to 5 pounds), cut up, or 4 to 5 pounds chicken wings and some giblets (about 1 pound), if available
> 2 medium onions, quartered
> 2 large carrots, halved
> 2 celery ribs, halved
> 1 medium green bell pepper, halved
> Generous handful of fresh parsley, including stems
> 6 whole cloves
> 2 bay leaves
> 1 teaspoon salt
> ½ teaspoon white pepper
> 3 to 4 quarts water

■ Place the chicken, including the neck and giblets (but not the liver), in a large stockpot with the remaining ingredients. The water should cover the chicken completely by 3 inches; if not, add a cup or two more. Cover, bring to a boil, and simmer for 2 hours, skimming off froth as it forms on top. Remove the chicken to a tray, allow to cool a bit, then remove the meat and skin, reserving the meat for another use. Return the bones and skin to the pot and simmer, covered, for 1 hour more.

■ Strain the stock through a sieve into a bowl, pressing the juices out of the solids with a rubber spatula. Chill the stock overnight and discard the fat that solidifies on the surface. Transfer to 1-quart containers and freeze for up to 3 months, if desired.

Beef Stock

MAKING YOUR OWN STOCK may sound like a lot of work, but this efficient method of simmering in the oven overnight does simplify matters. If you are in a hurry and have to buy beef broth, do not substitute beef consommé for this; consommé has gelatin added.

> 5 pounds beef soup bones, cut into 6-inch lengths
> 6 medium carrots, scrubbed and halved
> 3 large onions, unpeeled and quartered
> 6 celery ribs, including the leaves
> 1 turnip, scrubbed and quartered (optional)
> 3 bay leaves
> 12 whole cloves
> 12 black peppercorns
> Large handful of fresh parsley, including stems
> 5 quarts water

■ Preheat the oven to 400° F. Place the bones in an oiled 12 × 17-inch pan and bake for 30 minutes. Add the carrots and onions, and bake another 30 minutes, turning the vegetables and bones with tongs at least once during the last cooking period. When the bones are deeply browned (and this may take a few minutes longer), transfer them along with the browned vegetables to a large stockpot. Pour the fat out of the pan, then deglaze with a little water using a wooden spoon to scrape up the browned bits, and add this to the stockpot. Add the remaining ingredients, cover, and bring to a boil. Place in a 140° F. oven for 12 hours (I like to do this overnight) or simmer on top of the stove for at least 12 hours.

■ Remove the bones and vegetables with a slotted spoon, then strain the stock through a fine sieve. (If you want a clearer broth, line the sieve with cheesecloth. I must admit, I generally skip that step.) Refrigerate for several hours or overnight, or until the fat rises to the top and forms a hard layer. Discard the fat and transfer the stock to 1-quart containers. It can be frozen for up to 3 months.

Greens for Salad

THIS TECHNIQUE CAN BE used for any leaf lettuce and spinach, but spinach leaves sometimes hold the soil, so be very thorough in your rinsing of it. Cleaned and stored in this manner, the greens will keep for several days. Allow one generous handful of greens per serving.

> Greens, any amount
> Cold water

■ Place the greens in a clean sink or pan and cover with cold water. Swish to loosen soil, then allow to stand for 5 minutes. Carefully scoop up the greens from the surface of the water; shake the greens off and transfer to a colander or salad spinner. Shake or spin off as much water as possible.

■ Layer the lettuce between a dish towel or paper towels, which will absorb the extra moisture. Place towels and greens in a plastic bag, squeezing out as much air as possible. Seal and refrigerate in the vegetable drawer until needed.

Really Good Tartar Sauce

Makes 1 ½ cups

I QUITE LIKE THIS Amish version of tartar sauce. It uses dill pickles instead of sweet ones. I add capers; the Amish would not.

> 1 cup mayonnaise
> 2 tablespoons finely chopped onion
> 2 tablespoons finely chopped dill pickle
> 1 ½ tablespoons prepared mustard (I prefer
>   horseradish style)
> 1 tablespoon capers (optional)
> 1 tablespoon minced fresh parsley

■ In a small mixing bowl, combine all the ingredients and mix well. Transfer to a jar and cover. Refrigerate until needed. This will keep up to 1 month.

Home-grown lettuce in the garden resembles a large, crisp green rose.

Toasted Nuts

TOASTING NUTS GIVES THEM a deeper flavor, and in some recipes this is a needed step. They can be toasted two ways: in the oven or in the microwave.

▓ OVEN METHOD: Preheat the oven to 375°F. Place the nuts in a shallow pan, such as a pie pan or jelly-roll pan. Drizzle a bit of oil over the nuts —about 1 teaspoon for each cup of nuts—then sprinkle lightly with salt. Bake the nuts until golden and fragrant, 5 to 8 minutes, depending on the type of nut, stirring occasionally. They burn quickly, so watch them carefully. Remove from the oven and cool.

▓ MICROWAVE METHOD: Place the nuts on a large paper plate or microwave-safe plate. Drizzle a bit of oil over the nuts—about 1 teaspoon per cup of nuts—then sprinkle lightly with salt. Microwave the nuts on high at 2-minute increments, stirring after each, until the nuts appear toasty and smell nutty. Remove from the oven and cool. The average time for 1 cup of nuts is about 6 minutes in my microwave, but this will vary from microwave to microwave.

Plumped Dried Fruits

MOST DRIED FRUITS, such as raisins, currants, and prunes, benefit from being reconstituted or "plumped," as my niece Mary Ellen says. Vary these amounts according to your recipe; you don't have to be too precise.

> ³⁄₄–1 cup raisins or other dried fruits
> ¹⁄₄ cup water or juice

▓ Measure the raisins into a glass measuring cup. Add the liquid. Cover with plastic wrap and microwave on high for 1 minute. Remove from the oven and allow the fruit to stand for 5 minutes. Drain off any remaining liquid and discard (or use as part of the liquid in the recipe). The fruit is now ready to be added to the recipe.

Perfect Pie Pastry

Makes enough for 2 pies with top crusts

THIS REMAINS MY FAVORITE pie pastry; it never, ever fails. It is prepared with an electric mixer and is ideal for the cook who has always been apprehensive about making pie crust, for it handles beautifully and comes out flavorful and golden every time. Make a double recipe and freeze the extra. One-fourth of this recipe is enough dough for one 8- or 9-inch pie shell; half of this recipe is enough for a 2-crust pie.

> 4 cups all-purpose flour
> 1 tablespoon sugar
> 2 teaspoons salt
> 1³⁄₄ cups butter-flavored solid vegetable shortening
> 1 egg
> 1 tablespoon cider vinegar
> ¹⁄₂ cup water

▓ Combine the flour, sugar, salt, and shortening in a large mixer bowl and blend until it has the texture of coarse crumbs. In a small bowl, whisk or beat together the egg, vinegar, and water. Drizzle over the flour mixture and mix thoroughly. Shape the dough into a patty, wrap in plastic wrap, and place in the freezer for 45 minutes, or refrigerate overnight.

▓ When chilled, form the dough into a long roll, then divide into fourths. Roll and use immediately, or wrap each portion separately and refrigerate or freeze.

Meringue Topping

Makes enough to generously cover a 9-inch pie

TO KEEP YOUR MERINGUE from "weeping," never add more than 2 tablespoons of sugar for each egg white used. Also, the pie filling should be warm or even hot when the meringue is swirled on top. This immediately starts to cook the bottom of the meringue, which is good. The oven temperature should not be more than 325°F. The addition of cream of tartar also gives the meringue extra stability. Be sure there are no specks of egg yolks in the whites or they will not beat properly. Egg whites are mostly water, and the cornstarch in this recipe helps absorb that moisture.

> 3 egg whites, at room temperature
> $1/4$ teaspoon salt
> $1/4$ teaspoon cream of tartar
> 6 tablespoons granulated or superfine sugar (see page 89)
> $1^1/2$ teaspoons cornstarch

▨ Preheat the oven to 325°F. (or reduce the temperature if you have just baked your pie). In a large mixer bowl, beat the egg whites, salt, and cream of tartar until soft peaks form. Gradually add the sugar, a tablespoon at a time, and continue beating until stiff peaks form and the mixture is glossy. Just before the beating is completed, sprinkle in the cornstarch and incorporate thoroughly. The peaks should not topple over when the beating is completed.

▨ Spread the meringue on the warm filling (this keeps it from shrinking away from the filling as it cools), clear over the edge of the crust. Swoop the meringue into attractive peaks. Bake for 15 to 18 minutes in the middle of the oven or until the peaks are golden brown. Cool the pie at room temperature until there is no warmth left in the meringue at all, then refrigerate the pie until needed.

Whipped Cream Topping

Makes 2 cups

EQUALLY GOOD as an alternative to meringue on pies or dolloped onto squares of gingerbread and other desserts, this topping has light corn syrup added to help stabilize it. Consequently, the cream does not go flat, but stays nice and perky for a couple of days (though most pies don't last that long). Sometimes cooks will complain that their cream doesn't whip. An older cream (check the date on the box) whips better than a newer cream, and the bowl and beater should be well chilled.

> 1 cup very cold heavy cream
> $1/4$ cup confectioners' sugar
> 1 teaspoon vanilla extract
> 1 tablespoon light corn syrup
> $1/8$ teaspoon salt

▨ Combine all of the ingredients in a mixer bowl and whip until the cream is stiff, with well-defined peaks. Don't walk away and leave this while it is beating, though, for the mixture can turn to butter in a matter of seconds. Serve immediately or cover tightly and refrigerate for a day or two.

Hot Lemon Sauce

Makes 2 cups

THIS SIMPLE TART yet sweet sauce is excellent poured over gingerbread, rice pudding, fruitcake, steamed puddings, and cake that is a bit past its prime. That particular combination is sometimes called cottage pudding. Doesn't that have a nice nostalgic ring to it?

> 1 cup sugar
> 2 tablespoons cornstarch
> $1/8$ teaspoon salt
> 2 cups boiling water
> $1/4$ cup ($1/2$ stick) butter
>   Grated zest and juice of 1 lemon
> $1/2$ teaspoon grated nutmeg

▦ Combine the sugar, cornstarch, and salt in a small saucepan. Gradually stir in the boiling water. Bring to a boil over high heat and boil, uncovered, for 3 minutes. Stir in the butter, lemon zest and juice, and nutmeg and cook 2 minutes longer. Serve warm.

Chocolate Fudge Frosting

*Makes enough for a large 2-layer cake
or an average 3-layer cake*

THIS REMAINS MY FAVORITE chocolate icing or frosting. I believe the original recipe came from the *Farm Journal* magazine light-years ago, and it still can't be improved upon.

> 1 pound confectioners' sugar
> $1/3$ cup plus 2 tablespoons cocoa powder
> $1/4$ cup ($1/2$ stick) butter, at room temperature
> 1 egg white
> 5 tablespoons evaporated milk
> 1 teaspoon vanilla extract
> $1/4$ teaspoon salt

▦ Combine all the ingredients in a large mixer bowl and beat on high speed for 1 minute, or until the frosting is light and creamy. Frost between the layers first, then the top and sides, forming decorative swirls with the tip of a knife.

Chocolate Glaze Frosting

Makes 1 scant cup

THIS IS A TERRIFICALLY easy and elegant frosting, enough for one 9 × 13-inch loaf cake or a 9 × 13-inch pan of bar cookies. It is enough for a skinny layer cake, but if your cake is large, and certainly this would include a Bundt-type cake, double the recipe.

> 6 ounces semisweet chocolate morsels
> ½ cup sour cream
> ⅛ teaspoon salt

■ In a double boiler, over hot but not boiling water, melt the chocolate. Stir in the sour cream and salt, and mix gently. Remove from the heat and immediately spread on the sides and top of the cake. Store the frosted cake in the refrigerator, removing before serving time to come just to room temperature.

Basic Butter Frosting

Makes 2 cups

HERE IS A VERSATILE frosting that is perfect on cookies and cakes. The flavor can be varied by adding fruit-flavored extracts, such as orange or lemon, and some grated zest of orange or lemon, or add almond or chocolate extract. It's a pretty adaptable recipe; play around with it.

> ½ cup (1 stick) butter, at room temperature
> 4 cups confectioners' sugar
> 3 tablespoons milk
> 1 teaspoon vanilla extract
> ⅛ teaspoon salt

■ In a mixer bowl, cream the butter on medium to high speed for 30 seconds. Gradually add 2 cups of the confectioners' sugar, beating until combined. Add the milk, vanilla, and salt; mix well. Gradually add the remaining sugar and beat until smooth. This can be made in advance and refrigerated.

Most Delicious Coconut-Pecan Filling and Frosting

Makes enough to fill and to frost a 2-layer 9-inch cake

A PLAIN LAYER CAKE can be all gussied up with this superb filling and frosting.

> 3 large egg yolks, slightly beaten
> 1 cup evaporated milk
> 1 cup sugar
> ½ cup (1 stick) butter
> 1 teaspoon vanilla extract
> 1⅓ cups sweetened shredded coconut
> 1 cup coarsely chopped pecans

■ In a medium saucepan, combine the egg yolks, evaporated milk, sugar, butter, and vanilla. Cook over medium to medium-low heat, stirring constantly, approximately 15 to 20 minutes or until the mixture thickens. Remove from the heat and stir in the coconut and pecans. Beat with a spoon until the filling has cooled and is of spreading consistency. Use one-third of the mixture for the filling, then frost the cake (sides first, then top) with the remaining mixture. Store the frosted cake in the refrigerator and bring to room temperature before serving.

Quick Streusel Topping

*Makes enough for a 9-inch pie topping
or 2-quart flat baking dish of fruit*

THIS RECIPE IS unapologetically simple. I make it in big batches, quadrupling the recipe, to have on hand for quick desserts. The original came written thusly: 2 parts flour, 1 part white sugar, 1 part butter. Here is my version, and certainly feel free to change it any way you want.

> 1 cup all-purpose flour
> ½ cup sugar
> ½ teaspoon grated nutmeg
> ½ teaspoon ground cinnamon
> ⅛ teaspoon salt
> ½ cup (1 stick) butter

■ In a medium mixing bowl, whisk together the dry ingredients. Cut in the butter with a pastry blender or fork until coarse crumbs form. Transfer to a tightly covered container and store in the refrigerator until needed.

NOTE: For apple crisp, combine 6 cups sliced, cored Jonathan apples, skin on. Place in a greased 2-quart flat glass baking dish. Pour over ½ cup cider or apple juice, sprinkle all of the topping on top of the apples, and bake at 375°F. for 1 hour. Leaving the skins on the apples makes this crisp an attractive pink.

Foamy Sauce

Makes 2 cups

RATHER LIKE A BEIGE, fluffy hard sauce, this lovely old recipe is an ideal embellishment for steamed puddings or apple and mincemeat pies. It melts immediately into the hot dessert; you'll love it.

> 2 tablespoons (¼ stick) butter, at room temperature
> 1 cup confectioners' sugar
> 1 egg, beaten
> 1 teaspoon vanilla extract
> ½ teaspoon ground cinnamon or grated nutmeg
> ⅛ teaspoon salt
> 1 cup heavy cream

■ In a mixer bowl, cream the butter and confectioners' sugar. Add the egg, vanilla, cinnamon or nutmeg, and salt; mix well and set aside.

■ In another mixer bowl, whip the cream until stiff and add a bit of it to the butter-egg mixture to lighten it, then gently combine both mixtures and chill. This should be done at least 3 hours before serving to give the butter time to firm up within the whipped cream.

English Pouring Sauce

Makes 1¼ cups

YOU MIGHT KNOW THIS as crème anglaise, but the Amish and Mennonites call it English pouring sauce, which is perfectly all right with me. It is a classic accompaniment to any number of desserts. I like to serve it in a pretty bowl with grated nutmeg sprinkled on top, to let everyone help themselves.

> 3 egg yolks
> 3 tablespoons sugar
> 1 teaspoon cornstarch
> 1 cup whole milk
> ⅛ teaspoon salt
> 1 teaspoon vanilla extract

■ In a mixer bowl, beat the egg yolks well. Gradually add the sugar and beat for 3 minutes. Beat in the cornstarch. In a medium saucepan, scald the milk over medium heat until bubbles form around the edges of the pan; do not boil. Gradually add the hot milk to the egg mixture, stirring with a wooden spoon, not a whisk (if you don't want to aerate the mixture).

■ Transfer the sauce back to the saucepan and cook over low heat, stirring constantly with the wooden spoon, until the mixture thickens. Remove from the heat and add the salt and vanilla. Transfer to a storage container. Place a piece of plastic wrap or wax paper directly on the surface of the hot sauce and allow to cool completely. Cover tightly, leaving the plastic wrap on top. (This keeps a skin from forming on top of the custard.) Refrigerate until needed. To serve, transfer to a bowl and sprinkle fresh nutmeg over the top. This sauce can be made 2 days in advance.

[Guide to Places to Visit]

❖

As we traveled about the country, we found some exceptional places to learn more about Amish and Mennonite country life, some very good shops, and other places that shouldn't be missed. Here is a partial list:

Indiana

AMISH ACRES
1600 West Market Street
Nappanee, IN 46550
800/800-4942

Historic Amish farm, with demonstrations, excellent restaurant, theater, and inns. Listed on the National Register of Historic Places. Write for information.

ANTIQUES FROM BRUCE CHANEY AT LONSDALE
10979 North Roanoke Road
Roanoke, IN 46783
219/672-9744

Charming shop filled with antique goodies, and Bruce Chaney can answer all your questions. Don't miss this place if you are in northern Indiana. No oak or Depression glass. Open daily by chance and any time by appointment.

CONNER PRAIRIE LIVING HISTORY MUSEUM
13400 Allisonville Road
Fishers, IN 46060
317/776-6600

Featuring an 1836 Indiana town with three historic areas, the museum also has a top-notch early quilt collection plus a good decorative arts collection and gift shop. There is an attractive dining room on the premises, but also consider The Classic Kitchen (page 282) in Noblesville.

COUNTRY SHOPS OF GRABILL
13756 State Street
Grabill, IN 46741
219/627-6315
Monday–Saturday 9–5, Sunday 12–5.

One of Indiana's larger antiques shops, over 30,000 square feet with sixty individual shops featuring some of the area's well-known antiques dealers.

FORT WAYNE MUSEUM OF ART
311 East Main
Fort Wayne, IN 46802
219/422-6467
Tuesday–Saturday 10–5,
Sunday 12–5, closed on Monday.

This elegant museum designed by Walter Netsch of Skidmore, Owings and Merrill has Amish quilts from the Pottinger Collection, among other fine things, plus a good gift shop.

GREENFIELD HERB GARDEN
Box 9, Depot and Harrison
Shipshewana, IN 46565
219/768-7110

Truly an excellent source of fresh and dried herbs, books, herb-related supplies, classes, and unusual gifts. Don't miss it.

GREEN MEADOWS GIFT AND ANTIQUE SHOP
State Road 5
Shipshewana, IN 46565
219/768-4221

Operated by Ruth Miller and her daughter, Gwen, this treasure-filled shop has folk art and local antiques. A couple of miles north of Shipshewana on Road 5.

INDIANA STATE MUSEUM
202 North Alabama Street
Indianapolis, IN 46204
317/232-1637

This museum has part of the Pottinger Collection of Amish quilts and artifacts; they are superbly displayed.

MENNO-HOF, MENNONITE-AMISH VISITORS CENTER
Box 701
Shipshewana, IN 46565
219/768-4117
Group and private tours available.

Located across from the auction, this is the place to start your tour of Indiana Amish country.

REBECCA HAARER ART AND ANTIQUES
Box 52, 168 Morton Street
Shipshewana, IN 46565
219/768-4787

Ms. Haarer is an Amish and Mennonite folklorist and an authority on Amish quilts. Her shop has excellent examples of local quilts and books, and also Christmas ornaments. And you can buy *The Budget* here, as well.

Directory of Mennonite Relief Sales, United States

FOR DETAILS, CONTACT:

Mennonite Central Committee, 704 Main Street, Box 500, Akron, PA 17501

STATE	CITY	DATE
California	Fresno	First Saturday of April
Colorado	Rocky Ford	Third Saturday of October
Illinois	Arthur	Fourth Saturday of August
Illinois	Peoria	Third Friday and Saturday of March
Indiana	Goshen	Fourth Saturday of September
Indiana	Montgomery	Second Saturday of July
Iowa	Iowa City	Memorial Day weekend
Kansas	Hutchinson	Second Saturday of April (unless Easter weekend, then first Saturday)
Michigan	Fairview	First Saturday of August
Missouri	Harrisonville	Second Saturday in October
Nebraska	Aurora	First Saturday of April (unless Easter weekend, then second Saturday)
New York	Bath	Last Saturday in July
North Dakota	Minot	First Saturday of April
Ohio	Kidron	First Saturday of August
Oklahoma	Fairview	Always the Friday and Saturday after Thanksgiving
Oregon	Albany	Second Saturday in October
Pennsylvania	Gap	Second Saturday of August
Pennsylvania	Harrisburg	First Saturday of April (unless Easter weekend, then second Saturday) A very large sale!
Pennsylvania	Johnstown	Fourth Thursday, Friday, and Saturday of October
Pennsylvania	Lancaster	Second Thursday of March, selling livestock and hay
South Dakota	Sioux Falls	Fourth Friday of August
Texas	Houston	First Saturday of November
Virginia	Fisherville	Last Saturday of September
Washington	Ritzville	First Saturday in October
Wisconsin	Jefferson	Second Saturday of August

Directory of Mennonite Relief Sales, Canada

STATE	CITY	DATE
Alberta	Tofield/Coaldale	July 17–18 weekend
British Columbia	Clearbroo	September 19 weekend
British Columbia	Kelowna	September 26 weekend
British Columbia	Prince George	October 3 weekend
Ontario	Black Creek	September 19 weekend
Ontario	Guelph	February 20 weekend; sells mostly cattle
Ontario	New Hamburg	May 30 weekend; a very large sale!
Manitoba	Brandon	August 15 weekend
Manitoba	Morris	September 19 weekend
Saskatchewan	Hague	June 13 weekend; sells mostly grain and farm supplies
Saskatchewan	Saskatoon	May 29–30 weekend

GENE STRATTON PORTER
STATE HISTORIC SITE
P.O. Box 639, 1205 Pleasant Point
Rome City, IN 46784
219/854-3790
Tuesday–Saturday 9–5, Sunday 1–5. Last guided tour of home starts each day at 4:30.
Twenty acres of woods with trails on the shore of Sylvan Lake, formal gardens, and picnic shelters. Grounds are open dawn to dusk. Her cabin has personal furnishings, artifacts, and library. Gift shop sells her books.

THE SUMMER HOUSE
Rural Route #4, Box 134
North Manchester, IN 46962
Kerry Hippensteel, prop.
219/982-4707

Comprehensive herb garden and shop, with attractive folk art and accessories. Call regarding hours.

TOPEKA CARRIAGE AUCTION
Box 279
Topeka, IN 46571
219/593-2522
Carriage auctions, June and October; horse auctions throughout year.

YODER'S DEPARTMENT STORE
AND HARDWARE
State Road 5 (across from auction)
Shipshewana, IN 46565
219/768-4887

Take a look at a real hardware and department store used by the Amish. If you need a 5-gallon ice cream freezer, this is the place to get it.

Maryland

YODER'S COUNTRY MARKET
61 Locker Lane
off of Route 669 North
Grantsville, MD 21536
800/321-5148
A large Amish and Mennonite market, filled with good things to eat. There is another store in nearby Cumberland. Call for information.

Ohio

LEHMAN HARDWARE AND APPLIANCES, INC.
One Lehman Circle, P.O. Box 41
Kidron, OH 44636-0041
330/857-5757

One of the best Amish hardwares I've seen. It is like stepping back into the nineteenth century. And they have a catalog!

SAUDER FARM AND CRAFT VILLAGE
State Route 2
Archbold, OH 43502
800/590-9755

Admission charged: Adults $9; Seniors $8.50; Students (6–16) $4.50.

An impeccably restored regional early pioneer village of the 1800s with a great restaurant and quilting supply shop. Send for brochure and map. Outstanding spring quilt festival.

Pennsylvania

BIRD-IN-HAND FARMER'S MARKET
PA 340 and Maple Avenue
Bird-in-Hand, PA 17505
717/393-9674

Authentic Amish and Mennonite farmer's market, with delicious regional specialties.

MENNONITE INFORMATION CENTER
2209 Millstream Road
Lancaster, PA 17062
717/299-0954

Be sure to start your exploration of Pennsylvania Amish country here. Call in advance to arrange for private guided tours.

READING TERMINAL MARKET
12th and Arch Street
Philadelphia, PA 19107
215/922-2317
Monday–Saturday 8–6, closed Sunday.

One of the oldest farmer's markets in the country. Amish merchants from Lancaster sell Wednesday through Saturday.

[Guide to Restaurants, Bed and Breakfasts, and Inns]

❖

HERE IS a partial list of places, either en route to or within Amish and Mennonite communities. For more information, consult tourist or Mennonite information centers or regional *Mobile Guides* for current information about lodging and restaurants.

Listed below is information on regional restaurants and accommodations. (R) indicates a restaurant only; (R, A) signifies both food and accommodations are available.

Indiana

Amish dinners served at an Amish Home, groups only. By advance reservation only.

LAVERN G. AND BETTY MILLER
0075 South, 1150 West
Middlebury, IN 46565 (R)
No phone; please write.

THE BUGGY WHEEL
RESTAURANT
Morton Street
Shipshewana, IN 46565
219/768-4444 (R)
Regional Amish and Mennonite dishes, and be sure to visit the bakery next door.

CHECKERBERRY INN
6244 County Road 37
Goshen, IN 46526
219/642-4445 (R, A)
Sophisticated country inn, nestled in Amish country. Superb cuisine, delightful place. I never tire of going there—one of the best inns in the country.

THE CLASSIC KITCHEN
610 Hannibal Street
Noblesville, IN 46060
317/773-7385 (R)
Tuesday–Saturday, lunch 11–2; dinner 6–9. Reservations requested.
Eclectic food with historical recipes made in-house with no preservatives or additives. Steve Keneipp has developed a charming, not-to-be-missed destination restaurant. You'll love it.

DAS DUTCHMAN ESSENHAUS
RESTAURANT AND INN
U. S. State Road 20
Middlebury, IN 46540
219/825-9471 (R, A)
Amish and Mennonite regional foods, marvelous pies, gifts galore, including a Christmas shop. One of the favorite and busiest restaurants this area. Reservations for large groups are necessary. The inn is new and very nicely done.

FREDERICK-TALBOT INN
13805 Allisonville Road
Fishers, IN 46038
800/566-2337
(A, with breakfast)
An outstandingly restored old house right across from Conner Prairie. The rooms are large, furnished with antiques, and the breakfasts, served in a sunny spacious dining room, are incredibly generous. This is real Hoosier hospitality.

HOME OF ELIAS RUFF
1791 Log Cabin Restaurant
13531 Main Street
Grabill, IN 46741
219/627-6312 (R)
Monday–Wednesday 11–3; Thursday 11–8; Friday–Saturday 11–9; Sunday 11–4. Reservations requested after 4 P.M.
Restored log cabin is very charming. The bread and pies are exceptionally good.

MOSAIQUE RESTAURANT
115 South Buffalo
Warsaw, IN 46581
219/269-5080 (R)
If you are in the area, the side trip to Warsaw to dine at the very sophisticated Mosaique is a must. Call for reservations and opening hours.

SONGBIRD RIDGE BED &
BREAKFAST
5350 North State Road 5
Shipshewana, IN 46565
219/768-7714
(A, with breakfast)
Five guest rooms, furnished with country folk art and antiques, Amish breakfast. Lovely view overlooking Amish farms. Close to Shipshewana Flea Market.

WHITE HILL MANOR
2513 East Center Street
Warsaw, IN 46580
219/269-6933
(A, with breakfast)
A most attractive place to stay about an hour from Amish country. English Tudor house, gracefully transformed into a bed and breakfast.

GREEN MEADOWS BED &
BREAKFAST
R #2, Box 592
Shipshewana, IN 46565
219/768-4221
(A, with breakfast)
The Millers, who own and operate this charming place, are unforgettably lovely people, and so is their bed and breakfast. Don't miss their gift and antiques shop.

OIL LAMP RESTAURANT
State Road 15
New Paris, IN 67884
219/831-4666 (R)
A bit off the beaten track, but Suetta Bechtel's giant cinnamon rolls make it worth the trip.

Iowa

LACORSETTE MAISON INN
629 1st Avenue East
Newton, IA 50208
515/792-6833 (R, A)
Elegant, yet comfortable mansion, with cozy nooks and alcoves, listed on the National Historic Register.

Kentucky

BEAUMONT INN
638 Beaumont Inn Drive
Harrodsburg, KY 40330
800/352-3992 (R, A)
Built in 1845 and located in the heart of Bluegrass country, redolent of Southern history, brimming with beautiful antiques and fascinating memorabilia. Listed on the National Register of Historic Places and located amid numerous historic sites and attractions.

Maryland

ANTRIM 1844
30 Trevanion Road
Taneytown, MD 21787
800/858-1844 (R, A)
Antebellum ambience together with genuine hospitality; one of Maryland's most renowned country inn resorts with fireplaces and Jacuzzis.

THE INN AT BUCKEYSTOWN
c/o General Delivery
3521 Buckeystown Pike
Buckeystown, MD 21717
800/272-1190 (R, A)
Victorian mansion in Buckeystown, which is a registered historic pre-Revolutionary village steeped in Civil War lore, near Battlefield Park.

Michigan

THE NATIONAL HOUSE INN
102 So. Parkview
Marshall, MI 49068
616/781-7374
(A, with breakfast)
A warm, beautifully furnished inn, nestled among the 850 structures of nineteenth-century architecture in Marshall, a National Historic Landmark District.

Minnesota

SCHUMACHER'S NEW
PRAGUE HOTEL
212 W. Main Street
New Prague, MN 56071
612/758-2133 (R, A)
See Bavarian folk painted furniture and eiderdown comforters in this inn known for its superb Czech and German cuisine.

Missouri

THE MANSION AT ELFINDALE
1701 South Fort
Springfield, MO 65807
800/443-0237
(A, with breakfast; lunch or dinner for guests upon request)
Step into the Victorian era and stay in a magnificent 1888 mansion decorated with period furniture. Experience an authentic afternoon tea with English pastries.

WALNUT STREET INN
900 E. Walnut Street
Springfield, MO 65806
417/864-6346
(A, with breakfast)
Just 30 minutes from Branson, this 14-room luxury urban inn is in the historic district and is within walking distance of museums, theaters, and restaurants.

Ohio

The Inn at Honey Run
6920 County Road 203
Millersburg, OH 44654
330/674-0011 (R, A)

Innkeeper Marge Stock has created one of the most beautiful and successful inns in the country. It is one of my very favorite places. Nestled in the rolling hills and woods of Holmes County, the inn's exquisite seclusion, extraordinary architecture, and good food make for an unforgettable experience.

Wisconsin

The American Club
Highland Drive
Kohler, WI 53044
800/344-2838 (R, A)

Luxurious Tudor-style, world-class, historical hotel listed on the National Register of Historic Places. Enjoy two PGA golf courses, tennis, and 30 miles of hiking in the 500-acre nature preserve, and nine different restaurants.

[Mail-Order Directory]

❖

Publications

THE BUDGET
P.O. Box 249
Sugarcreek, OH 44681
330/852-4634

Amish and Conservative Mennonite newspaper. Subscription price $30 one year (subject to change); call for current prices. Also available in Amish and Mennonite stores.

AMISH-COUNTRY COOKBOOK
The Dutch Corporation
P.O. Box 2608
Middlebury, IN 46540
219/825-9471, ext. 430

Favorite recipes gathered by Das Dutchman, Essenhaus Restaurant. Good regional cookbooks, with recipes from the staff of the Essenhaus. Three volumes available, each $11.50 plus $4.00 shipping and handling.

BALL BLUE BOOK, GUIDE TO HOME CANNING, FREEZING AND DEHYDRATION
Direct Marketing
Alltrista Corporation
P.O. Box 2005
Muncie, IN 47307-0005
317/281-5000

The definitive book on canning. Ball's instructions are precise and absolutely trustworthy. $4.95 plus $1.00 postage and handling.

PONDVIEW EMUS
5365 West Bachelor Road
Angola, IN 46703
219/833-1961

Write for information concerning emu meat, emu meat products, and emu oil. Material available on raising the birds as well.

HOLMES COUNTRY TRAVELER
P.O. Box 358
Millersburg, OH 44654
216/674-2461

A magazine about Amish country in Holmes County, Ohio, published five times a year. Subscription rates are $12.95 per year.

MARCIA ADAMS
  HEARTLAND JOURNAL
P.O. Box 40086
Fort Wayne, IN 46804

A quarterly newsletter chockful of ideas and suggestions for traveling, collecting, gardening, reading, entertaining, and preparing sumptuous dishes. Published four times a year, $18 per year. Great gift!

Fine Cookware and China

FANTES
1006 South Ninth Street
Philadelphia, PA 19147
800/878-5557

Superb kitchen equipment shop, and they have a good newsletter. Don't miss this place when in Philadelphia.

HAMMERSONG TINWARE
221 S. Potomac Street
Boonsboro, MD 21713
301/432-4320

Great cookie cutters of all descriptions. Send for the catalog.

LEHMAN'S NON-ELECTRIC CATALOG
One Lehman Circle, P.O. Box 41
Kidron, OH 44636
330/857-5757

Old-time country hardware serving the Amish community, plus a large illustrated black-and-white catalog filled with goodies. $3 for the catalog.

SUR LA TABLE
84 Pine Street
Pike Farmer's Market
Seattle, WA 98109
800/234-0852

Right across from the market, this shop is jammed full of dishes, cookbooks, cookware, and helpful people. A "must-see" when in Seattle. And they have a catalog.

WILTON ENTERPRISES
2240 West 75th Street
Woodridge, IL 60517
708/963-7100, ext. 320

Specialty baking pans of all descriptions. Cake and cookie pans, other baking supplies, including six-mini-star mold and four cavity mini angel food pans, as well as 10-inch and heart angel food pans.

THE WOODEN SPOON
P.O. Box 931
Clinton, CT 06413-0931

Deep metal pie pans, 8-, 9-, and 10-inch size. Get the pans; they are necessary for good pies. Write for their catalog.

Mail-Order Foods

KING ARTHUR FLOUR
BAKER'S CATALOGUE
P.O. Box 876
Norwich, VT 05055-0876
800/827-6836

Baking supplies, including flours, maple sugar, and extracts.

WHITE LILY FOOD COMPANY
P.O. Box 871
Knoxville, TN 37901

This fine southern soft wheat flour, perfect for biscuits and other southern breads, can be ordered by mail. Write for information.

VERNON MILLER,
THE CIDER PRESS
55514 County Road 8
Middlebury, IN 46540
219/825-2010

Boiled cider syrup, sorghum and maple syrup, plus regional jam and jellies.

RALPH SECHLER AND SONS
St. Joe, IN 46785
219/337-5461

The very best pickles and relishes on the market! Write or call for price list.

SWEET CELEBRATIONS
7009 Washington Avenue South
Edina, MN 55439
612/943-1661

Formerly Maid of Scandinavia, this is a terrific mail-order place for all esoteric baking needs, such as hartshorn powder or baker's ammonia ($4 for 8 oz.). Send for their catalog.

WILLIAMS SONOMA
P.O. Box 7456
San Francisco, CA 94120-7456
800/541-2233

Rose water ($8.50 for 7 oz.). For oils such as lemon, orange, lime, cinnamon, clove, and anise, call for more information and a free catalog.

THE VICTORIAN CUPBOARD
P.O. Box 1852
Old Chelsea Station
New York, NY 10113
800/653-8033

Victorian rose water & orange water duo, used for creating fragrant, floral-scented pastries and molded custards, or as a substitute for vanilla. Formulated especially for cooking. In 6-oz. cobalt blue bottles, $19.

WEST POINT MARKET
1711 West Market Street
Akron, OH 44313
216/864-2151 or
800/838-2156

Not only can you find extracts here, but everything else under the sun. The very best of the top grocery stores in the country. Worth a special trip to browse among the wines and cheeses, and stay for lunch. They will ship.

YODER'S COUNTRY MARKET
61 Locker Lane
off of Route 669 North
Grantsville, MD 21536
800/321-5148

Be sure to visit this comprehensive market if in the area. Catalog of Amish and Mennonite specialties: preserves, granola, canned meats, smoked meat, syrups, molasses, etc.

[Bibliography]

❖

Amish-Country Cookbook: Favorite Recipes Gathered by Das Essenhaus. Volumes I, II, and III. Elkhart, IN: Bethel Publishing, 1961.

Amish Struggle with Modernity, The. Hanover and London: University Press of New England, 1994.

Bial, Raymond. *Visit to Amish Country.* Urbana, IL: Phoenix Publishing, 1995.

———. *Amish Home.* Boston: Houghton Mifflin Company, 1993.

Boyertown Area Cookery or the Boyertown Housewife and Kitchen Efficiency Guide and Companion. Second Edition. Boyertown, PA: Boyertown Area Historical Society, May 1985.

Cornucopia—A Cookbook. Wakarusa, IN: Holdeman Mennonite Church, 1956.

Daily Bread. Bourbon, IN: North Main Street Mennonite Church, Nappanee, and Bourbon Mennonite Church Chapel, 1954.

Day in an Amish Kitchen, A. Greendale, WI: Reiman Publications, L.P., 1995.

Day in the Life of the Amish, A. Greendale, WI: Reiman Publications, L.P., 1994.

Dunkard-Dutch Cookbook. Lebanon, PA: Applied Arts Publishers, 1962.

Hark, Ann and Barba, Preston H. *Pennsylvania German Cookery: A Regional Cookbook.* Allentown, PA: Schlechter's, 1950.

Heller, Edna Eby. *Art of Pennsylvania Dutch Cooking.* New York: Doubleday, 1958.

Homemaker's Cookbook. Goshen, IN: Goshen College Mennonite Church, 1942.

Kraybill, Donald B., and Nolt, Steven M. *Amish Enterprise: From Plows to Profits.* Baltimore and London: Johns Hopkins University Press, 1995. Kraybill, Donald B., and Olshan, Marc A., editors.

Lee, Hilde Gabriel. *Taste of the States: A Food History of America.* Charlottesville, VA: Howell Press, 1992.

Our Swiss Pantry. Berne, IN: Women's Missionary Society of the First Mennonite Church, 1952.

Peek into Our Pantry. Goshen, IN: Women's Study Club of the Eighth Street Mennonite Church, 1946.

Showalter, Emma. *Mennonite Community Cookbook.* Scottsdale, PA: The Mennonite Community Association, 1957.

Wisler Country Cooking. Fairview Mennonite Church, Elkhart County, IN. Iowa Falls, IA: General Publishing & Binding, 1964.

[Credits]

❖

As I scan these names, every one brings back memories of happy and learning experiences. It is Dick's and my observation that everyone we have worked with has been helpful and courteous, and this so enhanced this book. We do appreciate the open-hearted cooperation we received in the Amish and Mennonite communities we visited.

Allen County Public Library, Fort Wayne, Indiana
Berlin Mennonite Church, Berlin, Ohio
Boyd and Wurthman Restaurant, Berlin, Ohio
Bread Box Bakery, Shipshewana, Indiana
The Budget
Bunker Hill Cheese Company, Millersburg, Ohio
Betsy Chapman
Julian Coblentz
Fanny and Lester Detweiler
Patricia Dozier
Fannie Erb
Gospel Heaven Mennonite Church, Millersburg, Ohio
Gordon Grabill
Heian Jogakuin College, Osaka, Japan
Irma Helmuth, Arthur, Illinois
Helping Hands Quilt Shop, Millersburg, Ohio
Alverna Hess
Holley Hobbs

Carol Hochstetler
Honeyville General Store, Honeyville, Indiana
Elton Hostettler
Vera Jess
Regina Johnson
Maribel Kraybill
Bruce Dun Lavey
Gaylen Lehman
Grace Leong
Cindy Lorbach
Janet Lord
John Martin
Laura McCaffrey
Dolores Medhoff
Menno-Hoff Mennonite-Amish Visitors Center, Shipshewana, Indiana
Mennonite Information Center, Berlin, Ohio
Mennonite Information Center, Lancaster, Pennsylvania
Amos Miller
Annie Miller's Bread and Pies, Middlebury, Indiana
Barbara Miller
Betty Miller
Dorcas Miller
Edna Miller
Edna Maye Miller
Elva Miller
Joe D. Miller
Leah Miller
Lou Jane Miller
Mary Miller
Ruth and Paul Miller
Alma Mullet

Mark Newman
Mr. and Mrs. Earl Nifong
Lucille Noble
Pondview Emu Farm
Ben and Verna Ramer
Effie Schlabach
Verna Schlabach
Schmucker's Produce Farm, New Haven, Indiana
Cynthia Sevier
Arlene Shanon
Ruth Shrock
Loudell F. Snow
Joe Springer, Mennonite Historical Library, Goshen College, Goshen, Indiana
Doris Stonestreet
Al Such
Lovina Swartzenburger
Mary Swartzenburger
Susie Swartzenburger
Pamela Thomas
Edna Troy
Effie Troy
Wana Cabinets and Furniture, Grantsville, Maryland
Harry Weaver
John Weaver, Kuntry Lawn Furniture
Kim Weiner
White Swan Antique Store, Millersburg, Ohio
Dale Yoder
Iva Yoder
Yoder's Popcorn, Shipshewana, Indiana
Mrs. Gene Zarger

[Index]

❖